Booker T. Washington and the Struggle against White Supremacy

Booker T. Washington and the Struggle against White Supremacy

The Southern Educational
Tours, 1908–1912

David H. Jackson, Jr.

BOOKER T. WASHINGTON AND THE STRUGGLE AGAINST WHITE SUPREMACY

First published in 2008 by
PALGRAVE MACMILLAN®
in the US—a division of St. Martin's Press LLC,
175 Fifth Avenue, New York, NY 10010.

Where this book is distributed in the UK, Europe and the rest of the world, this is by Palgrave Macmillan, a division of Macmillan Publishers Limited, registered in England, company number 785998, of Houndmills, Basingstoke, Hampshire RG21 6XS.

Palgrave Macmillan is the global academic imprint of the above companies and has companies and representatives throughout the world.

Palgrave® and Macmillan® are registered trademarks in the United States, the United Kingdom, Europe and other countries.

ISBN-13: 978–0–230–60652–4
ISBN-10: 0–230–60652–0

Library of Congress Cataloging-in-Publication Data

Jackson, David H.
    Booker T. Washington and the struggle against white supremacy :
    the southern educational tours, 1908–1912 / David H. Jackson, Jr.
        p. cm.
    Includes bibliographical references and index.
    ISBN 0–230–60652–0
        1. Washington, Booker T., 1856–1915—Travel—Southern States.
    2. Washington, Booker T., 1856–1915—Political and social views.
    3. Washington, Booker T., 1856–1915—Psychology. 4. National Negro
    Business League (U.S.)—History. 5. African Americans—Education—
    Southern States—History—20th century. 6. African Americans—
    Southern States—Social conditions—20th century. 7. Southern
    States—Race relations—History—20th century. 8. Southern
    States—Description and travel. 9. African Americans—Social
    conditions—To 1964. 10. United States—Race relations—History—
    20th century. I. Title.

E185.97.W4J33 2008   2008005345
370.92—dc22

A catalogue record of the book is available from the British Library.

Design by Newgen Imaging Systems (P) Ltd., Chennai, India.

First edition: October 2008

10 9 8 7 6 5 4 3 2 1

Printed in the United States of America.

*Dedicated to Sheila, David III, Daja,
and all present and future "Jacksonites"*

CONTENTS

FIGURES

Map Produced by Katherine Milla.

1 Washington and the coordinators of his five tours. Center: Washington, president and founder of the National Negro Business League. Top left: Charles Banks of Mound Bayou, Mississippi, coordinated Washington's Mississippi tour. Top right: Bishop George Wylie Clinton of Charlotte, North Carolina, coordinated Washington's North Carolina tour. Bottom left: Robert L. Smith of Waco, Texas, coordinated Washington's tour of Texas. Bottom middle: James C. Napier of Nashville, Tennessee, coordinated Washington's tour of Tennessee. Bottom right: Matthew M. Lewey of Pensacola, Florida, coordinated Washington's Florida of tour.

2 Top left: Washington working at his desk at Tuskegee Institute. Top right: Washington speaking. Center: Washington with bandaged head after Henry Ulrich assault in New York, March 1911. Bottom left: Washington speaking in Jacksonville, Florida. Bottom right: Washington in Copenhagen, Denmark.

3 Top left: Washington, president of Tuskegee Institute. Top center: Robert R. Moton led many of the "plantation songs" on Washington's tours and became his successor at Tuskegee Institute. Top right: Emmett J. Scott, Washington's loyal secretary. Bottom left: John Merrick, business leader in North Carolina and Washington supporter. Bottom center: Charles Banks, Washington's "Chief Lieutenant" for Mississippi. Bottom right: Charles Spaulding, a business leader in Charlotte, North Carolina, and Washington supporter.

4 Top left: Joseph Blodgett, businessman in Jacksonville, Florida, and Washington supporter. Top center: Elias Cottrell, Bishop of the CME Church and Washington supporter. Top right: Abraham Lincoln Lewis of Jacksonville, Florida. Business leader and supporter of Washington. Bottom left: Charles H. Anderson, businessman in Jacksonville, Florida, and Washington supporter. Bottom center: Distinguished scholar-activist W. E. B. Du Bois.

Bottom right: Matthew W. Dogan, President of Wiley College in Marshall, Texas.

5 Top: Charles Banks's home in Mound Bayou, Mississippi, during Washington's tour in 1908. Washington is standing at the front and center of the porch with Banks to his right. Bottom: Washington and associates at Bishop Elias Cottrell's home in Mississippi during his tour of the state in 1908. (Seated, left to right): Emmett Scott, Robert Moton, Washington, and (far right) Bishop Elias Cottrell. (Standing): William H. Holtzclaw (second from left) and Charles Banks (fifth from left).

6 Top: Washington and associates in Florida during his tour of the state in 1912. From left to right, (Back Row): Sumner A. Furniss, Emmett J. Scott, William T. Andrews, Matthew M. Lewey, and J. C. Thomas. (Front Row): James C. Napier, Washington, Samuel E. Courtney, John B. Bell, and Gilbert C. Harris. Bottom: Washington and associates in North Carolina during his tour of the state in 1910. From left to right, (Back Row): J. T. Saunders, George C. Clement, J. A. Dellinger, Nathan Hunt, C. S. Brown, R. W. Thompson, Silas A. Peeler, James B. Dudley, Henry L. McCrorey. (Middle Row): William S. Pittman, John H. Washington, James E. Shepard, Emmett J. Scott, William H. Lewis, Booker T. Washington, John Merrick, George W. Clinton, Charles W. Greene, R. B. McRary, G. W. Powell. (Front Row): Horace D. Slatter, D. A. Winslow, George F. King, Charles C. Spaulding, John A. Kenney, Charles H. Moore.

7 Top left: John Brown Bell's home in Houston, Texas. Top right: Elias Cottrell's home in Holly Springs, Mississippi. Bottom left: "The Oaks," Washington's home. Bottom right: John Merrick's home in Durham, North Carolina.

8 Top left: Masonic Temple in Jacksonville, Florida. Top right: Florida A&M College's Mechanics Arts Building. Middle right: Girl's Dormitory at Paul Quinn College, Waco, Texas. Bottom left: Florida A&M College's Carnegie Building. Bottom right: Rust University in Holly Springs, Mississippi, was attended by Charles Banks and Ida B. Wells-Barnett.

9 Top left: Original caption under photo reads: "Christ—The Son of God. Man was created in the image of God. Is the negro in the image of God's son—Christ?" Top right: Beastly depiction of black man with white woman. Caption under photo reads: "The Beast and the Virgin. Can you find a white preacher who would unite in holy wedlock, a burly negro to a white lady? Ah! Parents, you would rather see your daughter burned, and her ashes

scattered to the winds of heaven." Center: Negative depiction of black infant. Caption under photo reads: "The Virgin Mary and the Child Christ. Could the Child Christ possibly be of the same flesh as the Negro?" Bottom left: Negative depiction of black child. Caption under photo reads: "Adam and Eve in the Garden of Eden. Is the negro an offspring of Adam and Eve? Can the rose produce a thistle?" Bottom right: Black "brute" ravishes white woman. Caption under photo reads: "Natural Results. The screams of the ravished daughters of the 'Sunny South' have placed the Negro in the lowest rank of the Beast Kingdom."

Acknowledgments

To a large extent, this project began with a discussion I had ten years ago with my former mentor the late Dr. Theodore (Ted) Hemmingway. Back in 1986, he had published an essay on Booker T. Washington's tour of Mississippi and years later I wrote a study on Charles Banks, Washington's Mississippi lieutenant who coordinated that tour, so we discussed working together on a book that covered Washington's travels. I recall Ted's enthusiasm in saying we could call the book "Booker T. Washington and his Traveling Roadshow." Unfortunately, before he passed away in 2006, we never took time beyond that initial discussion to work on the project. Moreover, at that point, neither one of us really understood the *real* meaning behind the tours, and as it turns out Washington's travels were much more than just a "roadshow."

It took several years for this project to unfold during which time I traveled to numerous libraries and archives throughout the southern region of the United States. During that time, I incurred a number of debts and I owe a number of people for assisting me along the way with preparation of this work. Several of my former graduate students and mentees (self-proclaimed "Jacksonites") either worked in my office as research assistants or just volunteered their time to help me with this project, and I am very thankful for their assistance. A number of them have gone on to enroll in and/or complete doctoral programs since we met, including Anthony Dixon, Indiana University (2007); Sheena Harris, the University of Memphis; Will Guzman, the University of Texas (El Paso); Danton Wims, Indiana University; Darius Young, the University of Memphis; Ameenah Shakir, the University of Miami; Reginald Ellis, the University of Memphis; Jonathan Hutchins, the University of Mississippi; Shirletta Kinchen, the University of Memphis; Daleah Goodwin, the University of Georgia; Katrina Sims, the University of Mississippi; and Christina Davis, the University of Georgia. I would also like to express thanks to a few other former graduate students who assisted me with this work—Talibah Marin-Coleman and Attorney Alvin Benton.

Ralph Turner, the interim dean, and Keith Simmonds, the assistant dean of the College of Arts and Sciences, Florida A&M University (FAMU), encouraged me to continue my research while serving as the Chairman of the Department of History, Political Science, Public Administration, Geography, Social Science Education, and African American Studies at FAMU. Dr. Simmonds, who previously served as department chair, shared with me the difficulty in publishing while doing administrative work at the university, and he was correct! However, with persistence and tenacity, I somehow managed to complete this project.

I was the recipient of a Faculty Research Award Program (FRAP) grant, provided by Dean Chanta Haywood and the School of Graduate Studies and Research at FAMU, which helped to underwrite portions of my research. In addition, a number of colleagues provided moral support, read drafts of the manuscript, and gave me assistance at different points. For that I would like to thank Larry E. Rivers, president of Fort Valley State University, and professor Canter Brown, Jr., who reviewed early drafts of the study and provided me with meaningful feedback.

I am also grateful to my colleagues, Titus Brown and Juanita Gaston, for encouraging and assisting me in my scholarly endeavors. Another former colleague, Tameka Bradley Hobbs, read some of the early chapters of this work and gave me critical feedback and encouragement. My colleague and friend, Sylvester Johnson (now at Indiana University), read drafts of the manuscript and allowed me to bounce a number of ideas off him during our daily runs. He always remained supportive and provided insightful feedback as I shared different thoughts with him about this project.

During my travels for this study, a number of people provided support. Whenever I visited Nashville, George Bell allowed me to stay at his home and willingly chauffeured me from place to place. My big brother, Kever Conyers and his wife Jackie also opened their home to me in Memphis. I am also most indebted to Kever for assisting me with the photographs for this book, and I would like to thank Katherine Milla for preparing the map. I also offer a word of gratitude to Newgen Imaging Systems that made the final revisions to this work, and I am grateful to Christopher Chappell and the rest of the staff at Palgrave Macmillan for guiding this work to publication.

Last, I must acknowledge my father, the late David H. Jackson, Sr., who played a tremendous role in my life and accomplishments. Although he is no longer here physically, he continues to inspire me as I move onward and upward. And, my mother, Vera, my sisters,

Tammy and Belinda, and my mother-in-law, Gloria Merritt, have always been encouraging and believed in me and my work. Ultimately, none of my efforts would be possible without the patience and support of my wife, Sheila, and our children, David III and Daja. They continue to make big sacrifices, while still encouraging and inspiring me to succeed as I pursue my scholarly interests.

Notwithstanding the assistance I received from others with this study, all errors contained herein are mine.

Abbreviations

AME	African Methodist Episcopal
AMEZ	African Methodist Episcopal Zion
BTWP	Booker T. Washington Papers
BTWPF	Booker T. Washington Papers Microfilm
CME	Colored Methodist Episcopal
FAMC	Florida Agricultural and Mechanical College
FAMU	Florida Agricultural and Mechanical University
FSNBL	Florida State Negro Business League
HNIC	Head Negro in Charge
MIT	Massachusetts Institute of Technology
MSNBL	Mississippi State Negro Business League
NAACP	National Association for the Advancement of Colored People
NCSNBL	North Carolina State Negro Business League
NNBL	National Negro Business League
TSNBL	Tennessee State Negro Business League
TXSNBL	Texas State Negro Business League

Booker T. Washington's Southern Educational Tours: 1908–1912

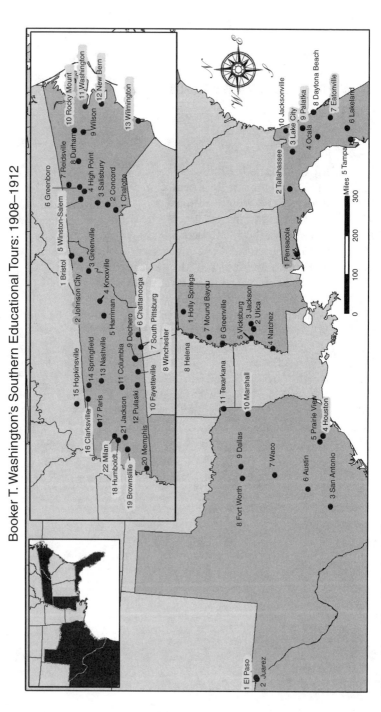

11 Washington
12 New Bern
10 Rocky Mount
9 Wilson
8 Durham
13 Wilmington
7 Reidsville
4 High Point
3 Salisbury
2 Concord
1 Charlotte
6 Greensboro
5 Winston-Salem
3 Greenville
1 Bristol
2 Johnson City
4 Knoxville
5 Harriman
6 Chattanooga
9 Dechero
7 South Pittsburg
8 Winchester
15 Hopkinsville
14 Springfield
13 Nashville
11 Columbia
10 Fayetteville
17 Paris
12 Pulaski
16 Clarksville
21 Jackson
22 Milan
18 Humboldt
19 Brownsville
20 Memphis

1 Holly Springs
7 Mound Bayou
6 Greenville
5 Vicksburg
3 Jackson
2 Utica
4 Natchez
8 Helena

11 Texarkana
10 Marshall
5 Prairie View
4 Houston
8 Fort Worth
9 Dallas
7 Waco
6 Austin
3 San Antonio

1 Pensacola
2 Tallahassee
10 Jacksonville
3 Lake City
9 Palatka
4 Ocala
8 Daytona Beach
7 Eatonville
6 Lakeland
5 Tampa

1 El Paso
2 Juarez

Miles
0   100   200   300

Map produced by Katherine Milla.

CHAPTER 1

Introduction

Born into slavery in 1856 to a black mother and white father he never knew, Booker T. Washington became the preeminent African American leader of his day. It can even be argued that he reigns as the most powerful black leader to ever live in America. Washington came from humble beginnings near Hale's Ford in Franklin County, Virginia. He worked as a servant during his childhood and lived through the Civil War; after which, he took up various jobs including working in the West Virginia coal mines, a very dangerous task. While working in the coal mines, he learned of a school designed to educate African Americans and Native Americans called Hampton Institute in Hampton, Virginia. Hampton had been founded by Samuel Chapman Armstrong, and he became Washington's mentor when the latter eventually arrived at the school with nothing but the clothes on his back.

Armstrong, however, held many of the same racist views as Southern racial demagogues. Although he believed that the average black person was inferior to whites in mind and body, he looked at Washington as an exception. He might have rationalized Washington's genius by attributing his talents to the "white blood" in his veins. Washington, nevertheless, took certain lessons from Armstrong that he would incorporate into his strategy of racial uplift for years to come. For instance, Armstrong encouraged the purchasing of land, which became a major part of Washington's philosophy.

In 1881, Armstrong recommended Washington to build and lead a school in Tuskegee, Alabama, built on the Hampton model of industrial education, and Washington agreed. When he arrived at Tuskegee there was little there from which to build a school, but he and his students, starting from scratch, eventually made their own bricks, designed their buildings, planted and cooked their own food, and so forth.

Washington built Tuskegee Institute into one of the finest black schools of the day. At a time when most black colleges were still run by white missionaries, Tuskegee had an all-black faculty and virtually an all-black student body. It is no accident that some of the leading black scholars in the country wound up teaching at Tuskegee. Perhaps the most famous is scientist George Washington Carver. Others such as architect Robert R. Taylor, a graduate of Massachusetts Institute of Technology (MIT), joined him. The academic faculty also included people with degrees from Fisk, Atlanta, Harvard, and Oberlin Universities. Washington boasted that Tuskegee employed the largest number of black college graduates in the country. In fact, W. E. B. Du Bois himself would have taken a job at the school had he not committed to a position at Wilberforce University eight days earlier. "It would be interesting to speculate just what would have happened, if I had accepted the last offer of Tuskegee instead of that of Wilberforce," Du Bois reflected in his autobiography *Dusk of Dawn*. Louis Harlan says that Tuskegee Institute became "the largest and best-supported black educational institution of his day, and it spawned a large network of other industrial schools." Washington, he continued, "offered blacks not the empty promises of the demagogue but a solid program of economic and educational progress through struggle."[1]

In 1895, Washington delivered his biggest address at the Atlanta Cotton States Exposition, which catapulted him into national fame. Ironically, Frederick Douglass passed away the same year, creating a vacuum in black leadership. The major reason Washington and other African Americans wanted to be included in the event was because "Negroes saw in the exposition a chance to demonstrate their progress since emancipation." During his speech, the Tuskegee leader told the mixed audience that when it came to social matters, blacks and whites "can be as separate as the five fingers, yet one as the hand in all things essential to mutual progress." These words, among others, resonated throughout the country and from this point on, many considered Washington, a gifted elocutionist, Douglass's rightful successor.[2]

Washington's educational tours of the American South in the early twentieth century, as this book explores, constituted remarkable organizational and inspirational efforts in the face of what at times seemed to be virtually insurmountable challenges. The details of these events help to make this point, but insight into the man and the circumstances that necessitated these tours brings the matter into sharper focus. History lay heavily upon the times and the man, and its layers formed the framework within which he acted. His words and deeds can resonate again with clarity, but only if they echo purely and truly as he had intended them to be understood. Washington won many followers and supporters by taking "educational tours" or "educational pilgrimages" through several states. Washington took these tours for four major reasons: first, to inspire, encourage, and show blacks that progress was being made and that they needed to continue to move onward and upward; second, to solidify his position as the Head Negro in Charge (HNIC) against black opposition such as the Niagara Movement and later the National Association for the Advancement of Colored People (NAACP); third, to counter prevailing white stereotypes that blacks were degenerating since the end of slavery and retreating into barbarism; and fourth, to show whites in the North and South that black people were advancing despite assertions by some to the contrary. In essence, these were not literally educational tours in terms of academic learning, but what Washington saw as an opportunity to educate himself, and more importantly others, about the progress of the black race. Thus, it should be understood up front that instead of focusing on how Washington struggled against Du Bois in a quest for leadership or revisiting the ideological debate between the two (which has already been written on extensively), this study emphasizes how Washington fought to undermine white supremacy, a much bigger problem and enemy to all African Americans.[3]

In his book—*White Supremacy: A Comparative Study in American & South African History* (1981)—historian George M. Fredrickson says that white supremacy can be defined as the "attitudes, ideologies, and policies associated with the rise of blatant forms of white or European dominance over 'nonwhite' populations. In other words, it involves making invidious distinctions of a socially crucial kind that are based primarily, if not exclusively, on physical characteristics and ancestry." Moreover, "in its fully developed form, white supremacy means 'color bars,' 'racial segregation,' and the restriction of meaningful citizenship rights to a privileged group characterized by its light pigmentation." White supremacy, Fredrickson continued, suggests "systematic and self-conscious efforts to make race or color a qualification for membership in the civil community." Another scholar has concluded that the goal of white supremacy is "none other than the establishment, maintenance, expansion and refinement of world domination by members of a group that classifies itself as the white 'race.'" Ultimately, under this system nonwhites, no matter how acculturated or how numerous, are treated as permanent outsiders, aliens, or as second-class citizens, and in one way or another, Washington worked to destroy this system during his lifetime.[4]

Washington began these particular statewide tours by traveling through Arkansas and the Oklahoma and Indian territories in 1905, and these tours won him much support for his agenda. However, his most successful tour early on featured Mississippi in 1908 and was directed by Charles Banks. It set the standard for the other tours the Tuskegean subsequently took throughout the South. Like a modern-day politician on the campaign trail, Washington traveled throughout the South promoting his platform, agenda, and strategies for racial uplift. On the Mississippi trip alone, he spoke to an estimated forty thousand to eighty thousand people. In total, Washington reached around 1 million black and white people through these campaigns over a five-year period. He said he took these tours to "meet the masses of my people and to instruct them as far as I can through speaking to help them in their industrial and moral life."[5] After his successful Mississippi tour, Washington traveled through nine other Southern states: South Carolina, Virginia, West Virginia, and Tennessee in 1909; Delaware and North Carolina in 1910; Texas in 1911; Florida in 1912; and Louisiana in 1915.[6]

Washington's tours were sponsored primarily by state and local affiliates of the National Negro Business League (NNBL). Washington founded the NNBL in 1900 in Boston. According to a program distributed at its third annual meeting in Richmond, Virginia,

> The object [of the league] is to inform, as best we may, the world of the progress the Negro is making in every part of the country, and to stimulate local business enterprises through its annual meetings and in any other manner deemed wise; to encourage the organization of local business for the purpose of furthering commercial growth in all places where such organizations are deemed needful and wise.[7]

Economic development, independence, self-help, and race pride were all encouraged by League members.[8]

The NNBL became an important component of the Tuskegee Machine. Organized in a pyramid structure, the NNBL placed Washington at the top, state presidents on the second level, local presidents below them, and the general members at the bottom. The local presidents reported to the state presidents and the state presidents reported to Washington. Men and women from numerous professions were members of the NNBL, ranging from businessmen and doctors to farmers and carpenters.[9] Significantly, the NNBL not only served as a stimulus for business in the black community, but it also served as an incubator for other black organizations such as the

National Negro Bar Association, the National Negro Bankers' Association, the National Association of Negro Insurance Men, the National Negro Press Association, and the National Negro Funeral Directors' Association. By way of example, the NNBL offered African American business owners an opportunity to network with black lawyers and enabled the lawyers to develop corporate law practices.[10]

This book follows a case study approach by focusing on five of Washington's Southern educational tours from 1908 to 1912 through Mississippi, Tennessee, North Carolina, Texas, and Florida. It explores the racial climate during that era in each state, analyzes the psychology and philosophy of Washington and his supporters, and culminates with a detailed discussion of the major stops he made. It also sheds more light on Washington's Tuskegee Machine, that "intricate, nationwide web of institutions in the black community that were conducted, dominated, or strongly influenced from the little town in the Deep South where Washington had his base." According to Harlan, the Tuskegee Machine was "broadly based throughout the black middle class, had powerful white allies and many recruits even from the Talented Tenth, [and] made rewards and punishments a central feature of its recruitment and retention of its followers." The study also reveals more on how the state and local chapters of the NNBL functioned and who some of their key players were.[11]

Furthermore, Washington's racial philosophy in action as it evolved over the years, along with the work of various state and local business leagues and the businessmen who comprised them, is examined. Various examples of black educational development in five Southern states during the height of the Jim Crow era are discussed, while Washington's appeal as a leader to Southern blacks and whites is gauged. It also compares and contrasts the racial setting in several Southern states and cities and illustrates how blacks in those areas responded to segregation and white oppression with different forms of agency. Moreover, a number of "unsung heroes" come to life in this book. Important biographical information on members of Washington's entourages along with other leading blacks in the various states will be explored. In addition, this work analyzes how Washington's admirers and critics responded to his tours and what it all meant in terms of his leadership. By examining these tours one starts to see the imperative of Washington using them to maintain his control over the Tuskegee Machine and black America.

It is also very significant to understand that Washington used these educational tours not simply to promote himself and his personal agenda. In a broader sense, he used them to address the

"Negro problem" and to counter white racist notions about blacks degenerating and retrogressing into barbarism since emancipation from slavery. Senator Benjamin Tillman, a white racist demagogue from South Carolina, was one of those who argued that the black race "had retrograded" since freedom. "Under slavery," Tillman said, "the Negro was exceedingly well behaved. The uplifting influence of that institution was so marked that there were 'more good Christian men and women and ladies and gentlemen' among the Southern slaves than in all Africa." Further, due to emancipation African Americans had become "inoculated with the virus of equality," he said, and turned into "a fiend, a wild beast, seeking whom he may devour." In an attempt to explain his paranoia that blacks were going to mistreat whites as they had been mistreated, Tillman argued that African Americans "planned to kill all the white men, marry their women, and use white children as servants."[12]

Moreover, Senator Tillman believed that when blacks received a "little smattering of education" the results were "enervating and destructive of the original virtues of the race." He continued: "'Over education,' on the other hand, by stimulating ambitions impossible of attainment, created discontent which resulted in crime, as in the city of Washington, where intensive efforts were made to educate the blacks. There the Negro criminal and illegitimacy rates were high and Negro public opinion did not frown upon open violation of the moral law." Tillman also said that "over education" would make black men desirous of white women. "Booker T. Washington, the outstanding example of the educated colored man of the times, was declared 'a humbug' whom a German was forced to chastise because Washington 'had been making goo-goo eyes' at the German's [Henry Ulrich] wife," said he.[13]

It is clear that Washington, along with other Bookerites, worked to subvert these theories. Despite these prevailing notions and ridiculous stereotypes about African Americans, the Wizard of Tuskegee undermined them by placing black doctors, lawyers, bishops, businessmen, educators, farmers, children, and the like on display, exposing the fallacy of these and other claims. Moreover, the Tuskegee leader displayed black manliness and character through these trips. Washington aimed to make it more difficult for racists to seize upon black suffering and oppression to perpetuate myths of white superiority. Through these trips, then, he demonstrated that black men were educated and successful in various endeavors, had black wives, and did not desire white ones. Washington showed that educated and successful blacks had nice homes and churches that were well maintained, and when left unmolested, African Americans could succeed in business and life just like anyone else. Indeed, this represented the Victorian definition of manhood. Washington aimed to publicize the incongruence between what people were hearing and what they were actually seeing; what some people were writing versus what African Americans were actually accomplishing. In a word, black progress made white men question their own manhood.

"Measuring racial progress," according to historian David Blight, "became a major preoccupation in black America around the turn of the century." Indeed, a number of black writers and editors joined Washington in compiling books that demonstrated black progress since emancipation, in their efforts to counter the type of misinformation put forth by white Southerners like Tillman. "A written defense was needed first to eradicate the negative stereotypes that had been circulated against the humanity of the black man," wrote historian Randolph Meade Walker. "If blacks were ever to be accepted as human beings, they had to set their case forth logically and methodically in print. Otherwise, it might be interpreted by the public as proof that the African American was incapable of meeting his opponent on the literary field of battle, thus, proving the black man's innate inferiority," Walker concluded.[14]

The books written by these authors differed from biographies like Washington's *Up from Slavery* published in 1901 that demonstrated the gospel of self-help. Several provided statistical data on advancements made by African Americans in property ownership, literacy, and many other categories. Others highlighted African Americans' participation in wars and other national affairs, the successful growth of black businesses, churches, colleges, and schools. There were more that contained biographical sketches on black women and men who had made significant achievements throughout the country. Even before the turn of the century, William Simmons published *Men of Mark: Eminent, Progressive, and Rising* (1887) that included sketches of 177 African Americans. Washington published *The Negro in Business* in 1907 and *My Larger Education: Chapters from my Experience* in 1911. John Edward Bruce wrote *Short Biographical Sketches of Eminent Negro Men & Women in Europe & the United States* (1910); William N. Hartshorn, *An Era of Progress and Promise, 1863–1910* (1910); Green P. Hamilton, *The Bright Side of Memphis* (1908) and *Beacon Lights of the Race* (1911); Monroe N. Work edited the *Negro Year Book and Annual Encyclopedia of the Negro* (1912); Clement Richardson edited the *National Cyclopedia of the Colored Race* (1919); and J. L. Nichols and William Crogman wrote *Progress of a Race* (1920). The broader historiographical aim of these books mirrored one of Washington's purposes for taking the tours discussed throughout this monograph—to show the world the remarkable progress black people had made since emancipation from slavery. Blight concluded: "these compilations were often informed by a Bookerite agenda of racial uplift and accommodationism, as well as by a general desire for pride and respectability."[15]

Historian Blight also posits that "the purpose of these works seemed to be to cheer the race on to higher aspirations, to emotionally empower the young; they were encyclopedic pep talks within the black community of memory. To read these volumes is to enter huge storehouses of uplift ideology, as though encountering thousands of anecdotes from Booker T. Washington speeches without a narrative line." Furthermore, "in schools, families, and among black youth, these books provided much needed reminders of black success, repositories of seemingly self-made achievement. By an almost endless array of measures, each book attempted to show how far black folk had come since, and in spite of, slavery," he concluded. Without a doubt, the racial progress rhetoric emphasized in these books gave black people hope.[16]

To be sure, Washington did not pioneer these speaking tours to publicize advancements made by the race. Other nationally recognized black leaders before him like Frederick Douglass and John Mercer Langston also took tours throughout the South for similar reasons. They spoke across the land espousing the virtues of education, training, owning land, and farming. They realized that someone needed to counter whites' negative image of the recently emancipated slaves. For example, Douglass arrived in Nashville in September 1873 to much pomp and circumstance. Newspapers publicized his arrival, a delegation of seventy-five persons and a fourteen-horse carriage awaited him, and as historian Bobby Lovett explains, "the trip from the depot became a parade, complete with a brass band and thirty blacks mounted on fine horses, traveling on Market Street to the Public Square." The processional later went to the fairgrounds where thousands of persons awaited its arrival. Importantly, as part of their addresses these spokesmen were expected to highlight the achievements of the black elite so they would leave a positive impression on white listeners.[17]

This study will enforce the theme of nationally recognized African American leaders speaking across the land on behalf of their oppressed race. In many ways it is a bottom-up, rather than a top-down, history as it gives a closer perspective of what occurred on the ground at the turn of the century among common African Americans who, as individuals, are not found on the pages of history books. In his seminal work on Washington, Harlan erroneously asserted that "to describe one of these state tours is to describe them all."[18] True, the events became staged in a similar fashion throughout the South, but there is much to be learned from each pilgrimage. First, these tours were a significant part of Washington's life story and by studying several of these trips, a bigger picture emerges that cannot be seen through examining just one of these visits. It becomes apparent that over time Washington used these tours to consolidate his base and to win over more support from blacks and whites in the North and South. The Niagara Movement that began in 1905 had met its demise by 1908, but was followed by the stronger interracial NAACP. Through espionage, Washington knew the happenings of both of these groups and he undermined their effectiveness. Simultaneously, he felt compelled to keep himself and his message at the forefront of American race matters and these educational tours helped him accomplish that.

Nonetheless, this monograph will demonstrate that although Washington and Du Bois were in a race for leadership during the Jim Crow era, both men understood they had common enemies—white racism and white supremacy. In fact, in the absence of Jim Crow oppression and white supremacy, there would have been no need for men like Washington and Du Bois in the first place. So while both men had different approaches for solving the race problem, those differences became secondary in importance to the overall uplifting of the race and the eliminating of white supremacy.

During Washington's day, public speaking served as a major form of recreation for blacks and whites. People did not have radios, televisions, and modern-day conveniences like computers and cellular phones. But Washington took control of the outlets that gave him the most exposure: newspapers, magazines, and books, and he orchestrated speaking tours throughout the South as we shall see.[19]

Although not the wealthiest African American, Washington became perhaps the most influential black leader in the history of this country, even to this very day. His tentacles extended throughout black America and into white America in ways that have not been repeated by any other individual African American. His control over the black press, his influence and support from the Talented Tenth and white philanthropists, his role as advisor to presidents Theodore Roosevelt and William H. Taft, his creation of Tuskegee Institute, the NNBL, the Tuskegee Farmer's Conference, as well as his close connections with black bishops, ministers, educators, and Masonic leaders all gave Washington an inordinate amount of power that has literally gone unmatched.

Washington understood that by gaining the endorsement of whites, especially influential ones, he would win over other blacks because many African Americans turned to whites for validation in terms of who their leaders should be.[20] Washington astutely traveled with Northern newspapermen because he realized that by having stories of his tours printed in Northern newspapers he could win over new supporters who would agree with his philosophy and people who could provide a gateway into new resources and philanthropy.

By touring the homes, schools, businesses, churches, and other institutions, Washington saw the lives of countless people more intimately. Thus, when people wrote him letters or approached him about philanthropy for their schools, for example, he was better qualified to vouch for their work. In at least one case, he even withdrew his endorsement of the East Tennessee Normal and Industrial Institute after he visited the school and felt disappointed with what he saw. "The school is not what it represents itself to be," Washington noted, and the principal John W. Ovletrea "does not have a good reputation for moral and sensible living in the community of Harriman and parts of Tennessee."[21] It behooved those who expected assistance from Washington to have things in order when he came to town.

The symbolism of these trips also went a long way for those interested in advancing the struggle for racial uplift. For instance, the fact that there were whites on the platforms at virtually all of Washington's stops, participating and giving praise to the Tuskegean, showed supporters what America could one day become, and projected an image of racial equality that, for some, created a sense of optimism. At the same time, this symbolic integration exacerbated the fears of white racists and xenophobes. Numerous Southern newspapers made sure they publicized segregation at these events to allay any fears among typical Southern whites that blacks were pursuing social and racial equality.

Ultimately, these trips represented a form of empowerment for African Americans, allowing them to display black material and educational progress among other things. Simultaneously, the tours served as a form of agency by Washington and the countless other women and men who worked with him to stage these affairs. Every little fiber of these trips needs to be dissected to understand their meaning for the Tuskegean and the people of the day. As we shall see, conditions brought about by white efforts to firmly establish white supremacy during Washington's lifetime necessitated these Southern educational tours.

CHAPTER 2

The Three R's: Reconstruction, Redemption, and Racism

During the holocaust of African enslavement, black people had very little control over their minds and bodies. The rapes, sadistic beatings, separating and selling of families, along with other features of the system, worked to dehumanize African people and break their spirit.[1] The notion of blacks one day controlling their own lives economically, socially, spiritually, and politically became an idea many whites could not conceive. Because of their exclusion from the political system, blacks had no influence in terms of decision making in Congress. However, as the abolitionist movement gained momentum and tension between the North and South came to a head, the voice of American blacks became heard. After the Civil War, which lasted only a few years, white Southerners' reality was turned upside down. Many of the things they never imagined they would see in their lifetimes concerning black people happened right before their eyes.

After the abolition of chattel slavery, Reconstruction set the tone of race relations in the country for years to come. During that era, black people participated in America's political system impressively and with much vigor. The political arena became the most immediate avenue blacks took to exercise their citizenship. No doubt, pursuing political over economic power appeared to be the most reasonable approach for blacks to take as they experienced their new freedom. In the immediate aftermath of chattel slavery, blacks remained on the plantations and began to sharecrop with very little opportunity for economic advancement. By contrast, African Americans all over the South won elected office with calculated Republican support. "It would appear that Republicans anticipated a real political advantage from the black vote in states that generally saw a close contest with the Democrats," George Fredrickson noted, therefore "the decisive factor which provided the necessary support for black enfranchisement was not a popular commitment to racial equality but a belief that Republican hegemony and the restoration of the Union on a safe and satisfactory basis could be accomplished only by subordinating racial prejudices to political necessities."[2]

Regardless of the motivation, this became the first serious effort to incorporate African Americans into the body politic. In Mississippi, for instance, blacks made a number of major political gains at the national level. Blanche K. Bruce and Hiram Revels served terms in the U.S. Senate, an accomplishment that would not be repeated for more than eighty years. At the state level, John Roy Lynch became the speaker of the house, Alexander K. Davis served as lieutenant governor, James Hill became secretary of state, and Thomas W. Cardozo presided as superintendent of education.[3]

North Carolinians also elected blacks to state and national office. John A. Hyman became the state's first black congressman. He served in the state senate from 1868 to 1874, and in 1874 was elected to the U.S. House of Representatives. In addition, 187 blacks served in the North Carolina legislature during Reconstruction. For the most part, even after Reconstruction, Tar Heel blacks continued to represent the "Black Second" congressional district until 1901, one year after Democrats implemented a state constitutional amendment disfranchising African Americans, ending the term of George H. White. In Texas, Matthew Gaines, George T. Ruby, Walter M. Burton, and Walter Ripetoe served in the state senate, while Norris Wright Cuney, Benjamin F. Williams, and numerous other African Americans served in the Texas House of Representatives during Reconstruction.[4]

Likewise, Florida produced a number of national and state political leaders like Josiah T. Walls, who served in the Florida House of Representatives, the Florida Senate, and later the U.S. House of Representatives. Jonathan Gibbs became Florida's secretary of state and state superintendent of public instruction, and his son, Thomas Van Rensselaer Gibbs, served in the Florida House of Representatives.[5]

African Americans in Tennessee made only meager political gains compared to the other states in this study. No Tennessee blacks served in Congress, and only a few were elected to the Tennessee General Assembly, starting with Sampson W. Keeble in 1872. Over a fifteen-year period, thirteen blacks served, among whom were Monroe Gooden, Samuel A. McElwee, and Styles Hutchins, who in 1887, became members of the Tennessee legislature and were the last African American members until the 1960s. Other blacks also held local offices as county commissioners, city councilmen, justices of the peace, magistrates, aldermen, and so forth, during Reconstruction.[6] All throughout the South, black people moved into the political arena and demonstrated their willingness and ability to wield political power. All told, over one thousand five hundred blacks held office throughout the South during Reconstruction.[7]

However, Washington, like most African Americans, did not anticipate the white backlash that resulted from the shock and awe of black political activities. Already humiliated by their defeat in the Civil War, white Southerners were outraged that African Americans claimed the same legal and political rights as theirs. Especially, they considered it ridiculous that former slaves, presumed to be subhuman, could hold political office and vote. Indeed, this fact generated pure alarm and consternation among whites since they could not accept black people making decisions that affected white lives. Consequently, many of them began to use the same arguments developed by proslavery advocates in the antebellum period to discredit black political advances. Through various means they also began a brutal campaign to "redeem" the South from what they imagined to be "Negro" political corruption and domination. According to Fredrickson, this new cause, defined as white supremacy, effectively "allowed Southern whites to reduce the freedmen to an inferior caste."[8]

After the Reconstruction governments began to flounder, many Northern whites began to turn their backs on African Americans in the South, arguing that "blacks had had their fair chance, had demonstrated their present incapacity for self-government, and could justifiably be relegated, for the time being at least, to an inferior status." North Carolina's carpetbagger judge, Albion W. Tourgee, adequately surmised the rather hopeless situation between Southern blacks and whites in his 1879 novel *A Fool's Errand*. He assessed that Northern leaders had failed to achieve anything close to black equality during Reconstruction.[9]

> After having forced a proud people to yield what they had for more than two centuries considered a right—the right to hold the African race in bondage—they proceeded to outrage a feeling as deep and fervent as the zeal of Islam or the exclusiveness of the Hindoo caste, by giving the ignorant, the unskilled and dependent race—a race which could not have lived a week without the support or charity of the dominant race—equality of political right. Not content with this, they went farther, and by erecting the rebellious territory into self-regulating and sovereign states, they abandoned these parties to fight out the question of predominance without the possibility of national interference.[10]

Given this scenario, one scholar concluded that "the Negro never had a chance in this struggle," as Tourgee's novel makes clear. "His ignorance and poverty made him no match for the white conservative forces."[11]

To the absolute horror of Washington and other blacks, members of the Ku Klux Klan and other Southern white terrorist groups began to murder black and white Republicans, destroy their crops, and burn their homes and schools. By 1875, white Mississippians, realizing that the federal government would no longer intervene with use of force against them, declared open warfare on its majority black population. Called the "Shotgun Policy," whites in the Magnolia State began terrorizing Republicans (most of whom were black) in an extreme manner even for Reconstruction. In 1874, nearly three hundred black men were hunted down and killed outside of Vicksburg, Mississippi; and in Clinton, Mississippi, thirty Republican officials, teachers, and church leaders were murdered by white mobsters. A Mississippi newspaper, expressing the opinion of most whites in the state, proclaimed that "*Mississippi is a white man's country, and by the eternal God we'll rule it*"[12] (emphasis mine). By 1915, black political influence in the national Republican Party had almost completely run out. As Herbert Clark concluded, "the party deemed it more advantageous to abandon the Negro's cause and allow the return of white Democratic rule in the South. By doing so, the Northern businessmen could win the cooperation of white Southerners in exploiting the cheap labor and natural resources of that region."[13] In light of the campaign of terror whites conducted against them, some blacks questioned if their immediate interest and accomplishments in politics had been the best course. In reality, no matter what route they chose to elevate the race, whites were determined to make life for African Americans a living hell.

Indeed, several decades after Reconstruction, most Southern whites still could not tolerate even the *thought* of blacks having political power. David Wark Griffith highlighted this sentiment with the release of his widely viewed 1915 movie *The Birth of a Nation*. Griffith based the movie on Thomas Dixon's 1905 violently antiblack novel *The Clansman*. Both the film and the novel purported to be historically accurate. In the film, the Klan wrested political power from black politicians in South Carolina during Reconstruction and rescued white womanhood from "black fiends" by attacking and killing blacks and mulattoes, and thus saving the day. This film was immensely popular, grossing $18 million dollars (the equivalent of over $300 million as of 2008). President Woodrow Wilson even had a private showing of the movie in the East Room of the White House and endorsed its storyline. According to John Hope Franklin and Alfred Moss, this movie "did more than any other single thing to nurture and promote the myth of black domination and debauchery during Reconstruction." As a result of the notoriously antiblack film, white violence against blacks increased. For instance, a white man in Lafayette, Indiana, became so enraged after seeing the movie that he killed a young African American man.[14]

The point to remember is that just the *thought* of black men having political power repulsed whites so much that it evoked them to kill or commit violence. Whether blacks actually held this kind of power in Congress or in any state did not matter, because whites *imagined* they did and then reacted to their imaginations. In hindsight, it is clear that that generation of Southern whites was not ready to accept black participation in the political system, especially at the national and state levels, and they went to the extreme to make sure blacks did not. "The granting of political rights, it was argued, had led to dreams of 'social equality' and had encouraged blacks to expropriate white women by force," one historian explained. Thus, black men's allegedly "overpowering desire for white women was often described as the central fact legitimizing the whole program of legalized segregation and disfranchisement."[15]

Washington lived during the time when Southern whites systematically started disfranchising blacks through numerous methods including literacy tests, poll taxes, gerrymandering, grandfather clauses, and stuffing ballot boxes. Any person convicted of theft, arson, bigamy, perjury, bribery, or burglary (crimes usually associated with blacks) lost their voting privileges. "White crimes," like murder, rape, and grand larceny, were not so exclusionary. This led one federal official who spent time in Mississippi to conclude that "white people down there are generally inclined to think that stealing is a baser crime than killing, and that breaking a man's head is not half so mean and contemptible as cutting his purse."[16]

"Political participation by black Mississippians seems to have been a major reason for whites lynching blacks in Mississippi during the 1870s," scholar Julius E. Thompson explains. Moreover, surviving data suggests that "83 percent of the lynching victims (686 individuals) in Mississippi were killed for political participation in the 1870s," according to Thompson. White Mississippians called a constitutional convention in 1890 for the express purpose of disfranchising blacks. Mississippi Senator James Zachariah George, the chief architect of what became known as the Second Mississippi Plan, explained the necessity of the matter: "Our chief duty when we meet in convention is to devise such measures...as will enable us to maintain a home government, under the control of the white people of the State." Furthermore, "the plan is to invest permanently the powers of government in the hands of the people who ought to have them—the white people," he said. James K. Vardaman (who served as governor of Mississippi from 1904 to 1908, and as a U.S. senator from 1913 to 1919) also commented that "there is no use to equivocate or lie about the matter," Mississippi's constitutional convention "was held for no other purpose than to eliminate the nigger from politics; not the 'ignorant and vicious,' as some of those apologists would have you believe, but the nigger...Let the world know it just as it is." Indeed, the convention produced the Second Mississippi Plan, under which white politicians constitutionally ended black political participation. Other Southern states, beginning with South Carolina in 1895, followed Mississippi's lead.[17]

Thus, after whites began to redeem the South, especially politically, it did not make sense for any Southern black leader of consequence to try to steer black people back into politics as their primary racial uplift objective. This is partially why Washington had more appeal to the masses of Southern African Americans than Du Bois, William Monroe Trotter, and Washington's other critics. Southern blacks had long memories and realized that political activism could still lead to death, even decades after Reconstruction ended.[18] It is worth noting that after being forced out of politics, black people in the South did not collectively regain the right to vote in the United States until the 1960s, nearly one hundred years after Reconstruction, and long after the vast majority of the people discussed in this study were dead.

Throughout Washington's lifetime, whites continued to use violence to control, intimidate, repress, and condition blacks into submission. Between 1889 and 1932, nearly four thousand people were lynched, averaging about three people each week for thirty years.[19] Black men were most often the victims of these lynch mobs that created sadistic rituals in which thousands of white Christians participated and witnessed. However, it must be remembered that the violence did not stop there. More often, small groups of whites would hunt down African Americans and shoot or hang them after a minor disagreement or argument, and these murders went either unrecorded or underrecorded. According to historian Grace Hale, "these lynchings in the night claimed many more victims than the open-air spectacles of torture that drew such large crowds." In addition, "white men continued in more private settings to rape black women and assault African Americans for 'reasons' ranging from black resistance and economic success to white hatred, jealousy, and fear." Although no one can say conclusively how many blacks were killed in the South, the estimates run high. Congressman Charles Williams "estimated as early as 1880 that 130,000 people had been murdered in the South for political reasons."[20]

Fredrickson asserts that "what white extremists may have confronted in the image of the black brute was not so much a Negro as a projection of unacknowledged guilt feelings derived from their own brutality toward blacks." Thus, whites developed a vested interest in demonizing blacks to assuage their consciences. "Otherwise many whites would have had to accept an intolerable burden of guilt just for perpetrating or tolerating the most horrendous cruelties and injustices. But in seeing blacks as bad enough to deserve what they got, racists undoubtedly conjured up a monster that was capable of frightening its creators and driving them to new frenzies of hatred." "In the end," he concluded, "even the most oppressed and rigidly subordinated black sharecropper could serve as a symbol of terror for the white-supremacist imagination."[21]

In addition to violence, whites sought to control blacks' economic future, which became a major focus of Washington. In this effort, they established black codes all over the South to ensure the presence of a stable labor force. Black codes designated employees as "servants" and employers as "masters," and prevented African Americans from vagrancy or loitering, effectively forcing blacks to work whether they wanted to or not. According to Franklin and Moss, in the postbellum South, "control of blacks by white employers was about as great as that which slaveholders had exercised. Blacks who quit their jobs could be arrested and imprisoned for breach of contract." Among other things, the black codes permitted corporal punishment, restricted blacks from using firearms or drinking alcohol, and limited the areas in which African Americans could rent or purchase property.[22]

Moreover, throughout the South, thousands of African Americans were arrested, tried, and convicted for any number of crimes. "The theft of a pig could now mean a few years of hard labor instead of a beating behind the barn," one scholar found. Southern politicians developed the convict-lease system in the late nineteenth century under which the state leased convicts to planters and businessmen to clear swamps, build railroads, tend cotton, and so on. The planter or company had to house, feed, and clothe the convicts, but did not pay them. The system proved to be quite profitable considering the state no longer had to house these inmates, but they still received income. In fact, the system became so remunerative that police officers were encouraged to charge blacks with any number of crimes to meet the demand. "Convict leasing was about profits, brutality, and racist ideas," David Oshinsky wrote in his book *Worse than Slavery: Parchman Farm and the Ordeal of Jim Crow Justice* (1996). "Before convict leasing officially ended, a generation of black prisoners would suffer and die under conditions far worse than anything they had ever experienced as slaves," he asserted.[23]

Furthermore, as white Southerners realized they could no longer buy and sell African Americans physically, they began to create black memorabilia, called "contemptible collectibles" by Patricia Turner, to satisfy their psychological craving and to take advantage of a new financial opportunity. In other words, this became the new way to buy, sell, and own black folks, figuratively speaking. Also from these efforts, whites created new stereotypes about African Americans that further perpetuated black myths and assuaged white consciences.[24]

Indeed, white Southerners romanticized the conditions of slavery leading them to create all sorts of Old and New South mythology. The notion of the happy docile slaves who loved their owners more than they loved themselves came out of the postbellum era. The popular image and perception of the black "mammy" is a case in point. D. W. Griffith utilized this image in his film *Birth of a Nation*. White audiences cheered when the plump, dark-skinned mammy in the film defended her master's house during attacks from black and white Union soldiers. She remained loyal to this white family throughout the movie, refusing to take advantage of her newfound freedom.[25] However, Catherine Clinton, in her book *The Plantation Mistress: Woman's World in the Old South* (1982), asserts that the existence of the antebellum mammy is highly unlikely:

> This familiar denizen [the mammy] of the Big House is not merely a stereotype, but in fact a figment of the combined romantic imaginations of the contemporary southern ideologue and the modern southern historian. Records do acknowledge the presence of female slaves who served as the "right hand" of plantation mistresses. Yet documents from the planter class during the first fifty years following the American Revolution reveal only a handful of such examples. Not until after Emancipation did black women run white households or occupy in any significant number the special positions ascribed to them in folklore and fiction. The Mammy was created by white Southerners to redeem the relationship between black women and white men within slave society in response to the antislavery attack from the North during the

ante-bellum period. In the primary records from before the Civil War, hard evidence for its existence simply does not appear.[26]

After Reconstruction, whites imagined history and tried to attribute these and other characteristics to blacks in an attempt to make them fit a certain profile. In other words, through stereotyping they tried to make black people into whom and what they wanted them to be, often portraying African Americans as inferior and subhuman. On the whole, these black collectibles were universally derogatory and had deprecating racial features. These items helped to "prove" that African Americans were not only different but inferior as well. In this way, these "contemptible collectibles" provided a tangible and physical reality to the idea of racial inferiority. These props helped reinforce newly created racist ideology that emerged after Reconstruction. Leon Litwack concluded that "to count the lynchings and burnings, to detail the savagery, the methodical torture prolonged for the benefit of spectators, to dwell on the voyeuristic sadism that characterized these ritual murders and blood rites in the name of enforcing deference and submission is to underscore the degree to which many whites by the late nineteenth century had come to think of black men and women as less than human."[27]

Thus, the type of material culture that developed around these objects during Washington's lifetime helped whites forge a common identity around the idea of "whiteness." It also served the race and class interests of the white aristocracy by helping working-class whites, who could not identify with the elite's economic background, identify with their race. Moreover, in this age of racist demagoguery, the objects served a political purpose in that they reinforced Old and New South mythology, making sectional reconciliation much more palatable.[28]

The objective of these acts was to conduct psychological warfare against African Americans in an effort to make them accept racist ideology. Kenneth Goings has astutely explained this effort in *Mammy and Uncle Mose: Black Collectibles and American Stereotyping* (1994):

> By producing and using in advertising everyday items that clearly depicted African-Americans as inferior, as objects worthy of torment and torture, manufacturers and consumers were giving a physical reality to the racist ideology, thus confirming what the racist demagogues were saying. Items from this period were dominated by folk art pieces, sheet music, advertising motifs, tourist souvenirs, and some housewares. African-Americans, male and female, were portrayed as

very dark, generally bug-eyed, nappy-headed, childlike, stupid, lazy, deferential, *but happy.* This last characteristic was an important dimension of the collectibles: African-Americans could not simply be second-class citizens, they had to actively acknowledge their subordinate position by smiling, by showing deference, and, most important, by appearing to be happy even as they were treated horribly.[29]

Furthermore,

> The Old South theme played to the interests of the southern white elite who wanted to reenter the nation on their own terms, and who wanted a free hand to deal with the darkies as they saw fit. The Old South collectibles made the idea of cooperation between the races based on class a distinct impossibility for working-class whites. Some whites may have been as poor as African-Americans, but they were not as depraved or animalistic. For poor whites in the North as well as in the South, these collectibles "proved" that African-Americans were indeed different and subhuman. Hence, white society justified barbaric punishments such as torture and lynching, meted out to African-Americans who overstepped their boundaries. After all, it wasn't as if a real human being were being burned; moreover, if African-Americans could and deserved to be dealt with in such a manner, then they certainly did *not* deserve such civilized rights as voting or serving on juries.[30]

Other scholars have written about the effort of those in the postwar South to make a cult out of being "white." The desire to control how blacks and whites perceived "blackness" became a preoccupation, conscious and unconscious, for many whites. Hale in her book *Making Whiteness* (1998) adds: "white southerners sought to found their own racial identity within the maintenance of an absolute color bar."[31] This inextricably tied whiteness to the derogation and oppression of blacks. Another capstone of this whiteness movement came with the legal sanctioning of segregation. In the case of *Plessy v. Ferguson* (1896), the Supreme Court decided on the issue and ruled legal the principle of "separate but equal." This helped validate and legalize racial differences; moreover, "Whites created the culture of segregation in large part to counter black success, to make a myth of absolute racial difference, to stop the rising," Hale wrote.[32] As Washington observed, signs and signals emerged all over the South codifying the system. There were "white" and "colored" water fountains, bathrooms, cemeteries, schools, hotels, banks, books, and so on. Making the segregation system even worse, in most instances the facilities blacks were forced to use were not only separate, but most times inferior to those of whites. For instance, while whites had adequate indoor lavatory facilities at places of public accommodation, blacks oftentimes had to go to the back of buildings where both men and women shared the same shabby toilets, if there were any at all. Every time this occurred, at least part of the objective was to make black people resent being "black"—the opposite of "white." In the aftermath of the Civil War, a full-scale psychological war commenced—a concerted effort to make black people hate themselves in deference to whites and to have an inferiority complex. Under this system, through equating better facilities and access with whiteness, blacks were supposed to spurn blackness and hopelessly desire to be white, and some did. But most African Americans merely wanted to gain access to the amenities that whiteness provided, not change their color or race. So if it appeared to some that blacks wanted to be white, it could simply be that they equated whiteness with having access to restrooms, hospitals, and other benefits that came with "white privilege."

Simultaneously, segregation demonstrated the need and provided the path for white people to validate their cult of whiteness. Another good example of this cultic whiteness movement can be seen through white efforts to segregate and provide second-class service to black train riders. Contrary to arguments put forth by whites, "the problem of black middle-class riders in first-class cars...was less that whites feared 'racial pollution' than that the visible dress and deportment of these travelers belied any notion of southern blacks' racial inferiority," according to Hale. She continued:

> Whiteness itself was being defined in the late nineteenth century first-class train cars. When middle-class blacks entered the semi-public spaces of railroads, they placed their better attire and manners in direct juxtaposition with whites' own class signifiers. Because many whites found it difficult to imagine African Americans as anything other than poor and uneducated, finely dressed blacks riding in first-class cars attracted their particular ire.[33]

We might add that it also worked to shatter their fictitious, stereotypical image of blackness.

Meanwhile, white psychologists, criminologists, historians, and social workers, specializing in "scientific racism," engaged in efforts to win control over the perception of blacks throughout most of Washington's life. Some of their ideas emerged from British scientist Charles Robert Darwin's theories of evolution and "natural selection." Darwin argued that God did not determine people's destiny, but "a random process dominated by the fiercest or luckiest competitors" did.[34] Unlike many of his colleagues, and to his credit, Darwin believed that all human beings were part of a common species. However, he relied on racist descriptions of whites and nonwhites to argue this idea. He surmised, for instance, that "nonwhites inevitably declined or disappeared in the wake of contact with whites because inferior races, like women, were ill-equipped to deal with sudden change or complex developments. They were naturally given to a primitive state of thinking or being." Furthermore, he felt that indigenous people "disappeared" because of their inferior capacity to adapt. Unwittingly, this sort of reasoning had the effect of "rendering invisible the history of genocidal campaigns that white governments (including the American colonial and U.S. governments) waged against native nations," scholar Sylvester Johnson has correctly concluded.[35]

William Graham Sumner and Herbert Spencer, sociologists, took Darwin's evolution theory and applied it even more so to people. Their theory, known as Social Darwinism, maintained that through a process of natural selection the strong would survive and the weak would falter. Life, in fact, was a struggle and only the fittest would survive. For white racists, this became the scientific basis for explaining why African Americans, Native Americans, and immigrants were at the bottom of society, and why the white Anglo-Saxon remained at the top—they were most fit. This also allowed whites to disregard the social and legal system that worked to oppress other groups, especially blacks, and blame their condition on the group's supposed innate inferiority. While even the most liberal Southern whites thought that blacks could be made substantially better, they still rejected the notion that blacks could ever rise to become their equal.[36]

The discourse of "civilization," which included Darwinistic thought, also developed during this time and consisted of elements of race and gender. White men found very effective ways of linking male dominance to white supremacy. For example, upper- and middle-class white men utilized "civilization" to maintain their racial, class, and gender authority. They used "civilization" to legitimize their claims to power and supremacy. According to Gail Bederman, by 1890 the discourse of civilization had developed around three specific meanings. They were race, gender, and millennial assumptions about human evolution. "Human races were assumed to evolve from simple savagery, through violent barbarism, to advanced and valuable civilization," she informed. "But only white races had, as yet, evolved to the civilized stage. In fact, people sometimes spoke of civilization as if it were itself a racial trait, inherited by all Anglo-Saxons and other 'advanced' white races."[37]

In addition to racial characteristics, gender became an essential component of "civilization."Civilized men and women had evolved pronounced sexual differences. Civilized women were womanly; that is, spiritual, delicate, and devoted to the home. Civilized men were the most "manly" creatures ever evolved, manifesting self-control, good character, and protection of their women and children. By contrast, and on the opposite end of the spectrum, were the savage woman and man. "Savage women," says Bederman, "were aggressive, carried heavy burdens, and did all sorts of 'masculine' hard labor. Savage men were emotional and lacked a man's ability to restrain their passions." Savage men did not provide for their children or protect their families, and engaged in behaviors unthinkable for civilized men.[38]

In brief, manliness became the highest form of manhood, and "civilization" became the highest form of humanity. The most advanced races were the ones that had developed perfect womanliness and manliness. Based on these beliefs, black men and women, presumed to be racial primitives, could never be as manly and womanly as white men and white women, no matter how hard they tried. In fact, they did not even have the biological capacity to develop advanced characteristics of womanliness and manliness because their ancestors had never evolved that capacity.[39]

Many white interlocutors made the case for black inferiority. A Southern army officer named Dr. Robert W. Shufeldt added to the argument. In 1907, he published *The Negro: A Menace to Civilization* in which he claimed that black men and women "are almost wholly subservient to the sexual instinct...They copulate solely for the gratification of the passion—for the erotic pleasure it affords them. In other words, negroes are purely animal." Shufeldt believed that blacks had a deep desire to have sexual relations with whites, so he warned all white women and children to be wary. He cautioned that black fiends might even "increase the size of the genital fissure by an ugly outward rip of his knife, a common practice among negroes when they assault little white girls." Like other racists, Shufeldt did not believe African Americans could change because they were "deteriorating morally every day...It is their nature, and they cannot possibly rid themselves of that, any more than skunks and polecats can cast away their abominable scent glands and the outrageous odor they emit."[40]

Charles Carroll weighed in on the subject in 1900 with his 382-page book *The Negro a Beast or In the Image of God*. The author informed his readers that it took him fifteen years to complete his "study." As the title indicates, Carroll sets out to prove that African Americans were subhuman and were made more in the image of "beasts" than of "God." He includes ten illustrations in his book depicting black children and adults with exaggerated features, to the point that they do not look human compared to the white images they are juxtaposed against. In an effort to dismiss miscegenation and the racially mixed offspring resulting from such liaisons, Carroll concluded that "the Negro belongs to the flesh of beasts, from the fact that his offspring by man, though mated continuously with negroes will not revert to the Negro, but approximates a lower grade of animal. Further evidence of this is found in the fact that the mixed bloods frequently develop characters which are never found in either the pure white or the pure Negro, but which are peculiar to lower grades of animals."[41]

Injecting God and the Bible into his racist ideology, Carroll went on to argue that "the great intellectual qualities which the men of this and preceding ages have displayed, are the result of inheritance from Adam, upon whom they were a divine bestowal. Hence, they are transmittable." However, "the low order of the Negro's mentality—his lack of inventive skill—is demonstrated by his meager accomplishments in his undomesticated state, which, has been shown, are confined to the fashioning of a few rude weapons of stone; while the greater achievements of the domesticated Negro are due solely to the influence of man." Of course, he meant the "white man." Then he concluded: "if from any cause he [blacks] is relieved of this influence and is thrown upon his own resources in the forest, he soon relapses into savagery and descends to the use of stones for weapons." This typified the argument Southern whites made against blacks suggesting that blacks benefited from slavery and had begun to degenerate since freedom. They saw slavery as redemptive, not exploitative.[42]

Similarly, Buckner Payne, a Nashville publisher, wrote in his postbellum work *The Negro, a Descendant of Ham?* that black people were neither descendants of human beings nor descendants of Ham. Instead, they were beasts. While "God had long before determined, that the Japhetic race should govern the world," he wrote, African Americans were destined to be at the bottom of society as evidenced by their history that "is as blank as that of the horse or a beaver." Payne went on to assert that blacks, unlike whites, had no souls. "The Negro, in fact, was an animal, the noblest beast of creation, but a beast, nevertheless. Because Negroes, like all other animals, must have been on the ark, and because Noah's all-white family were the only human beings on the ark, then the Negro must have been created along with the other beasts in the Garden of Eden," he reasoned.[43]

Like Payne, white ministers did not wait for "science" to prove black inferiority; they simply used the Bible to make their case. As explained by Johnson in *The Myth of Ham in Nineteenth-Century American Christianity: Race, Heathens, and the People of God* (2004), these preachers had long argued that people of African descent were subhuman. Amazingly, they took modern-day racial designations and read them back into biblical stories that existed years before there were any "races." Nonetheless, white clergymen came to argue that the races descended from Noah's three sons: Ham, Shem, and Japheth through whom the earth was repopulated after the great flood destroyed the remainder of mankind. Shem represented the Israelites (Jews); Japheth represented the white Anglo-Saxons (Gentiles), who in the late 1800s and early 1900s considered themselves to be a superior race; and Ham represented Africans, an inferior race. Based on their reading of the Bible, Shem and Japheth were blessed and promised an auspicious future, while Ham's descendants were supposedly *cursed* because Ham accidentally saw his father drunk and naked, and he laughed at him. They called this the "curse of Ham."[44]

"Race discourse concerned narrations that associated God with a *people*. Some people were people of God. Others were not; they were heathens," continued Johnson.[45] Furthermore,

American religious themes were founded upon the biblical story, and explanations of race identities were a subset of that worldview. The Bible in the post-Reconstruction era was, after all, just that—*the* Bible—not a collection of disparate ancient texts but a singular document comprising one continuous narrative...The Bible, furthermore, was not merely a book. It was the lens for understanding the world and the looking glass for glimpsing social (i.e., collective) selves. This is why black and white authors cited biblical narratives and genealogies to explicate (the fiction of) their racial histories. And they did so without the slightest hint of irony or qualm.[46]

Religious scholar Philip Schaff, a professor of church history and biblical literature at the Reformed Church in Mercersburg, Pennsylvania (later Lancaster Theological Seminary) and later a professor of church history at Union Theological Seminary in New York City around the turn of the twentieth century, believed that blacks were inferior to whites and that "God alone...will settle the Negro question." Reflecting on the past, he preached that slavery itself was a beneficent and absolutely necessary institution. As "a training school for the universal religion of the Gospel," Schaff averred, "slavery itself was controlled by God and would work to benefit

Ham's posterity in America." In fact, it had already lifted blacks "from the lowest state of heathenism and barbarism to some degree of Christian civilization." And, "if allowed to run its course, it would affect Ham's children's 'final deliverance from the ancient curse of bondage.'"[47]

These and other arguments chagrined African Americans of all classes and backgrounds. In 1891, Frederick Douglass became so disturbed by the claims that he asserted: "the Christianity of this country as exhibited in the Church is not the Christianity of Christ. It is a man-degrading and Negro-hating Christianity...and in its presence today, the Negro is robbed, lynched and murdered without rebuke or remonstrance from these Christian pulpits." Surely, large numbers of African Americans shared Douglass's sentiments and some whites recognized their dismay. For instance, Charles R. Winthrop, a white minister, lamented to prominent black clergyman Francis J. Grimke' that it had become very hard to persuade many young college-educated Negroes "that they can hope for much from Christianity." Thus, historian Jaqueline Moore correctly concludes that blacks found it "hard to stay involved with a church that did not recognize the rights of the race."[48]

Along with theologians, white medical doctors weighed in on the issue arguing that the condition of African Americans could be explained based on their anatomical and physiological inferiority. "Medical candor expressed racial contempt by promoting an image of the black as a degenerate and dilapidated creature whose improvement appeared to be a hopeless task, even for modern medicine and other agents of white benevolence," John Hoberman cogently explained. Moreover, Hoberman asserted that from the beginning, ideas about black inferiority have served "slave-based or colonial societies that formulate them by assigning certain capacities to blacks and denying that they possess whatever other capacities would enable them to transcend their lowly or even subhuman status. White characterizations of black racial biology have thus been a balancing act that concedes to slaves or servants the aptitudes that make them functional members of the social order they serve while withholding aptitudes that are reserved for whites alone."[49]

An example is found in an assertion by Dr. S. W. Douglas of Eudora, Arkansas, that blacks were too lazy and indolent to "take proper exercise." These types of claims by Southerners contradicted common knowledge that most black Americans survived only by hard labor, and that many performed countless feats of endurance and strength in their daily avocations. These contradictions

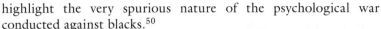

highlight the very spurious nature of the psychological war conducted against blacks.[50]

Furthermore, the idea of African American infirmity became deeply rooted in the racist system that prevailed in the United States by the end of the nineteenth century. Although the black population continued to grow, one of the most pervasive myths in American and some European anthropological and medical circles was that African Americans were becoming extinct. Auguste Laugel, a French geologist, sympathetic to Radical Republicanism, opined that the black race was "destined to disappear in the South." Frederick L. Hoffman, who published one of the most influential studies on the race question, believed "the time will come, if it has not already come, when the negro, like the Indian, will be a vanishing race." Similarly, Charles Gayarre', an unreconstructed Creole aristocrat from New Orleans, predicted that blacks would "die out in the end... of weak lungs and from want of congenial air in the more elevated regions to which he has been raised, and to which he cannot be acclimated...." And Paul B. Barringer, professor of medicine at the University of Virginia, concluded that "all things point to the fact that the Negro race is reverting to barbarism with the inordinate criminality and degradation of that state. It seems, moreover, that he is doomed at no distant day to ultimate extinction." White demagogues viewed this as a natural progression for an inferior race of "feeble exotics."[51]

Hoberman argues that "the extinction thesis served to establish the disastrous consequences of emancipation for the black population." It seems that belief in these ideas about blacks served a psychological and emotional need of white people. It suggested that as blacks disappeared, the "Negro problem" would eventually go away.[52] Clearly by 1900, Darwin's ideas had provided the basis for racist concepts that would prevail in the twentieth century.

To match all of that, one of the most insidious examples of the dehumanization of African people occurred, not in the South, but in New York City. On a "specimen gathering mission" for the World's Fair committee in the early 1900s, Samuel Phillips Verner, a white missionary, minister, and explorer, found Ota Benga, a young man in Congo, Africa, and brought him to the United States. First, he placed Ota on display at the Saint Louis Fair in 1904. Benga proved to be a real attraction with his shaved head and sharpened teeth. Some observers thought his teeth verified the practice of cannibalism among Africans. In September 1906, William T. Hornaday, director of the Bronx Zoological Gardens, placed Ota Benga on exhibit at the Bronx Zoo in New York City and caged him with an orangutan in the

"Monkey House" where he became an even bigger attraction. Bones were scattered around the cage to create the impression of savagery, danger, and cannibalism. A sign posted outside the cage read:

The African Pygmy, "Ota Benga,"

Age, 28 years. Height, 4 feet 11 inches.

Weight 103 pounds. Brought from the Kasai River,

Congo Free State, South Central Africa,

by Dr. Samuel P. Verner,

Exhibited each afternoon during September.

To a generation raised on Darwinist thought, some people described Ota as being the "missing link" in the table of evolution. According to the *New York Times*, "the pygmy was not much taller than the oranguatang and one had good opportunity to study their points of resemblance. Their heads are much alike, and both grin in the same way when pleased."[53]

Thousands of visitors came out to see the "Pygmy in the Zoo," helping to boost fledgling sales at the park. On September 16 alone, forty thousand visitors came to the park to get a glimpse of Ota. "Nearly every man, woman, and child of this crowd made for the monkey house to see the star attraction in the park—a wild man from Africa," the *New York Times* reported. "They chased him about the grounds all day, howling, jeering and yelling. Some of them poked him in the ribs, others tripped him up, all laughed at him." To add to the excitement, park keepers often coaxed Ota into charging the bars of the cage and opening his mouth wide to show his sharp teeth, all to the delight of the crowd.[54]

Fortunately, black ministers in New York and others came together and vehemently protested. They realized that the image Ota projected lent credence to scientific racists' argument that Africans and their descendents were subhuman. Reverend R. S. MacArthur, pastor of the Calvary Baptist Church, asserted in utter disgust that "the person responsible for this exhibition degrades himself as much as he does the African. Instead of making a beast of this little fellow we should be putting him in school for the development of such powers as God gave him...We send our missionaries to Africa to Christianize the people and then we bring one here to brutalize him." Another black clergyman, James H. Gordon, superintendent of the Howard Colored Orphan Asylum in Brooklyn and head of the Colored Baptist Ministers' Conference, asserted: "Our race, we think, is depressed enough without exhibiting one of us with the apes. We think we are worthy of being considered human beings, with souls." Due to these and other protests, along with the "unmanageable" behavior Ota began to manifest, park officials took Ota off display and removed him from the zoo before the end of the month. Ultimately this young man committed suicide before he could be transported back to Africa.[55]

African Americans responded in a number of ways to white efforts to exterminate them physically. Likewise, they resisted white attempts to assassinate their character, image, and manhood on a daily basis. Some blacks fought violence with violence, while others simply left the South and emigrated to the North, the West, and to Africa. William Monroe Trotter, Du Bois, and others organized protest groups while still other blacks lashed out through various newspapers and books of their own.

Recognizing that whites viewed Reconstruction as the menace to black advancement, Du Bois attacked this position in his study *Black Reconstruction in America: 1860–1880* (1935). Du Bois titled the last chapter of his book "The Propaganda of History," in which he exposed a number of writers and their antiblack Reconstruction histories. Du Bois convincingly argued that those histories were more emotional than scholarly. By contrast, his revisionist work showed that African Americans made a number of contributions during the era, but white American historians overlooked, misinterpreted, or refused to recognize them.[56] Du Bois certainly exercised the power of the pen in a most erudite fashion to defend black people's humanity.

Like Du Bois, Washington and his supporters, called Bookerites, responded to the challenges African Americans faced in a variety of ways. The following chapters will illuminate some of the ways they addressed these matters. However, first, it is essential to have a clearer understanding of the language used by Washington and his associates as they toured the South. A psychohistorical evaluation of how the Tuskegee Machine operated is also provided, adding further clarification to the meaning behind the message of Washington's educational tours.

CHAPTER 3

Booker T. Washington and the Psychology of "Black Survivalism"

We Wear the Mask

We wear the mask that grins and lies,
It hides our cheeks and shades our eyes,—
This debt we pay to human guile;
With torn and bleeding hearts we smile,
And mouth with myriad subtleties.

Why should the world be over-wise,
In counting all our tears and sighs?
Nay, let them only see us, while
We wear the mask.

We smile, but, O great Christ, our cries
To thee from tortured souls arise.
We sing, but oh the clay is vile
Beneath our feet, and long the mile;
But let the world dream otherwise,
We wear the mask!
                    Paul Lawrence Dunbar[1]

DIPLOMACY

In the broader sense, diplomacy means the thoughtful and careful consideration of words and ideas expressed to reduce the words and ideas to the level of being the least offensive, while they carry the force of what is desired to the maxim.

To be a diplomat, one has to be very careful in his expressions before indulging in them. He must think seriously and calculatingly so that his thoughts and words may have the desired effect without

arousing suspicion or inviting hostility. You must first be a very
skillful thinker and psychologist to be a diplomat. A diplomat
never reveals his true state of mind. He never reveals his hand in
dealing with a situation. He always keeps a line of defense for
whatever he says or does in reserve.

—*Marcus Garvey*[2]

The impact and role of Washington's contributions to racial uplift have been badly misunderstood, mostly because he operated in a fashion that is epitomized in Dunbar's "We Wear the Mask" poem and Marcus Garvey's teachings on diplomacy. Unfortunately, as Harlan wrote, "Washington's public image, which in time became a deception, was fixed in the minds of his generation by two highly publicized events, a speech and a book." People during his era knew Washington by his Atlanta Cotton States Exposition Address given in 1895 and his magnum opus, *Up from Slavery*, published in 1901. In the mid-1950s, Frenchman Edmund Bartelemy likened Washington to an Uncle Tom, labeling *Up from Slavery* "a new *Uncle Tom's Cabin*, equally captivating, but more modern and truer." This misperception gained currency by the 1960s, and black activists along with others assumed that Washington had been a sellout, a person willing to flush his own people down the drain for the betterment of whites. While nothing could have been further from the truth, most people have not taken time to study the subject sufficiently to learn otherwise. Only a few voices called out to the contrary. Washington's associate, William H. Lewis, for one, declared that the "Tuskegean was trying to bring the wooden horse inside the walls of Troy," showing that, during his era, Washington's allies at least understood his psychology and strategy. Today, however, many people, especially college-educated African Americans, tend to identify more closely with the "radical" teachings of Du Bois.[3] The writer's experience has been that many of these same individuals stubbornly refuse to modify their misperception of Washington, even when the evidence clearly shows a man who does not conform to an "accommodationist" model.

This common perception of the Tuskegean springs partly from seeds he planted himself. By the time he finished his studies at Hampton Institute in 1875, Washington believed that the problems facing blacks mostly would be solved through a program leading to economic independence. "It should be our highest ambition," he once declared, "to make the negro, first of all a property-holding, industrious, intelligent, virtuous citizen, and a Republican, or Democrat afterward."[4] These characteristics squared with late nineteenth- and early twentieth-century Victorian notions of manhood. If blacks produced goods and services that whites needed, the Tuskegee leader concluded, whites would patronize those blacks regardless of their color. Washington also thought that Southern whites needed to be persuaded that educating blacks served the interests of the South. He taught that African Americans should be law abiding and cooperative with whites when it came to maintaining peace. In addition, the Tuskegean believed that industrial education would provide blacks with an economic niche in the country that would not threaten or antagonize white Southerners.[5]

Many whites, then, misinterpreted the meaning of these beliefs by assuming that Washington condoned segregation and black inferiority. Southern whites also stretched the sense of his public pronouncements that minimized political and civil rights and higher education for blacks. Similarly, they thought that by discouraging political and social activism, Washington essentially encouraged blacks to stay in an inferior economic and social position in the South. By way of contrast, Northerners believed that Washington's teachings made for peaceful relations between the races in the South, while providing blacks with economic stability and the overall economic development of the Southern economy.[6]

Importantly for true understanding of the man, Washington knew firsthand the oppression and violence blacks experienced because of their race. Thus he, along with other members of the Tuskegee Machine, practiced what this writer calls a "black survival strategy" whereby they acted deferentially and in a conciliatory manner toward whites on the surface while keeping close their true thoughts, feelings, and various motives. According to Harlan, "While Washington publicly seemed to accept a separate and unequal life for black people, behind the mask of acquiescence he was busy with many schemes for black strength, self-improvement, and mutual aid." Bobby Lovett added, "Washington was masterful when playing on whites' racial prejudices. He knew which of their strings to pull; which ones to leave alone; and which battles to fight." Donald Calista reached a similar conclusion. "There was a drastic difference between Washington's public pronouncements and his private activity," he recorded, "and as he glad-handed likely white contributors for a Negro cause he surreptitiously worked towards undermining the American race system."[7]

Washington's approach should be judged for its results, rather than on grounds of deception. Washington and other blacks, Mel Watkins explained, "milked whites' egos and pocketbooks with ingratiating postures and affirmations of satisfaction with their inferior positions [because] outward accommodation of bigotry was a common means of circumventing restricted opportunities." Watkins went on to observe that

> For most ordinary people...such accommodation (as it had been during slavery) was often required for survival. Those employed as domestics almost universally adhered to a pragmatic philosophy of deceit that reaffirmed employers' views of blacks as an unambitious, simple (if not simpleminded), and contented lot. The façade not only elicited small favors but brought some measure of status in the black community; there the domestics' access to white society's material comforts was envied, and tales of employers' gullibility and arrogance were cherished as *a source of private humor*.[8] (emphasis mine)

Watkins illuminates the fact that blacks commonly understood this "private humor" while those outside of the community did not. He gave the following example to illustrate his point:

> Rufus Thomas, the black disc jockey and rhythm and blues singer, mirrored a common attitude among blacks when he recalled his tactics as a waiter in Nashville during the twenties. "During that time, the white fellow was quite boastful...he'd say all these things. But he'd pay well, pay well. At the end of the night, I had the money. I won't say that he was broke, but he'd splurged and I had the money. And so you ask yourself: 'Hell, who's the fool or who's stupid?' Because I had the money at the end of the night and that was what I was working for."[9]

In this period of ascendant Negrophobia, Washington and other Bookerites made comments about "good and harmonious relations" between blacks and whites in the South strictly for white consumption. These men did not believe the words, but understood that to survive in the South and make some advances, especially along economic lines, they had to play certain games and "wear the mask." As a result, while Washington oftentimes would finance efforts to undermine legal segregation, peonage, and other forms of black exploitation behind the scenes, he acquiesced publicly on these issues at times as a strategy to keep the support of the white majority and possibly for his own protection.[10] Indeed, "although only a few influential white men and women within the Tuskegee inner circle knew of it at the time," David Lewis concluded, "historians have now unearthed the Wizard's impressive record of secret civil rights maneuverings."[11]

On at least one occasion, Washington rescued a black man from danger, even when his decision to do so could have spelled disaster for

Tuskegee Institute. On the night of June 8, 1895, Thomas A. Harris, a black Tuskegee lawyer seen as a "militant" by local whites, ran to Washington's house on Tuskegee's campus fleeing a white mob out to kill him. Later, when the mob arrived at Washington's home, torches and guns in hand, his response was "characteristically devious." "He appeased the local whites by publicly seeming to turn the man away, while privately like a house servant fooling the master he helped the man to safety and a doctor," Harlan wrote. The Tuskegee leader knew that to survive "he had to be an artful dodger" and this incident "unquestionably deepened Washington's commitment to a life of duplicity, the only kind of life by which he could achieve his goals of power, influence, and security," Harlan concluded. Unsuspecting whites and even some blacks never thought that "ole Booker" was capable of such deception, trickery, and radical behavior, but those close to him fully understood his strategy and also practiced it.[12]

In explaining how African Americans in Mississippi survived the horrors of the Jim Crow era, Julius Thompson asserted that blacks "developed a 'mask' to wear for white society. A black minister might, for example, advise his congregation on ways to outwit the white man. But if the preacher met that man on the street, he would be outwardly polite and respond with 'Yes, sir' and 'No, sir.' There was one social self for whites and a real self shared only with other blacks," Thompson continued. "Resentment, however, ran deep among many blacks." Indeed, "this state of affairs would run deep in the black Mississippi psychological state of consciousness for many years to come."[13]

Certainly, these "secret maneuverings" and/or black survivalism did not begin during the Age of Booker T. Washington and was not peculiar to blacks in Mississippi. African Americans utilized all sorts of "tricksterism" during slavery for the same reasons they would during the Jim Crow era—to navigate the horrors of the peculiar institution and to secure the most they could from the system. Men such as Frederick Douglass, William Wells Brown, Lunsford Lane, and countless other blacks understood these traits. Douglass noted that while "the master studies to keep the slave ignorant, the slave is cunning enough to make the master think he succeeds." Lucy Ann Delaney asserted that enslaved blacks lived behind an "impenetrable mask" and wondered "...how much of joy, of sorrow, of misery and anguish have they hidden from their tormentors!"[14]

This practice so prevailed among African Americans that historian John Blassingame in his magnum opus *The Slave Community* (1979) concluded that most blacks carefully masked "their true personality traits from whites, while adopting 'sham' characteristics when interacting with them." Furthermore, "on innumerable occasions the slaves' public behavior contradicted their private attitudes." For example, in 1842, Charles C. Jones, a Georgia planter, conceded that "persons live and die in the midst of Negroes and [k]now comparatively little of their real character." Likewise, South Carolina planter Edward A. Pollard expressed astonishment at "how little the slaveholders of the South, despite their supposed knowledge of the Negro, really knew of what was in him."[15]

During the holocaust of African enslavement, slaveowners experienced firsthand frustration at the level of deception they encountered with their bondsmen. "To survive in an oppressive society," James Cone surmised, "it is necessary to outsmart the oppressors and make them think that you are what you *know* you are not." He commented further: "It is to make them believe that you accept their definitions of black and white." One black song puts it like this: "Got one mind for the boss to see; Got another mind for what I know is me."[16]

Indeed, blacks used both animal and human folktales to convey their methods of survival. Many a trickster tale emerged in the late 1800s and early 1900s when African Americans lowered the veil of secrecy that existed during slavery. In the tales, "John" (also called Golias, Jack, Nehemiah, Pompey, or Brer Rabbit) oftentimes outsmarted his slaveowner, thereby receiving better food, clothes, or other rewards. He also prevented some imminent calamity, foiled attempts at punishment for different indiscretions, or secured his freedom.[17]

An example helps to make the point. In one story "Ole Massa" had decided to hang "'ol' uppity John." So John (considered to be "one smart nigger") had another slave climb a tree and light a match each time John said: "let it lightning." When the owner took John to the tree, John's owner agreed to let him pray first. John then said, "O Lord...if you're gointer destroy Ole Massa, tonight, with his wife and chillum and everything he got, lemme see it lightnin." The slave in the tree lit a match, creating a lightning effect. Then Massa told John to stop praying, but he continued and the same thing happened again: the match illuminated the skyline. After John repeated the prayer a third time, "Ole Massa started to run. He gave John his freedom and a heap of land and stock." The story concluded: "he run so fast that it took a[n] express train running at the rate of ninety miles an hour and six months to bring him back, and that's how niggers got they freedom today."[18]

Many a tale portrays the strategy's success. "So deceitful is the Negro that as far as my own experience extends I could never in a single instance decipher his character," an antebellum Georgia planter complained. "We planters could never get at the truth." No doubt, slaves lied regularly to their owners to manipulate them and get things they wanted, even though some Massas never realized it. Most slaveowners, though, took slave deception as suggestive of reality and, consequently, believed blacks were really content. Thus, they failed to comprehend this seeming contentment as a black survival strategy. Lawrence Levine recounts one of these tales as reported by Jake Green, a former Alabama slave. Green said that a slaveowner once boasted to a visitor that his slave, John, "ain't never told me a lie in his life." So the traveller bet the man a little over $100 that John would lie to him.[19] The story continued:

> The next morning after breakfast, he put a live mouse in a covered dish and instructed the master to inform John that he could eat whatever food was left over but that he must not open the covered dish. The white men left and when they returned the master asked John if he had obeyed his orders. John swore he had, but when the traveler lifted the cover off the forbidden dish the mouse was gone. "See dere," he said triumphantly, "John been lyin' to you all de time, you jes' ain't knowed it." "An," [Jake] Green quickly added, "I reckon he right, 'caze us had to lie.'"[20]

In another folktale, John's owner did not realize that John had been eavesdropping outside his window, hearing his plans for the next day, then recounting what he had heard under the guise of fortune telling. John also hid things and then "discovered" the items when the owner needed them, thereby gaining a privileged position on the plantation. One day, John's owner boasted to another slaveowner about his slave's fortune telling powers, but the other man did not believe it and asserted that "dat nigger can't tell no fortunes. I bet my plantation and all my niggers against yours dat he can't tell no fortunes." On the day of the contest, the men hid a raccoon under a huge iron wash pot, after which Ole Massa said: "John, if you tell what's under dat wash pot Ah'll make you independently rich. If you don't, Ah'm goin' kill you because you will make me lose my plantation and everything I got." Fearing, at last, that his deceptions were going to be discovered, John, sweating profusely, walked around and around the wash pot, tapped it, put his ear to it, then confessed despairingly: "Well, you got de old coon at last." John's owner jumped for joy, while the other planter fell to his knees. "John, you done won another plantation fo' me. That's a coon under that pot sho 'nuff." John received a saddle horse and a new wardrobe, and he quit telling fortunes after that. Because of arrogance, misinterpretation, and misreads, the slaveowners never fathomed being manipulated by their "inferior" slaves.[21]

Long tradition thus stood behind Washington, who had spent his early years in slavery (along with Bookerites, and blacks in general), when he said things for white consumption. He (like Green) "had to lie." Harlan describes Washington as "neither a black Christ nor an Uncle Tom but a cunning Brer Rabbit, 'born and bred in the brier patch' of tangled American race relations. Here both white and black enemies were made to feel the secret stiletto of a Machiavellian prince." Clearly the support Bookerites received from white philanthropists, politicians, lawyers, and others would have been terminated if they had shown their true intentions, so the task of deceiving became a natural one for Bookerites as blacks had been using this strategy to manipulate whites for years. "Life itself seemed to prepare him [Washington] to wear this mask..." one writer on the subject opined, "but what went on behind this mask?" The writer added, "One thing seems certain—beneath his ingratiating manner boiled a man filled with contempt for the injustices done to his race by whites." The same author noted that "even his rival, Du Bois, remarked, 'actually Washington had no more faith in the white man than I do.' And how little that was."[22]

Historians have generally declined the opportunity to conduct extensive psychohistorical analysis of Washington's speeches and writings to determine their deeper meaning. To the contrary, scholars too often have taken a literalist approach to reading Washington, the Wizard of Tuskegee. Washington clearly used metalanguage (coded messages) that others have misinterpreted over the years.[23] Evelyn Brooks Higginbotham makes a compelling argument that by understanding these coded messages, we can analyze race and gender relations more adequately. She illustrates the point by discussing discrimination on Jim Crow railroads. First-class railcars also were called "ladies" cars. "Indeed, segregation's meaning for gender was exemplified in the trope of 'lady,'" Higginbotham writes. "Ladies were not merely women; they represented a class, a differentiated status within the generic category of 'women.'" She adds: "Nor did society confer such status on all white women. White prostitutes, along with many working-class white women, fell outside its rubric. But no black woman, regardless of income, education, refinement, or character, enjoyed the status of lady."[24]

A person reading African American history without that basic understanding obviously could draw erroneous conclusions. If they took "lady" for its dictionary meaning, African American women would qualify. However, when race is injected into the equation, black women become totally disqualified under any and all circumstances, reshaping the entire meaning of the word. By the same token, people who read the speeches and words of Washington without understanding his metalanguage have drawn erroneous conclusions. "Race impregnates the simplest meanings we take for granted," Higginbotham asserts. "It makes hair 'good' or 'bad,' speech patterns 'correct' or 'incorrect.'" Furthermore, she adds, "racial meanings were never internalized by blacks and whites in an identical way. The language of race has historically been...a double-voiced discourse—serving the voice of black oppression and the voice of black liberation." She concludes, "blacks took 'race' and empowered its language with their own meaning and intent, just as the slaves and freedpeople had appropriated white surnames, even those of their masters, and made them their own."[25]

Many times when Washington gave speeches during his Southern educational tours, he spoke of behaviors in the past tense that he wanted to see in the present and future. Oftentimes he and his supporters talked about white Southerners being black people's "best friends" and whites "doing all they could to help Negroes," but they said these things strictly for white consumption. By using this kind of metalanguage Washington wanted whites *to behave* in the manner he described, to live up to the expectation, and make it become a self-fulfilled prophecy. Psychologists Robert Rosenthal and Lenore Jacobson called this phenomenon the Pygmalion effect or the self-fulfilled prophecy "because a prophecy about behavior is often fulfilled." For instance, Rosenthal and Jacobson observed, "If teachers communicate the 'prophecy' that certain students will behave intelligently, those students may behave in the expected manner." If their theory is correct, the same could hold true for adults. Indeed, Washington and other Bookerites gave suggestive messages filled with "prophecy." Thus, their speeches remained a coded but tactful way of placing demands on whites without breaching the line of racial etiquette and insulting them outright by telling them what to do. This simply became another method of black survivalism used by African Americans to navigate the perils of Jim Crow, a way of trying to get white Southerners to live up to higher standards of decency. This is why Washington's speeches went over so well with blacks and whites.[26]

Washington naturally surrounded himself with Bookerites, people who shared his views and philosophy on racial uplift. An examination of how these men dealt with whites and what they said in their speeches and writings reveals a striking similarity between their comments and Washington's. John Merrick, a Bookerite and successful barber in North Carolina, clearly wore a mask of deception when dealing with whites. While cutting their hair he laughed at darkey stories and sometimes told his own. Nevertheless, according to Walter Weare, *African Americans understood* that Merrick could with "great poise, tip his hat to the white man and at the same time call him a son-of-a-bitch under his breath."[27] Speaking with forked tongues—flattery followed by displays of disrespect and contempt—provided a psychological release creating a false sense of equal footing. Nevertheless, this shows that blacks realized (even if whites did not) the necessity of employing black survivalism to advance in the South.

An analysis of the life of Charles Banks, Washington's "chief lieutenant" for Mississippi, provides an even more poignant example. Publicly, Banks asserted that whites who lived near him in the all-black town of Mound Bayou laid "no barriers in the way of the effort to build up a substantial and creditable Negro town and colony."[28] He once stated that, because of economic reasons, "the whites of [Mississippi] show a disposition to encourage and help this town and community." Banks believed that the people who learned about relations between blacks and whites in the South from newspapers and politicians "fall far short of knowing what really is possible for the Negro in the South." Moreover, "if there is any preference shown to Negroes any where, it seems to be to us [here in Mound Bayou]." Likewise, in a document Banks wrote on the history of Mound Bayou, he related that "the best feeling exists in this section between the races and always has."[29] When Banks penned these comments, however, he was writing to white men. His tone on similar issues differed sharply when he communicated with his black friends such as Washington and Emmett Jay Scott, Washington's personal secretary. Banks realized the advantages of wearing the mask of deception; thus, when dealing with whites, he made these remarks for white consumption only.[30]

A second Banks story illustrates the use of deception to accomplish specific goals. In that instance, Banks dealt with a white man named W. L. Park, vice president and general manager of the Illinois Central Railroad. Banks announced that "the Negro problem…is being…well handled by the white man in the south" and "the thoughtful and right thinking Negro co-operates [with the white man] necessarily." Banks also told Park that if he studied the work taking place at Mound Bayou, he would "most likely conclude that it has not only been worth while to the Negroes who have done the work here, but to the white neighbors as well who encouraged and helped us to gain this footing." In this case, like in numerous others, Banks knew that most Southern whites did everything but "encourage" and "help" them. However, his motive was not to reveal to Park his true feelings about race relations in the South but to convince him to invest in one of his enterprises at Mound Bayou.[31]

On yet another occasion, Banks illustrated to Washington how he could manipulate the thinking of whites to suit his own purposes. While on a trip giving an interview to a white reporter, the white man offered him money to cover his expenses. Banks did not take the money, however, telling the reporter that he "felt it would be out of place, or unjust to...accept." Finding an African American who would refuse money shocked the interviewer, especially since the "Southern Negro had been pictured to him as loving the coin so well." Banks noted, "As Franklin says in his Almanac, I may have paid a high price for the 'whistle' but I think it worth the while." He had not refused this money just because he thought it the proper thing to do. He felt that by doing so he could alter this white man's views of Southern blacks. Banks, commenting on the effectiveness of his strategy, asserted to Washington that the results were "drammatical and just what I aimed to do."[32]

Given a literal interpretation of his public statements, one could argue that Banks really believed that whites in Mississippi entertained genuine concern about progress in Mound Bayou. However, this interpretation seems fallacious. It is more likely that Banks used this strategy to pacify whites and keep them from raiding Mound Bayou.[33] If the townsmen could stay on the good side of influential whites, he reasoned, the all-black town would benefit in the long run. The examples of Tulsa, Oklahoma and Rosewood, Florida illustrate how white fury and vengeance could result in total destruction of black communities. In both cases, white mobs overran and ravaged these communities for crimes allegedly committed by only one African American.[34] It seems that some whites looked only for an excuse to eliminate these communities because they became a source of economic competition.

The white patronage strategy followed by Banks allowed him to accomplish many goals. Whites never came into Mound Bayou and molested the townsmen. However, the possibility of a white assault on the town occurred about 1913 when an unknown African American in Mound Bayou shot and killed Riley Griffin, a white man. Griffin and his son had been drinking, and they attacked the black man, who had been selling tickets at the town carnival. According to the *Memphis Commercial Appeal*, "Wednesday night was one of feverish anxiety among the negroes of this town, who feared nearby towns would attempt to retaliate." Fortunately, whites agreed that the killing had taken place in self-defense, and "both Negroes and white citizens of this county have joined to suppress any intimation of violence since the crime." Mound Bayou's leaders also requested the protection of the sheriff.[35]

At that point, Banks's carefully designed strategy paid off. While African Americans and whites rarely joined together in such a situation, a more "unusual happening for the south—a really unheard of thing [then occurred] in Mississippi." At Griffin's graveside, "just before 'ashes to ashes and dust to dust' was solemnly said, the white minister called upon Isaiah Montgomery [founder of Mound Bayou] to make some remarks which he did, speaking appropriately." In addition, many prominent blacks from Mound Bayou attended the funeral and Mound Bayou's Mayor B. Howard Creswell assisted in digging the grave at the request of the Griffin family. According to the newspaper, after the burial, "peace and tranquility" returned to Mound Bayou and the surrounding towns, "and the best white people and the best negroes are working harmoniously together for mutual good and mutual progress."[36] To understand the strategy of Mound Bayou's leadership, we need only recall the "black survival strategy" employed by Washington where he kept the support of his white patrons, while behind the scenes he vigorously fought against segregation.[37]

As a result of using this strategy, Banks and other Mound Bayou leaders won the respect of a number of influential whites, and they could count on an unheard of level of confidence when dealing with whites in general. In addition, a number of "good whites" supported Mound Bayou's leaders. For instance, Thomas Owen, a prominent white attorney in Cleveland and Rosedale, Mississippi, stated that the work carried on by Banks and others "meets the approval of the best white people and unquestionably is calculated to do great good among the negroes." Owen thought that Banks's approach to racial uplift would make Negroes "more useful citizens and [allow them] to engage in work that they are qualified to do as well as qualifying them for the work they will have to do." Supporting his earlier comments about the approval given to Banks by "the best whites," he closed by stating that "it is useless for me to say that the better class of white people of the state will endorse and do endorse the work that you are doing."[38]

Owen was not the only local white man to hold such opinions. L. K. Salsbury, president of a business in Memphis, said that he had high regard for Banks's judgment when it came to issues related to financial matters and as it related to "the needs of the negroes in the South." Salsbury continued, "I consider your judgment and ability and high standing not on[ly] with the colored people but [also] with the white people in the South" and believe that your leadership "is equal to, if not greater, than is that of Booker Washington." He went on to say that Banks's work at Mound Bayou and throughout the South aimed "to harmonize the white people and the negro, and to show to each that it is to their interest to teach the negro not only to farm scientifically, but to save his money and plan ahead for a rainy day...and is working wonders along that line."[39]

These statements help to explain why the leaders and residents at Mound Bayou did not have to worry about night riding or other assaults against them in their "Negro Metropolis." For their purposes, currying favor proved a successful strategy because ultimately they achieved their desired results in terms of staving off white assaults and gaining the support of good whites in their various endeavors. Many of the leaders in Mound Bayou such as Banks, consequently, managed to deviate from their "place" on a frequent basis. They had nice homes, carriages, clothing, and a number of other things that made them appear "uppity." These acts amounted to a serious breach in the code of racial etiquette and would not have been tolerated at all if they had lived in many predominantly white communities in Mississippi and most other places throughout the South.[40]

It should be noted specifically that Washington and other Tuskegee supporters did not view themselves as Uncle Toms or accommodationists. They believed in creating "policies and programs to deal with the imposition and problems of racism, rather than react with mere words or with the threat of retaliation" and "viewed their task as constructing a community and carving out space in a country inclined to keep them at the bottom of the social, political, and economic ladder." Ultimately, Washington and his supporters concluded that individual uplift, personal achievement, and steadfast allegiance to the struggle for black advancement would result in uplifting themselves and the race. Washington felt that the time had come for blacks to be less dependent on whites. "In fact," Donald Calista observed, "Washington's major concern was directed towards lifting the Negro personality out of its demoralized state by fighting to make the Negro more independent and self-reliant." He added, "So as the Tuskegee philosopher played his tune to the tempo of Southern temperament he carefully laid the foundation for the destruction of social inequality for Negroes." Calista further concluded that Washington, due to his emphasis on the separation of blacks from whites, "may even be thought of as a supporter of militant Negro nationalism." Washington became so successful in selling his racial philosophy to Southern whites that George Fredrickson concluded: "it would not be far from the mark to call them white Washingtonians."[41]

Among the signature features of Washington's Southern educational tours were the "plantation songs" sung at each venue, normally led by Major Robert R. Moton of Hampton Institute. Under Moton's direction, school choirs, quartets, and blacks in the audience joined in singing in ways that "only negroes can sing." The plantation songs, also called plantation melodies, sorrow songs, slave songs, and spirituals, were developed by African Americans during the holocaust of enslavement just like the trickster tales.[42] The Fisk Jubilee Singers, under the direction of George White, became internationally renowned for singing these songs. Many of White's students, like other blacks just a few generations from slavery, wanted to distance themselves from these plantation melodies. Ella Sheppard, who sang with the Jubilee Singers, recalled that the group had no intention of singing slave spirituals. "The slave songs ... were associated with slavery and the dark past, and represented things to be forgotten," she wrote. But at the same time she realized that "they were sacred to our parents who used them in their religious worship and shouted over them."[43] Sheppard described how her view of the songs changed.

> We finally grew willing to sing them privately ... We did not dream of ever using them in public. Had Mr. White suggested such a thing, we certainly had [sic] rebelled. After many months we began to appreciate the wonderful beauty and power of our songs; but continued to sing in public the usual choruses, duets, solos, etc. Occasionally two or three slave songs were sung at the close of the concert. But the demand of the public changed this order. Soon the land rang with our slave songs.[44]

Indeed, as the Fisk Jubilee Singers traveled around giving performances to raise money for their school, they were greeted with cordial applause. However, when they sang spirituals at the end of their concerts, they received much greater enthusiastic applause. It did not take long for White to determine that the patrons, most of whom were white, wanted to hear these songs, so he gave them what they wanted. This allowed him to raise the much needed funds for Fisk.[45]

A study of these plantation songs by religious historian James Cone reveals interesting insights. He argues that these spirituals were coded and meant one thing to whites but something totally different to blacks. Certain understanding and interpretation of these songs could only be comprehended by those who shared and participated in the experience that created them. "Black music must be *lived* before it can be understood," Cone asserted. While he did not deny that any scholar could analyze "objective" data on black music and history, he contended that "there is a deeper level of experience which transcends the tools of 'objective' historical research. And that experience is available only to those who share the *spirit* and participate in the *faith* of the people who created these songs." Amiri Baraka made a similar point: "The God spoken about in the black songs is not the same one in the white songs. Though the words might look the same. (They are not even pronounced alike.) But it is a different quality of energy they summon." Along the same lines, James Haskins asserts that "the slaves learned to give double-meaning to the religious songs they sang. Quite a few Negro spirituals contain messages that white slave masters did not suspect and certainly did not anticipate."[46]

These spirituals were functional for blacks, and their aims and purposes were directly related to black consciousness. "Black music is unity music. It unites the joy and the sorrow, the love and the hate, the hope and the despair of black people," Cone said, "and it moves the people toward the direction of total liberation." John Lovell adds to our depth of understanding of black spirituals by demonstrating that they were essentially social, not merely religious. Lovell suggests that spirituals were "the slave's description and criticism of his environment" and "the key to his revolutionary sentiments and to his desire" to become free.[47] According to Cone,

Lovell's concern was not to question the integrity of slave religion but to relate it to the social life of the black slave striving for freedom in this life. He perceived three central themes in the black spiritual: (1) a desire for freedom; (2) a "desire for justice in the judgment upon his betrayers"; and (3) "a tactic battle, the strategy by which he expected to gain an eminent future."

Drawing upon these themes, Lovell interpreted references to Satan, Jesus, and heaven as concrete possibilities for earthly freedom. Satan was "the people who beat and cheat the slave," and King Jesus was "whoever helps the oppressed and disfranchised or gives him a right to his life." "Hell [was] often being sold South," and "Jordan [was] the push for freedom." In the spirituals "I Got Shoes," "When I Get to Heaven," "Swing Low," and "My Lord Delivered Daniel," the black slave was "tearing down a wreck and building a new, solid world, and all along we thought he was romanticizing."[48]

Cone and Lovell agree that these plantation songs represented "the story of black people's historical strivings for earthly freedom, rather than the otherworldly projections of hopeless Africans who forgot about their homeland." Hence the spiritual "Steal Away," sung in the early 1800s, became a coded message for enslaved Africans to convene secret meetings. In the song "Go Down Moses," a message of struggle, hope, and liberation arises out of the lyrics, and when blacks sung the song they thought of themselves, not the Israelites.

> Go down, Moses
> Way down in Egypt land,
> Tell ole Pharaoh, to let my people go.
>
> When Israel was in Egypt land:
> Let my people go,
> Oppressed so hard they could not stand,
> Let my people go.

During the Jim Crow era, "Pharaoh" meant white politicians, white policemen, white women, white lawyers, white judges, white businessmen, and white Southerners in general.[49]

According to Cone, black spirituals tended to focus on biblical passages that stressed "God's involvement in the liberation of the oppressed people." Thus, when blacks sung about Moses leading the Israelites out of bondage and Daniel in the lions' den, they were emphasizing "God's liberation of the weak from the oppression of the strong, the lowly and the downtrodden from the proud and mighty." Cone concluded: "The spiritual, then, is the spirit of the people struggling to be free; it is their religion, their source of strength in a time of trouble. And if one does not know what trouble is, then the spiritual cannot be understood."[50]

So it was for those African Americans turning out to hear Washington speak. Because of their shared experience, blacks identified with and decoded Washington's messages in ways virtually impossible for whites and others outside of their cultural experiences to understand. For whites to fully accept that blacks commonly carried out this type of trickery and deception would mean they would have to lessen their inflated egos and reconsider their ideas of superiority. Instead, they would have to concede that not only did blacks have the capacity, but also the tendency to engage in this type of ruse, and that reality remained difficult, if not virtually impossible, for them to accept.

Nonetheless, blacks utilized all of these survival mechanisms reflexively during the era of Jim Crow. The children and grandchildren of ex-slaves learned how to adapt to their situation and make the most of their lives, which meant learning how to survive the obstacles of the South. Some whites who attended Washington's speeches on these tours were elated to hear the "ol' darkeys" singing plantation songs as they thought that blacks were reminiscing about the "good old days" of slavery. Generations of white children in the South remembered being sung to sleep by these spirituals by the black women who raised them, and many were pleased to see new generations of blacks joining in with singing these plantation melodies.[51]

The songs were a salve for the white heart and mind, and they greased the way for Washington. But white Southerners did not understand that these melodies constituted protest instruments. Spirituals gave blacks hope that better days were coming and that God was on their side against the tyranny and terror of white oppression. Even after slavery, these spirituals remained songs of freedom, protest, and liberation to be used against peonage, lynching, black codes, disfranchisement, educational inequality, and other injustices that came with Jim Crow. In a word, they offered another component of black survivalism used by Washington.[52] No doubt, the Tuskegean was practical and calculating; he perfected the art of wearing the mask.

Most Southern blacks, understandably, did not welcome anyone coming into their communities intent upon stirring up strife among the races. Washington insisted that he took educational tours of the South to "bring about more helpful relations between white men and black men in the communities [he visited]." Black leaders who took more aggressive approaches and openly denounced whites risked being killed or chased out of town before sundown. The experiences of outspoken preacher-activist Bishop Henry McNeal Turner makes the point. Turner wrote inflammatory essays and gave "seditious" speeches at his own risk during this era. He even encouraged African Americans to arm themselves for self-protection. According to his contemporary and first biographer, Mungo M. Ponton, Turner became "the most fearless and outspoken Negro of his times or any other times." Moreover, "no man of our race has ever said so many harsh, unvarnished and biting things about the white American and lived to repeat it. There have been times when it seemed that his radicalism meant death to him," Ponton concluded.[53]

These assertions by Ponton contained merit. Indeed, to avoid becoming a lynching victim, a contemporary recorded, "Turner slept in the woods, [to avoid] mobs after him." The man added: "Mobs have stood under trees that he had climbed to hide himself. He has jumped ditches and been covered with mail sacks; he has stood in the woods on the side of the railroad that he might flee for his life."[54] Once when Turner traveled to Opelika, Alabama, to help establish an African Methodist Episcopal (AME) Church, he received a tip that a lynch mob planned to kill him when he exited the train. To avert this, the wily Turner, a light-skinned man, successfully joined the mob and helped its members to look for their intended prey.[55]

Washington, adopting an approach that differed markedly from Turner's, mastered the art of double-talk because he realized that for blacks to survive in the South, they had to understand white psychology and behavior. Naturally, powerless people tend to adjust to those who are in power in order to ensure their own survival. In *My Larger Education* published in 1911, Washington spoke to the point. In a chapter entitled "What I Have Learned from Black Men," he observed that supporters such as Moton "know more about the Southern white man than anybody else on earth." In other words, the experiences blacks shared gave them special insight when dealing with whites. "This thorough understanding of both races which Major Moton possesses," the Tuskegean commented, enabled him to give "the sort of practical and helpful advice and counsel *that no white man who has not himself faced the peculiar conditions of the Negro could be able to give*" (emphasis mine). On another occasion, he asserted that blacks knew certain things that were "rarely known or understood by any one outside of the Negro race." This clearly illustrates Washington's belief that blacks were "privileged" to certain understanding, incomprehensible to whites, just by virtue of living as African Americans.[56]

In his Pulitzer winning autobiography of W. E. B. Du Bois, David Lewis asserts that " 'Pitchfork Ben' Tillman, Tom Watson, James Vardaman, and the South's other redneck populists went to their graves never suspecting that much of the organized resistance to the extinction of the African-American as a civil being originated in the upstairs study of Tuskegee's principal."[57] This assertion, however, is not totally accurate. Ironically, outspoken racial demagogues—men such as Senators Ben Tillman of South Carolina, Hoke Smith of Georgia, James K. Vardaman of Mississippi, and novelist Reverend Thomas Dixon, Jr.—came close to piercing Washington's veil of deception. This may account for some of the vitriolic hatred they felt for the Tuskegee principal. Once an apprehensive white Southerner wrote that "whenever Professor Washington aspires for the negro a place not inferior in some sense to the humblest white man's place, he challenges the embattled, inflexible and on this point, absolutely unmerciful Anglo-Saxon." On another occasion, when a reporter asked Vardaman what he really thought of Washington, he called the Tuskegean "a smart man." However, in the next breath he said he viewed Washington as "a fraud & a liar." Vardaman then asserted, "BTW has one practice in the South another in the North—showing him a hypocrite."[58]

In 1905, Washington conceded as much. "When in the South I conform like all colored people to the customs of the South," he explained, "but when in the North, I have found it necessary...to come into contact with white people in the furtherance of my work in ways I do not in the South." Other white supremacists agreed that if blacks followed Washington's philosophy of racial uplift, they ultimately would become less dependent on whites. One white critic of Washington's in Mississippi contended all along that if blacks followed the Tuskegean's advice to buy homes and property, secure an education for themselves and their children, and so forth, they would become equal to whites.[59]

Surprisingly, Reverend Thomas Dixon, Jr., author of the popular novel *The Clansman*, actually pierced Washington's veil of deception, describing him as a "little ragged, barefooted picaninny who lifted his eyes from a cabin in the hills of Virginia, saw a vision and followed it." Dixon gave a fascinating critique of the Tuskegean's racial uplift strategy. In an August 1905 magazine article entitled "Booker T. Washington and the Negro: Some Dangerous Aspects of the Work of Tuskegee," Dixon argued that "Washington is not training Negroes to take their place in any industrial system of the South in which the white man can direct or control him. He is not training his students to be servants and come at the beck and call of any man." Even worse, "he is training them *all* to be masters of men, to be independent, to own and operate their own industries, plant their own fields, buy and sell their own goods, and in every shape and form destroy the last vestige of dependence on the white man for anything," Dixon warned. Dixon also cautioned that the independent black nation hoped for by Washington would be dangerous and eventually would lead to the fall of America. The reverend maintained that blacks were brought to America for one reason—to work for Southern white men. But, he lamented that "every pupil who passes through Mr. Washington's hands ceases forever to work under a white man. Not only so, but he goes forth trained under an evangelist to preach the doctrine of separation and independence."[60]

Dixon wondered if Southern white men would continue to disregard his assertions. "Does any sane man believe that when the Negro ceases to work under the direction of the Southern white man," Dixon queried, that "this 'arrogant,' 'rapacious,' and 'intolerant' [white] race will allow the Negro to master his industrial system, take the bread from his mouth, crowd him to the wall and place a mortgage on his house?" Then the clincher: "Competition is war—the most fierce and brutal of all its forms. Could fatuity reach a sublimer height than the idea that the white man will stand idly by and see this performance? What will he do when put to the test? He will do exactly what his white neighbor in the North does when the Negro threatens his bread—kill him!"[61] Just as amazing as these extremist attempts to pierce the Tuskegee leader's secret veil is the fact that for some people Washington's deception holds fast even today, nearly one hundred years after his death.

In the end, white extremists' hatred for blacks remained so strong that although some may have pierced Washington's veil of secrecy and realized his approach to racial uplift would be "dangerous" to white supremacy, they would not endorse the strategy advocated by the Tuskegean or his detractors because they felt threatened by both philosophies. However, as strange as it may sound, Dixon and men of his ilk could have viewed some of the positions argued by the Tuskegean's adversaries as being more tolerable. For instance, unlike Washington, many assimilationists and integrationists urged blacks to work within the system for political and civil rights. Some racist demagogues considered this approach less threatening because they understood that in pursuing those rights, whites would be the final arbiters. In other words, these "rednecks" believed that as long as African Americans took that posture, whites would be in the dominant position to determine their fate. By contrast, and based on comments by Dixon and others, they remained suspicious of Washington believing that his approach would liberate African Americans economically and thus make them less dependent on whites.[62] Indeed, several decades passed before whites in Congress, after considerable pressure from the black community, decided to extend civil and voting rights to African Americans.[63]

With that said, by 1915, the year that he died, not only had Washington begun to speak out more boldly against lynching, he also had disavowed segregation and its negative consequences completely. In an article published posthumously by the *New Republic*, Washington asserted, "Personally I have little faith in the doctrine that it is necessary to segregate the whites from the blacks to prevent race mixture." Then he gave six reasons why he felt that way: "1) It is unjust. 2) It invites unjust measure. 3) It will not be productive of good, because practically every thoughtful negro resents its injustice and doubts its sincerity. 4) It is unnecessary. 5) It is inconsistent. 6) There has been no case of segregation of Negroes in the United States that has not widened the breach between the two races."[64]

Although Washington underestimated the grip of white supremacy in thinking that economic uplift would lead to political rights for African Americans, Robert Norrell has concluded correctly that the Tuskegean "worked too hard to resist and overcome white supremacy to call him an accommodationist, even if some of his white-supremacist southern neighbors so construed some of his statements." The "protest-versus-accommodation dichotomy," Norrell continued, "has functioned as virtually a Manichaean divide in writing about African American leadership. The tendency to make protest leaders the good guys and accommodators the bad guys reflects the sentiments at large in society since the Civil Rights Movement." Indeed, few African American leaders have failed to engage in some form of protest. However, "it is only by comparing degrees of protest commitment, or preferring certain styles of protest to others, that distinctions are drawn (and often overdrawn)," Norrell explained.[65]

The substance of Washington's actions, when compared with the protest agenda put forward by the NAACP, appear fundamentally similar. Washington publicly protested against lynching, discriminatory funding in education, discrimination on trains, discriminatory voting systems, segregated housing laws, and labor union discrimination. Moreover, he personally arranged or partially financed lawsuits challenging jury discrimination, peonage, and disfranchisement. Simultaneously, he vigorously worked to counter the pernicious images projected in popular culture and the media about blacks, including the 1915 film *Birth of a Nation*, based on *The Clansman*. This provides one reason why Washington worked so diligently to persuade the public that African Americans were progressing, not degenerating.[66]

Following Du Bois's interpretations, many historians have confused the style with the substance of Washington's program, just as much as they have missed the point of his lectures. According to Norrell, "historians have shown a narrow-mindedness about black leaders' styles: African American leaders must always be 'lions' like Frederick Douglass, Du Bois, Martin Luther King Jr., or Jesse Jackson. They cannot be 'foxes' or 'rabbits,' else they will be accused of lacking manhood." He argued further that "on the level of sound logic, historians must be honest in recognizing that protest has yielded the desired results more episodically than consistently. Other strategies for change have worked better at times, and external influences have also been the prime determinant of change at some points." Therefore, Norrell concluded, "It is misleading to teach that change is the result exclusively, or even predominantly, of protest."[67]

Washington embarked on educational pilgrimages as part of the orbit of the Tuskegee Machine, not only for himself, but also for the race. He desired to publicize the good and bad conditions that blacks faced throughout the South, in order to prod those who could to act. He yearned to place black progress and black manhood on display at a time when white Southerners and Social Darwinists claimed that blacks were drifting backward into barbarism. His active role in promulgating the counterimage of the "Negro as beast" is unmistakable. His ability to double-talk made Washington's presentations a smashing success. If nothing else, the Tuskegee leader's appearances in small hamlets, towns, and cities throughout the South added to the quality of life for blacks by stimulating African American business and educational development, and providing real live examples of black progress and manliness. No doubt, these things caused some whites to experience anxiety and self-doubt. Although white men established a system to reinforce their position of social, economic, and political supremacy, black progress made some white men in particular question their own manhood. The chapters that follow demonstrate these facts.

CHAPTER 4

Tour of the Magnolia State, October 1908

African Americans suffered extreme terror in the Magnolia State around the turn of the century. Neil McMillen called Mississippi the "heartland of American Apartheid." Racial discrimination so prevailed in Mississippi at the end of Reconstruction that some whites there did not see the need for Jim Crow legislation. Blacks and whites in the state were separated in private and public hospitals and did not use the same entrances to state-funded healthcare facilities. Black and white criminals were not even incarcerated in the same prison cells. In Mississippi, racial segregation largely became a matter of custom, and the state "seems to have had *fewer* Jim Crow laws during the entire segregation period than most southern states," noted McMillen.[1]

There were some instances, nonetheless, in which black and white Mississippians worked closely together in the post-Reconstruction period. When William C. Handy, father of the blues, visited Clarksdale, Mississippi, in 1903 he marveled that the white Clarksdale bank had a black assistant cashier. He noted that he "had never seen [anything like this] before in all my travels." Such situations, however, were the exception rather than the rule. In most cases, the "place" of black Mississippians was carefully proscribed and fully understood by both races.[2]

Indeed, wherever they turned, African Americans in Mississippi faced segregation. More often than not, Jim Crow customs required not merely separation but exclusion. At funerals, public facilities, weddings, courtrooms, and other places of social gathering, habit dictated the races would never integrate. The racial code prohibited any form of interracial activity that might have implied equality. Nevertheless, blacks were not as concerned about integration as they were about having access to the facilities.[3] McMillen asserted that the years between 1889 and 1919 were "among the most repressive in

Mississippi history."[4] On numerous occasions, a breach in the code of racial etiquette by African Americans led to swift and irrevocable punishments. Blacks in Mississippi met with "indescribable cruelties" from white mobs. Some were drowned, torched, bludgeoned, dragged to death behind automobiles, tortured to death with hot irons, and publicly burned at "Negro Barbecues." Blacks were also victims of whitecapping in Mississippi where night-riding whites burned and shot into their homes, trampled their crops, and forced them off of their own land, especially African Americans who sought economic independence. Whitecaps beat, maimed, burned, and lynched black people without reservation.[5]

Between 1900 and 1909, 144 African Americans were lynched in Mississippi, 3 of whom were women. In early 1904, a most horrendous lynching occurred in Mississippi. Whites suspected Luther Holbert, an African American sharecropper, of murdering a white plantation owner near Doddsville, close to Sunflower County. Holbert and his wife tried to escape but were captured. With more than one thousand spectators witnessing, some drinking whiskey, lemonade, and eating hard-boiled eggs, the Holberts were inhumanely tortured before they were barbecued.[6] After being tied to a tree,

> [They] were forced to hold out their hands while one finger at a time was chopped off [and] distributed as souvenirs. [Their] ears were cut off. Holbert was beaten severely, his skull was fractured, and one of his eyes, knocked with a stick, hung by a shred from the socket...The most excruciating form of punishment consisted in the use of a large corkscrew in the hands of some of the mob. This instrument was bored into the flesh of the man and woman, in the arms, legs, and body, and then pulled out, the spiral tearing out big pieces of raw, quivering flesh every time it was withdrawn.[7]

Economically, African Americans were confronted with conditions similar to those they faced during slavery. At the start of the twentieth century, Mississippi was one of the poorest states in the Union, and the old planter class worked diligently to maintain an economic system that kept black people dependent. Through sharecropping and peonage, this is precisely what happened. In short, the economic situation for blacks remained about as bleak as it had been before the Civil War.[8] After 1877, African Americans' political rights were taken away through fraud, intimidation, and outright murder. In 1890, Mississippi legislators called a constitutional convention and disfranchised blacks. They imposed poll taxes, literacy requirements, and prohibited voting for those who had been convicted of perjury, theft, bribery, arson, or burglary. Following Mississippi's lead, other Southern states began enacting similar laws to deny suffrage to African Americans.[9]

Mississippi's Governor James K. Vardaman affirmed the position of most white Mississippians when he wrote that he opposed "the nigger's voting, it matters not what his advertised moral and mental qualifications may be. I am just as much opposed to Booker Washington's, with all his Anglo-Saxon reinforcements, voting as I am to voting by the cocoanut-headed, chocolate-colored typical little coon, Andy Dotson, who blacks my shoes every morning. Neither one is fit to perform the supreme functions of citizenship." Vardaman even wanted to repeal the Fifteenth Amendment, which, he said, "gave the nigger the right to pollute politics."[10]

The educational picture looked just as bad for blacks in the Magnolia State. Although African Americans paid a disproportionate share of public school expenses, they received little in return. Mississippi held the shameful distinction of being the Southern state that spent the least amount of money on black education. In 1900, African American children received only 19 percent of the state's funds for education although they accounted for at least 60 percent of the school-age population. Whites believed that if they could limit the educational achievements of blacks, they could also stifle their political, economical, and social aspirations.[11]

Washington visited Jackson, Natchez, Vicksburg, and Greenville in early October 1901 at the request of the trustees of the John F. Slater Board. While there, he discussed the importance of education, proper relations between the races, correct moral habits, securing land, building decent homes, and practicing economy, thrift, and industry. Although he went to Mississippi intending to speak only to African Americans, whites surprised him by attending every meeting. Numerous blacks impressed Washington with the progress they were making at the time of his visit; for instance, Natchez businessman Louis Kastor owned the city's largest saddle and harness store; Greenville had an African American on the police force. In Vicksburg, the Tuskegean stayed at the home of Wesley Crayton, an African American liquor dealer who had served as a delegate to the first NNBL convention in 1900. "I had not been in this home five minutes before the lady of the house asked me if I would not like to inspect her kitchen and pantry," Washington mused. "And I found everything in the kitchen as neat and intelligently arranged as one would expect to find in a home in New England." He met with successful black lawyers in Vicksburg and Natchez who told him "they feel their color does not prevent them from being treated with fairness in the courts." In Jackson, Washington saw African Americans conducting all sorts of business and found them owning "their own homes more largely than is true of any other city I have visited."[12]

These experiences deeply impressed Washington and reinforced his belief that economic uplift would be the most feasible path to political and social justice for his race. The successful businessmen he met during his visit "cast their votes without question, and have them counted," he said. Washington therefore reasoned that

> these few colored men really exercise more influence in politics than the masses who voted without restraint a few years ago, for the reason that their votes were in most cases freely counted out or in some way gotten rid of.[13]

Then the clincher,

> I may be mistaken, but I am led to feel that gradually, as our people get property and intelligence, become conservative, and learn the lesson of casting their fortune in every honorable way with their neighbors, they are not going to be refused an opportunity to vote.[14]

Until his death, Washington continued to cling to the efficacy of economic uplift expecting it to eventually lead to full political participation.

While in Mississippi, Washington received an invitation from President Theodore Roosevelt that would forever enhance the Tuskegean's image among most blacks, while damaging his reputation with many whites. Roosevelt invited the Tuskegee leader to dinner at the White House. According to Harlan, this dinner "was the final crown of success that secured his [Washington's] position as virtual monarch of the black people in the United States." On October 16, Washington wired his reply to Roosevelt: "My dear Mr. President—I shall be very glad to accept your invitation for dinner this evening at seven-thirty."[15] The Tuskegean hurried off to Washington, DC, and went to the home of Whitefield McKinlay, a local African American friend and realtor. McKinlay handed Washington Roosevelt's invitation for dinner that actually began that evening at eight o'clock.[16]

As news of this dinner became public, the media swarmed around this story like bees on honey. The president had breached the South's code of racial etiquette, and some vowed to never forgive him. Lerone Bennett asserted that the two major taboos in the Jim Crow South were interracial eating and interracial marriage. "Anything approaching interracial eating was proscribed. Anything which might by any stretch of the imagination lead to intermarriage was interdicted…" Why? Bennett concluded that "the root rationalization for all this was sex."[17] One Mississippian affirmed Bennett's point about these taboos in 1901 arguing that by having dinner with Washington, Roosevelt had "given his stamp of approval to social equality, and proclaimed to the world that the son of Booker Washington is good enough to be the son-in-law of Theodore Roosevelt."[18]

White Mississippians certainly lashed out at Roosevelt and Washington for this affair. The *Biloxi Daily Herald* asserted that "the most damnable outrage which has ever been perpetrated by any citizen of the United States was committed by the president when he invited a negro to dine with him at the white house."[19] Some saw clear political implications in the dinner. "After such an incident a respectable Republican party in the South is out of the question," one Mississippian wrote. "The South must remain as it has been solidly Democratic, and it may be that there are respectable Republicans in the North who will resent the attempt to force social equality upon them, and will repudiate the President who practices it, and his party."[20] Mississippians informed Roosevelt that any future effort to woo Southern converts to the Grand Old Party (GOP) would be futile and racial demagogue Vardaman, a Democratic leader, "accused Roosevelt of coddling a 'nigger bastard' for political advantage."[21] Another perturbed white Southerner wrote: "I have more respect for the blackest, rankest-smelling chicken thief in Mississippi than I have for the occupant of the White House. He has put himself so low in my estimation that he would disgrace the funky smell of an unwashed corn-field nigger."[22]

White Southerners expressed the same vitriol toward Washington. They felt betrayed by the Tuskegean, as he had always spoken out against social mingling. They recalled the one line in his Atlanta speech when he said that in matters social "we can be as separate as the five fingers." "I am surprised that the invitation should have been extended," one Southerner admitted, but "I am more surprised that the nigger should have accepted it. I thought better of Booker." Then in an effort to expose what he considered Washington's true objectives, this person wrote: "It shows the aim, ambition and end of Booker Washington's work. I have contended all along that social equality was the end to which Washington and his pusillanimous ilk were striving. He has advised the members of his race to so live, accumulate property, educate themselves, and when they should become fortified and entrenched that they could then enforce the recognition of their rights, etc." Ultimately, this writer could not believe Roosevelt "had no more decency than to take a nigger into his home." This white man felt betrayed by Washington because he believed "that nigger had too much sense to be caught in such a trap."[23]

These criticisms soon turned to talk of violence with Mississippians predicting "the feasting of Booker Washington by the President will be the cause of many darkies getting into trouble..."[24] Others thought the dinner "will simply result in the death of a score or more Negroes, who emboldened by the mad act of a fool President will presume to make demands that will be answered with pistol shots. And the blood of these misguided creatures will be on Roosevelt's hands."[25] Finally, another person wrote that "the action of President Roosevelt in entertaining that nigger will necessitate our killing a thousand niggers in the South before they will learn their places again."[26]

In 1906, several years after the White House incident, Charles Banks, president of the Mississippi State Negro Business League (MSNBL), began urging Washington to return to his state.[27] Washington eventually agreed and in October 1907, asked his chief lieutenant for the state, Banks, to coordinate the tour. Washington knew of Banks's superior organizational skills, which is one reason he frequently solicited his support when it came to organizing different efforts. Born in Clarksdale, Mississippi, in 1873 to parents who were slaves, Banks became the most powerful African American in the state by 1910. He received his early education in the Coahoma County school system and later attended Rust University (now Rust College) in Holly Springs, Mississippi. Banks started his first business, a mercantile operation, at the age of sixteen and remained self-employed throughout his life. In fact, he excelled so much in business that one of his contemporaries penned that "he always liked the jingle and clink of the dollars of commerce, and their sound is as pleasing to his ears as the rhapsody of a Beethoven sonata."[28]

A Republican Party leader in his state, Banks also founded the Bank of Mound Bayou in 1904 and worked as its cashier. He cofounded the Mound Bayou Oil Mill and Manufacturing Company and became its general manager, and he owned a blacksmith shop, a cotton brokerage company, a laundry, a mercantile business, a land speculation business, and more. In addition, he held considerable property in Mississippi, Tennessee, and Arkansas. Washington was so impressed with Banks's business savvy that he called him "the most influential Negro businessman in the United States," and although there were eleven black-owned banks in Mississippi at the time, Washington considered Banks "the leading Negro banker in Mississippi." Banks and Washington first met at the inaugural meeting of the NNBL in Boston in 1900; after which, he became third vice president, then first vice president of the NNBL, second in command only to Washington. Banks also founded the MSNBL in 1905, reputedly the strongest league in the association, and served as its president for almost two decades.[29]

Banks serves as a prototype of the kind of leaders with whom Washington affiliated and to whom he entrusted the success of his program of racial uplift. Washington and his "lieutenants," like Banks, shared the same philosophy of racial uplift and dealt with whites the same way; that is, they often "wore the mask." For instance, once when Banks invited whites to a ceremony in Mound Bayou, the town where he resided, he expressed conciliatory views toward them in a circular letter. He noted that while blacks in the town were making progress and doing positive things, "the thinking ones among us realize that this progress could not have been made without the aid, indulgence, kindly feelings and help of our white friends." Moreover, he said, "in many respects what we have done here is as much a compliment to the white man under whose supervision and direction we are, as it is to the *negro*" (emphasis mine). However, Banks deliberately used a lowercase "n" when spelling the word "Negro" in this circular because it went to whites. He generally did not do this when writing to blacks or "white friends."[30]

Some historians have mistakenly interpreted words and acts like these by Bookerites as "accommodation." However, an analysis of many personal and confidential letters written by Banks indicate that he said many of these things for white consumption only, and evidence suggests he really did not believe them. He used these tactics to manipulate whites and to achieve his goals. This can be called a "black survival strategy" and it was often Janus-faced. The approach may have been Machiavellian, but as long as the end justified the means, Banks considered it proper. In explaining to Washington the reason he often courted whites, sometimes wearing a mask of deception, Banks asserted: "I have adopted the policy of making the white man feel that he shares in the credit of what the Negro has done here at Mound Bayou." Further, he wanted the white man to feel "that it is as much a compliment to him as it is to the Negroes of Mound Bayou for us to have been able to accomplish as much here as we have." Many of these same points resonated throughout the Tuskegean's speeches on his tours throughout the South. However, Banks left no doubt as to his motives for employing this strategy. Banks said he adopted a policy of conciliation simply "to strip him [the white man] of any fear or suspicion of what such progress means to him." Banks and Washington knew that many whites, when threatened by African Americans' success and progress, would go to any extreme to hamper them. So this was not accommodation, but a well-thought-out strategy.[31]

Banks began to collect information on each city he scheduled Washington to visit and gave him the names of prominent people who lived there. Banks told Washington about Thomas W. Stringer of Vicksburg who served as a presiding elder of the AME Church. Briefings about him included information that he served as the leader in the state in church and lodges and founded the Masonic order in Mississippi and also the Knights of Pythias. Then Banks told Washington that "a reference to him is easily a great hit anywhere in Mississippi, and especially Vicksburg." In addition, Banks provided Washington with key landmarks in the state.[32] All of these things were done to ensure the success of Washington's trip. Banks also negotiated reduced rates from the railroad company to points at which Washington was to speak. This took a tremendous amount of bargaining with the railroad company, but in the final analysis, he secured very inexpensive round trip fares. Furthermore, those interested in hearing Washington could receive 25-cent fares from stations within a fifty-mile radius of each point at which he spoke.[33]

Banks became the major promoter of this trip, which ultimately brought publicity to himself and Mound Bayou. "Get hold of the leading white papers in every community where I am to speak," Washington told Banks, and "arrange for the attendance of as many white people as you possibly can at the places where I am to speak."[34] Banks, of course, accommodated the request and began writing to newspaper editors asking them to publicize Washington's trip in their papers.[35] Banks also wrote Perry Howard, his protégé in Jackson, requesting that he use his influence to make sure the leading white people were invited to hear the address of "Dr. Booker T. Washington."[36]

Banks wanted to show Washington that he and other Mississippians appreciated him coming to their state. Therefore, although Washington did not plan on charging a fee for the trip, Banks began soliciting money from his fellow citizens in the state. He asked them to have their "local committees raise and tender to him [Washington] a purse equivalent to the amount expended by him in going from place to place." The amount Banks estimated each committee would need to raise ranged from $75 to $100. Banks made it clear, however, that he was requesting this money without Washington's "knowledge or consent...because I believe it right and proper...[and]

I understand that similar courtesies were shown him on similar trips."[37]

When Washington found out about Banks's actions, however, he told him point blank "Don't do this." Even Emmett Scott, Washington's secretary, reiterated the point to Banks on two occasions. The first time Scott told him that "the Doctor very earnestly objects to propositions of purses being raised by local committees." The second time the tone was stronger and sufficient for Banks to realize that he should stop his pursuits. Said Scott: "the Doctor rather feels that no obligation should be put upon the people to tender him a purse of any kind…Will you call off the whole business at once?" To express the urgency of this exigency, Scott related further that Washington had suggested that he wire this information to Banks instead of writing him, which would have taken longer.[38]

After receiving this stern letter, Banks felt compelled to explain his actions to Washington and let him know why he started the "movement for the purse" in the first place. Banks told him:

> The railroad will require fares paid for eighteen [people] in addition to the charge for tourist sleepers. As we will have to get about ten or twelve more besides those who will come with you, and they must be selected and invited, I thought to have them feel that they were your guests on the car in full, and at the same time have our local committees raise amounts equivalent to the entire expense of the car.[39]

After reflecting on his plan, Banks noted that he felt "inclined to think this method would give color, rather than detract from the beauty of the trip." Nevertheless, he assured Washington that he had annulled his fundraising efforts and explained to Washington that although he canceled his requests for money from the local committees, the railroad company would be expecting a payment of fares for eighteen people from each place. Thus, he wanted to know how Washington planned to handle this matter.[40]

Banks apparently had more insight as to what was needed to defray as many expenses as possible for the trip, and probably had thought out the matter more thoroughly than Washington or Scott. Only six days after Banks wrote Washington about canceling the purse, Scott sent him a letter requesting money to help fund the trip. He asked: "Will you not, at your convenience, let Dr. Washington know at Tuskegee, just exactly what you and the local league of Mississippi can do in the way of bearing any part of these expenses…. We wish to know this," Scott continued, "as far in advance as possible so that we shall know just exactly what to depend upon."[41]

Banks became a little puzzled by Scott's request and although Scott asked him to keep his request secret from Washington, Banks decided to go directly to the latter—against the wishes of Scott—and tell him that he was "somewhat at sea regarding Scott's letter." This gave Banks an opportunity to display that his plans were correct in the first place. "Mr. Scott asks what the local league of Mississippi and myself would do in the way of helping out on the R. R. expense," he said, but "you will doubtless remember wiring me to recall my letter requesting local committees to...cover your expenses." Banks went on to say that while he had initially received favorable responses from those people he had written, he immediately wrote them stating that they would not have to cover any other expenses after he received the telegram. Therefore to keep his credibility as a leader, Banks said he could "hardly now go back to them with the suggestion as given me by Mr. Scott."[42] Banks made it known, however, that he would still personally give as much as possible. Eventually, Washington solicited funds from other sources; for instance, J. T. Harahan, president of Illinois Central Railroad, was asked if he would do anything to help reduce his expenses.[43]

Although Scott and Banks were close friends, the former really placed Banks in a precarious situation by asking him to go behind Washington's back and begin soliciting funds again from the local committees. However, Banks stood up for himself and addressed the matter directly with Washington. Although he wrote his letter to Washington, he sent Scott a copy (even though Scott had already told him that he did not want Washington to know about it). This gesture showed Scott that Banks did not intend to undermine him by going behind his back on this matter. At the same time, it is possible that Scott could have intercepted Banks's letter and prevented Washington from ever seeing it. Nevertheless, Banks continued to make preparations for the trip. By mid-1908, he had organized a fairly intense schedule ensuring that as many Mississippians as possible, both black and white, would be exposed to Washington. His schedule was as follows: Holly Springs, October 5; Utica and Jackson, October 6; Natchez, October 7; Vicksburg, October 8; Greenville, October 9; Mound Bayou, October 10; and Helena, Arkansas, October 11.[44]

In August 1908, just a few months before Washington's Mississippi trip, one of the nation's worst race riots erupted in Springfield, Illinois, a northern town. An African American man named George Richardson, who had been working in the area, was falsely accused of raping the wife of a streetcar conductor, a white woman. The sheriff safely extricated Richardson from town and the woman admitted that a white man had assaulted her. Still, an angry mob turned on the small black community, lynching two blacks, injuring dozens, shooting six dead, and destroying thousands of dollars of black businesses and homes. Another two thousand African Americans in that town were forced to flee their homes. This event proved a shocker for the nation and forced many apathetic Northern whites who had been straddling the fence in terms of racial problems to become more actively involved in the issue. This event ultimately led to the creation of the NAACP in 1909.[45]

When Washington embarked on this educational tour, he understood the racial climate in Mississippi and potential risks to his life. One person even equated Washington's bravery in going to Mississippi to a religious personage. "Booker T. Washington in Mississippi during this widespread mob oppression of his people is not unlike Moses at the Red Sea saying to his persecuted people: 'Fear ye not, stand still and see the salvation of the Lord.'" Indeed, J. Matony of Cynthia, Mississippi, wrote the Tuskegee leader on September 22, 1908, pleading with him not to come to the state. "Please do not make your visit to Jackson, Miss., on the 4th of October, 1908, and no other month," he begged. "It has been said that you will never leave in peace but in corpse or some other way, but not like you came. Take heed in the name of the Lord you may be safe . . ." Also prior to the trip, rumors circulated that the railcar Washington and others were traveling on would be blown up while in Jackson. The men were advised not to sleep in the car at night, and to change their schedule. Washington became so concerned about these threats that he hired F. E. Miller, a private detective with the Pinkerton Detective Agency, to accompany him on the tour.[46]

Washington remained concerned about his safety in Mississippi, especially in Jackson, the capital and home of the "White Chief," Vardaman. Emmett Scott had detective Miller assess the sentiment of people in Jackson concerning Washington's visit before the entourage arrived. Miller went ahead of the party and interviewed both black and white people in Jackson and reported that "the colored all were very much pleased" to have Washington visit them. And while Miller found some whites who would not openly state their opinions, he "found a great many anxious to see and hear him" and "he did not find any one who was opposed to his visit." Nonetheless, this shows the conditions of terror under which Southern blacks lived. It also illustrates how conscious Washington and his supporters were of the environment in which they lived.[47]

A distinguished coterie accompanied Washington on his trip. Among those with him were Emmett Scott, his personal secretary; Nathan Hunt, his stenographer; Major Robert R. Moton, Commandant of Hampton Institute, Hampton, Virginia; Hightower T. Kealing, editor of the *A.M.E. Church Review*, Philadelphia, Pennsylvania; Roscoe C. Simmons, editor of the *National Review*, New York City; Josiah T. Settle, attorney at law, Memphis, Tennessee; Charles Stewart, newspaper correspondent, Chicago, Illinois; Wayne W. Cox, cashier of the Delta Penny Savings Bank, Indianola, Mississippi; Willis E. Mollison, attorney and president of the Lincoln Savings Bank, Vicksburg, Mississippi; Elias Cottrell, Bishop of the Colored Methodist Episcopal (CME) Church, Holly Springs, Mississippi; A. P. Bedou, photographer, New Orleans, Louisiana; and of course, Banks. The fact that these people accompanied Washington showed their support for his agenda and demonstrated that he enjoyed the endorsement of progressive blacks in the country who comprised the Talented Tenth.[48] It also verified the existence of a civilized rising black professional class.

Washington and his entourage traveled on a private Pullman tourist car, which allowed them to avoid the humiliation of Jim Crow travel. African Americans of all ranks deeply resented paying for first-class train tickets but receiving second-class accommodations. T. Thomas Fortune, a Washington supporter at the time and editor of the *New York Age*, commented on the Tuskegee Wizard's travel arrangements through Mississippi. "In order that he and his party may travel as people, and not as beasts, proscribed in labeled coaches," Fortune wrote, "Dr. Washington was compelled to arrange for a special coach for himself and his party."[49]

Washington arrived in Holly Springs on Monday, October 5, 1908 at about ten o'clock in the morning and was received by a crowd of around three thousand people. Holly Springs was the home of the late Hiram R. Revels, a former U.S. senator, and the late James Hill, former secretary of state and member of the Republican National Committee for Mississippi (both African Americans). A committee of around thirty people received the party in carriages and took them to the Baptist Normal College, founded by Alex Teague, pastor of the Holly Springs Baptist Church, where Washington spoke for a few minutes. Next, they went to Rust University, a school run by the Methodist Episcopal Church, where the Tuskegee leader inspected different buildings. After that they went to the Mississippi Theological and Industrial Institute founded by Bishop Elias Cottrell of the Colored (now Christian) Methodist Episcopal Church. Cottrell, who had been a bishop since 1894, started the school after Governor Vardaman abolished the State Normal School for Training Negro Teachers in Holly Springs. Vardaman vowed to eliminate the "coon problem" by abolishing Negro education and opposed spending any money for that purpose. "The only effect of educating him is to spoil a good field hand and make an insolent cook," he sneered. This is why reporter Hightower Kealing snubbed Vardaman, stating that the governor's attitude had sparked the new school's creation. Kealing then boasted that Cottrell's school was "considerably larger in every way" and consisted of "splendid buildings all paid for by the colored people themselves at a cost of some $60,000."[50] This point demonstrated that blacks were willing to work for themselves to ameliorate their educational situation.

The party then went to Bishop Cottrell's residence, described by one observer as a "mansion which is one of the most spacious and beautiful homes owned by one of our race in all of America," where they dined and waited for the main address of the day. Having nice homes among elite blacks like Cottrell was important because of the status that came along with it. Oftentimes, they used their homes to host small dinners, receptions, weddings, and the like. Moreover, since many prominent blacks could not receive hotel accommodations in the South, they stayed with leading African Americans while traveling. Washington and his party took a picture outside of Cottrell's home and the Tuskegee Wizard even published a picture of the mansion to display the remarkable progress of his race.[51]

Later that day the party went back to Rust, the school attended by Banks and Ida B. Wells, where Washington spoke to a crowd of about one thousand eight hundred people, with an even larger crowd waiting for him outside the assembly room. W. W. Foster, president of Rust, presided over the program, and Ephraim H. McKissack, Grand Treasurer of the black Odd Fellows in Mississippi and professor at Rust, introduced Washington. The Tuskegean spoke for an hour and fifteen minutes and gave basically the same speech he would give in all the cities he visited. Throughout his orations, he was frequently interrupted by bursts of applause, which affirmed that his audience agreed with his views on race relations, education, and economic development. Washington started his speech at Rust slowly as he did on many occasions. "In accepting the invitation of Charles Banks and other prominent citizens of the State of Mississippi...I have but one object in view in coming here and that is to see for myself some of the progress of my own race," he noted, "and to say what I could...in the direction of helping to improve their industrial, educational, moral, and religious life and to strengthen friendly relations between the white race and the black race."[52] Indeed, one of the major reasons for the tour was not only to see black progress himself, but also to put black progress on display for the rest of the country to see.

After this, Washington moved into the substantive portion of his speech responding to claims that blacks had been degenerating since the abolition of slavery.

> Judging by what I have seen on former visits and from what I have heard from those who live in this State, I feel quite sure that the Negro in Mississippi is making progress. And when we consider all that has taken place during the last forty years I believe that we have every reason to congratulate ourselves that matters have gone as well as they have and that they are no worse.
>
> Both races in the South suffer at the hands of public opinion in one respect and that is by reason of the fact that the outside world hears of our difficulties, hears of crime, hears of mobs and lynchings, but the outside world does not hear of, neither does it know about the evidences of racial friendship and good will which exist[s] in the majority of the communities of Mississippi and other Southern states where black and white live together.
>
> As I have said we have done well, but there is no reason why the Negro in Mississippi as elsewhere, cannot make himself still more useful than he has in the past.[53]

One observer who enjoyed the presentation commented that "Dr. Washington delivered plain, inspiring, and practical talks which the people warmly received" throughout the state. Later that evening, Washington and his distinguished entourage once again attended a dinner and reception at the home of Bishop Elias and Catherine Davis Cottrell, this time sponsored by the Holly Springs Negro Business League. The *Indianapolis Freeman* publicized the role black women played at this reception. A genteel performance was expected of the wives of elite blacks along with other women who participated in these affairs. After serving the main course, the party ate ice cream and "iced cakes in the form of bricklets, bearing the initials of…B.T.W" for desert. Mrs. C. Gillis, Jr., served punch while Mrs. Alexander and Mrs. Payne were hostesses. After dinner, all the guests went to the parlor where "little Miss Beulah Cottrell" and Miss Georgia Hatter "sang in graceful and fearless tones 'Farewell' and 'Our Hero,'" the latter song arranged by Mrs. Gillis who accompanied the duo on the piano. According to the same paper, "every feature of the reception was a success" and "Mrs. Cottrell was the recipient of many hearty congratulations for the ease and soberness in which every feature of the great event was performed." This served as one of the highest compliments that could be paid to black Victorians of that era.[54] It also displayed class and refinement that contradicted the image of the black savage.

The next morning on October 6 they traveled to Utica and had breakfast at Utica Normal and Industrial Institute in Hinds County, founded by William H. Holtzclaw, a graduate of Tuskegee. There were around forty thousand black people in Utica, and they outnumbered whites by a margin of seven to one. Utica Normal, founded on October 27, 1903, consisted of a 1,500-acre farm, 3 large buildings, and 11 smaller buildings used for schoolrooms, shops, and homes, all valued at around $75,000. During his talk, Washington declared that African Americans needed all forms of education and warned whites that "no power on earth could stop the Negro from acquiring an education of some kind, and it was to the interest of all classes to see that he secured a good one." Whites took "education of some kind" to mean industrial education and the education of the hands. Blacks, however, interpreted these words as a call for industrial and liberal arts education, longer school terms, better school facilities, and a fairer distribution of state school funds.[55]

Washington made a colorful stop in the capital, Jackson, the same day. Perry W. Howard, a well-known attorney, chaired the local committee. Howard graduated from Rust University and earned a law degree from the Illinois College of Law (now De Paul Law School). In addition to his law practice, he served as president of the Mississippi Beneficial Life Insurance Company, as national chief counsel for the Elks, and later as president of the National Negro Bar Association. He also became very influential in Republican politics for decades.[56] From one o'clock until four o'clock, Washington visited different businesses, schools, churches, clubs, and homes maintained by Jackson's black community. Publicizing these venues served as a way of illustrating black progress and manhood to countless critics of the race. Later that day, the Tuskegean spoke at the Liberal Arts building managed by the State Fair. Louis K. Atwood, another African American attorney in Jackson, presided. After a prayer by Reverend E. W. Smith, Perry Howard made remarks. Washington spoke to a group of about five thousand people, of whom around one thousand were "the best white men and women of that section." Some of the best whites included Governor Edmund Favor Noel (1908–1912); Lieutenant

Governor Luther Manship; Reuben W. Millsaps, reputedly the wealthiest man in Mississippi; United States Marshal, Edgar S. Wilson; and Bishop Charles B. Galloway of the Methodist Episcopal Church (South). As with Holly Springs, Washington impressed the crowd there.[57]

Interestingly enough, about three minutes after he concluded his speech, a regrettable incident occurred. "The big audience jumped to its feet and started for the doors. Just then a twenty-foot section of the gallery, which runs all around the building gave way and some fifty persons, among them Bishop Charles B. Galloway, were dropped to the first floor," the *Indianapolis Freeman* reported. "One man had an arm broken and a woman had a hip dislocated. Many others were injured in a less degree," the paper concluded. With a slightly different version Pinkerton detective Miller reported that the "gallery gave way and fell to 1st floor" and about fifteen people, some of whom were white, sustained injuries, the most serious being a few broken limbs. After this, pandemonium erupted in the auditorium, some people broke down doors to get out and others jumped from windows. Ultimately, no one ever found this to be an act of sabotage, and Washington received no injuries and exited the building with very little inconvenience.[58]

As they left this venue, the Jackson Negro Business League organized a parade. Washington and his party were placed in decorated carriages and were taken past different businesses, homes, and schools, all of which were decorated. About two thousand children from the Smith Robinson Public School waited for Washington to pass, and they waved American flags, sang songs, and presented him with a huge bouquet of flowers. Washington stopped and gave a few brief comments to the children. That night, Washington's group attended a banquet at the home of a prominent black baker and restaurateur, H. T. Risher, who paid for all expenses himself. Washington stayed at Risher's home until the next morning.[59]

White supremacist Vardaman, Mississippi's governor from 1904 to 1908, disapproved of Washington's visit. He became one of the few white Southern political leaders who openly expressed his distrust and hatred of the Tuskegean. Vardaman often spoke disparagingly of African Americans in general and Washington in particular, calling him a "nigger bastard." He said that blacks were "lazy, lying, lustful animals[s]" whose behavior "resembles the hog's." When he won the governor's race, he boasted that his victory benefited blacks and whites because the whites remained on top and African Americans remained alive. Had he lost, Vardaman warned that whites "would have had to kill more Negroes in the next twelve months in Mississippi than we had to kill in the last twenty years."[60]

While Vardaman proclaimed that black behavior resembles the hog's, the fact that the Tuskegean actually demonstrated and publicized black progress and manliness made his claims seem all the more incredulous. Clearly, the sage of Tuskegee, and other progressive blacks, caused Vardaman to experience anxiety and self-doubt. Washington wrote letters to Francis J. Garrison and Oswald G. Villard on October 10, describing an encounter he had with Vardaman. "When I went to Jackson, the home of Vardaman, one newspaper there that sympathized with him urged the white people not to attend the meeting," Washington mused with some bravado, "but they came out by hundreds, both men and women. As we were driving to the hall where the meeting was held, Mr. Vardaman, unfortunately for him, happened to meet the procession going to the hall. You can imagine his embarrassment." The Tuskegean asserted that Mississippi's African Americans were "determined in spite of the opposition of demagogues like Vardaman and others to let nothing discourage them..." Another observer with Washington's party wrote in the *Baltimore Afro-American Ledger*: "I wish you could have seen Vardaman looking out the window on one side of his face, at Dr. Booker T. Washington."[61] This sentence is an example of racial metalanguage by this African American writer. His words clearly signified a form of disrespect under the norms of Jim Crow. He breached the code of racial etiquette by not using any courtesy title while referring to "Vardaman." By contrast, in the same sentence he deliberately refers to Washington with the esteemed title of "Doctor."[62] Southern whites recognized these overt acts of rebellion and openly criticized them. The *Hattiesburg Mississippi News* scoffed at newspapers that published stories " 'Doctoring' and 'Mistering' negroes," concluding that "certainly there is nothing elevating in it for the white man, and it simply makes a fool of the common, ordinary every day negro."[63]

The Tuskegee leader moved on to Natchez on Wednesday, October 7. He participated in a corner-stone-laying at Natchez Baptist College for a building that cost around $20,000. About two thousand and four hundred people gathered in the school's chapel for these exercises. Later that night, he spoke at the Baker Grand Opera House, where the white people were so interested in hearing him that they offered to pay for the opera house in which he spoke. The audience filled to capacity. Whites sat on the main floor and the "colored people" sat in the balcony and gallery. Washington's guests sat on the stage with him. Elias Camp Morris, president of the

National Baptist Convention, delivered a short address. Afterward, Samuel Henry Clay Owen, president of Natchez Baptist College, introduced Washington, calling him "the accepted leader of his people and one of the chief figures of the present." During his speech the Wizard of Tuskegee said the "Negro was in the South and in the South to stay, and that if he desired to leave, the white man would prevent his departure." His remarks were followed by several minutes of applause. After this talk, Natchez's Mayor Benbrook and a large group of whites made their way to the rostrum to welcome the Tuskegean and thank him for his address.[64] That evening J. B. Banks, M.D., with assistance from several others, entertained Washington's group at his home.[65]

On Thursday, October 8, at about noon, the Tuskegee leader arrived at Vicksburg escorted by T. V. McAllister, Mississippi's black receiver of public monies. They were met by members of the local business league who paraded them through town, then to black businesses like the Union Savings Bank led by Taylor G. Ewing Jr. and the Lincoln Savings Bank headed by Willis E. Mollison. Ewing graduated from Walden University in 1897 and practiced law in Mississippi and Tennessee before becoming a banker. He also served as manager of the New Life Printing Company and secretary and treasurer of the Vicksburg Undertaking Company. Mollison received his education at Fisk University and Oberlin and became a lawyer, politician, and banker. He served the Republican Party as a delegate to the Republican national conventions from 1892 to 1908. Later that day, the entourage visited the National Military Cemetery, the National Military Park, and other local attractions. At Vicksburg, Washington spoke at the Clay City Skating Rink that night. So many people attended that hundreds still could not fit into the large rink. Several well-known white attorneys from Vicksburg such as Marye Dabney, R. L. McLaurin, W. J. Vollor, and H. H. Coleman shared the stage with Washington. Children from the black public school opened the program singing "America." After a prayer, the Brook's Band provided music. The distinguished African American physician, Dr. John Arthur Miller, a graduate of Williams College and the University of Michigan, served as master of ceremonies and Willis Mollison introduced Washington.[66]

The Tuskegean commented on the "bugbear" (social equality) during his address in an effort to allay white fears of miscegenation:

> I am perfectly aware of the fact that there is an element of our white
> friends who often refrain from helping the negro to the extent that

they otherwise would, on account of the bugbear of what is sometimes referred to as social equality.

I am constantly mingling among members of my own race, North and South, and of all subjects discussed that is very rarely referred to. Let me say as emphatically as I can, that judging by my observation and experience with my race, nowhere in this country is it seeking to obtrude itself on the white race, and especially here in the South. I think you will find that the more sensible the negro is and the more he is educated, the more he finds satisfaction in the company of his own race.[67]

In a state that so brazenly neglected black education, Washington couched within his language the rationale that the more education blacks received, the less likely they would be to "obtrude itself on the white race." Washington also explained to whites more realistic concerns of blacks: "The Southern negro wants land, wants a house with two or three rooms in it, wants some furniture, books, newspapers, education for his children, wants to support the minister and the Sunday school." Furthermore,

we must increase his wants, we must arouse his ambition, we must give him something to live for, to hope for, and just in proportion as his wants are multiplied, are increased in many directions so that he will want better homes, better furniture, better churches, better schools, more books, more newspapers, in the same degree will he be led to work with more regularity and a longer number of days in order that the increased wants may be satisfied. The mere matter of paying a high wage to an individual, unless his wants have been increased along sensible and rational lines, does not solve the problem...In order to secure satisfactory labor we must make the individual in a degree intelligent, must arouse [his] ambitions and his hopes.[68]

Once again, Washington's speech went over well and the local white paper, the *Vicksburg Daily Herald*, endorsed it. After the program, the Wizard's party went to the home of Edward P. Jones, District Master for the Odd Fellows of Mississippi, where a banquet was held in their honor; after which, T. V. McAllister gave them another reception at his home.[69]

In Greenville, a crowd of approximately six thousand people met Washington at the depot. The Tuskegean's party toured the town viewing the homes and businesses of African Americans. They were then entertained at the home of Mr. and Mrs. H. C. Wallace. Later that day, Bishop Edward W. Lampton, of the AME Church, presided over the program and introduced the Tuskegee Wizard. Born in Hopkinsville, Kentucky, on October 21, 1857, Lampton moved to

Mississippi after pastoring several AME congregations in Kentucky, Mississippi, and Washington, DC, and he became a leader of the black masons, serving as Grand Master for Mississippi. Lampton unsuccessfully tried to start a pro-Washington newspaper while living in Washington, DC, and in 1908, he became bishop, presiding over the Mississippi and Louisiana districts. Although people in Greenville liked Lampton, he later got into trouble when one of his daughters offended a telephone operator by insisting that she call her "Miss" as with white phone patrons. When Lampton joined the argument on the side of his daughter, the phone company removed his phone. Afterward, threats were made against his family, so they fled to Chicago.[70]

Washington spoke at the courthouse, but so many people were in attendance that, at the sheriff's request, he gave a second speech to a large crowd that had formed on the outside steps. That night, the entourage attended a banquet sponsored by the Greenville Negro Business League at the Pythian Temple led by John W. Strauther, reportedly "the most successful affair of the kind ever given in Greenville."[71]

Washington stopped at all-black Mound Bayou last. One person asserted that "the capstone was put on at Mound Bayou. This was the only place where a band of music met us..." The Tuskegee leader arrived in the town at about eleven o'clock in the morning on Saturday, October 10. Isaiah T. Montgomery and his cousin Benjamin Green had founded Mound Bayou in 1887 and by 1912, it had become the largest all-black town in the United States. Approximately one thousand people lived in the town proper and another eight thousand lived around its periphery. Mound Bayou became a place of refuge for many blacks fleeing "whitecapping" and rampant discrimination in the state. The town had twenty-two dry goods and grocery stores that made at least $600,000 per annum. Mound Bayou also had its own newspaper (the *Demonstrator*), three restaurants, three shoe shops, two real estate companies, a hotel, a cemetery, a brick factory, a post office, an ice plant, two sawmills, six gins, a cottonseed oil mill, a bank, three schools, and six churches. In terms of professions, the town had a photographer, physicians, attorneys, a dentist, an undertaker, a tailor, and several seamstresses. However, the most impressive feature of Mound Bayou, one man observed, was that "the Railroad and Express Agent, Post Master, Mayor, Alderman, and Marshal, like all the rest of the citizens, are Negroes, and each serving their station with credit."[72]

In this cotton-producing Delta town, local committee members and city residents constructed a huge arch using cotton bales estimated at a cost of $10,000 through which the entourage traveled as they toured the town. People had their produce and other displays out for Washington to see. All of the male citizens wore signs attached to their hats that read: "Welcome, Booker T. Washington Day, Mound Bayou, Saturday, October 10, 1908." When the program began, Isaiah Montgomery introduced Washington. The Tuskegee leader described his audience in Mound Bayou as being so large that it "extended out in the surrounding fields as far as my voice could reach." He gave two speeches there, one at a church and the other at the local oil mill site where six thousand people were in attendance, of whom about four hundred were white. That night, the townsmen put on fireworks. Washington later asserted that "the largest and most successful meeting of the trip was held at Mound Bayou." That evening, Banks hosted a reception at his home. "We found 5 cows and 16 hogs slain and laid on the altar to be devoured by the people and they did work on it," J. O. Midnight wrote. "They were barbecued, and willingly gave up their lives for the hungry multitude..." Not surprisingly, Washington stayed with Banks during his visit to the town, and Banks's wife, Trenna, "was the busiest woman" as she rolled out the red carpet for the guest of honor. Washington's endorsement of the all-black town was major because it showed that blacks, when left unmolested, could develop and progress on a large scale just as anyone else. The symbolism of Mound Bayou's progress went a long way in undermining white supremacist arguments of black retrogression.[73]

In addition to his visits to particular towns in Mississippi, Washington made a few whistle-stops at places such as Leland, Port Gibson, and Shaw, where he spoke to voluminous crowds from the balcony of the train. Other people could only catch a glimpse of Washington as he passed by on the train and very graciously waved at them. Although little is known about the stop, he ended the tour by visiting Helena, Arkansas.[74]

Even after a successful tour, the lynching of Frank and Jim Davis at Lula, Mississippi, on October 11, reminded African Americans of the Southern climate in which Washington's lectures had taken place. The Davis brothers had gotten into an altercation with J. C. Kendall, a white train conductor for the Yazoo and Mississippi Valley Railroad, and one of them allegedly shot Kendall two times during a scuffle with his own gun. Although Washington is often described as a harmless accommodationist, one newspaperman believed his speeches had "incited" the men to kill. Although the Davis brothers escaped initially, it did not take long for them to be captured and incarcerated in the local jail in Lula. Shortly afterward, an irate mob of white citizens stormed the jail and lynched the two inmates. The victims' bodies were left hanging all night on Sunday by the mob, supposedly so Washington could see them as he passed through the state.[75]

Emmett Scott teased Banks a little about this incident when he got back to Tuskegee. "I was rather amused at the way you scampered home after that lynching happened," Scott said jokingly. "We were afraid that we would receive a warm reception from the citizens of Lula," continued Scott, and "to be frank with you, I was rather happy when I found myself in the confine of Memphis." After Scott got past the humor, he complimented Banks on the splendid job he had done in organizing and promoting the trip throughout his state.[76]

In the end, the trip proved to be a stunning success. Sources estimated that Washington addressed from forty thousand to eighty thousand people during his journey through Mississippi.[77] Banks received thank-you notes from numerous attendees from in and out of the state. Banks certainly pleased Washington with the way he organized and promoted this tour. After the visit, he told Banks: "I cannot find words to express the deep feeling of gratitude which all of us owe you for the magnificent manner in which you planned and carried out this trip through Mississippi." Furthermore, "no one could have done it better."[78] In addition, the overall progress blacks were making in the Magnolia State pleased Washington. He commented that he believed more had been accomplished by African Americans in Mississippi in the past ten years than had been done during the previous period since the Civil War. He went on to say that "the colored people have learned that in getting land, in building homes, and in saving their money they can make themselves a force in the communities in which they live" and these points were totally in line with his philosophical ideals.[79] By illustrating to the country the progress black Mississippians were making, Washington concretely continued his assault on white supremacist claims of African American degeneration.

"The trip through Mississippi was a splendid ovation for the Doctor from beginning to end," Scott told Banks. As can be surmised from his remarks, Scott remained enthused about the success of the trip and he expressed these sentiments to Banks: "You more than met every expectation and simply overwhelmed the Doctor with a series of receptions not to be duplicated anywhere close in all the country." Even more impressive is the fact that "every detail seemed to have been worked out and the various incidents occurred with clock-like precision." An editorial in the July 9, 1908 issue of the

New York Age stated that even black people in the Northern states like New York, Illinois, Massachusetts, and Connecticut could not equal the progress of their brothers in the Magnolia State. A later edition of the paper asserted that Banks "has the unstinted praise of our people everywhere for having brought about this important visit."[80] There were other write-ups and editorials published about the trip in numerous newspapers and magazines such as the *Christian Recorder, Charleston West Virginia Advocate, Birmingham Age-Herald, Montgomery Advertiser, New York Evening Post, Star of Zion, Vicksburg Daily Herald, Memphis Commercial Appeal, New Orleans Picayune, Odd Fellows Journal, Southern Workman, and A.M.E. Church Review,* to name a few. By covering the trip, these sources publicized black progress throughout the country. Perhaps Roscoe C. Simmons, editor of the *National Review,* best summarized the general opinion on Banks's organizing and hosting of the trip when he told Banks that he wanted to express appreciation for the wisdom he had shown in organizing and directing this tour. In short, "we all feel greatly helped and inspired by all we have seen and heard during this instructive and delightful tour," Simmons continued.[81] Banks received national exposure from various newspapers for coordinating this trip, which benefited him and Mound Bayou.[82]

The success of this particular trip helped Washington realize the potential of these tours in solidifying and strengthening his leadership within the black community as he promoted his agenda for racial uplift. More importantly, he realized that he could counter criticism of the black race by actually placing African American progress on display. From that point on until his death, Washington took several tours and used them to combat white supremacy and consolidate his power within the country. The trips became part of the orbit of the Tuskegee Machine. With the potential of such displays in mind he charted his next steps.

CHAPTER 5

Tour of the Volunteer State,
November 1909

After completing a very successful Mississippi tour, Washington realized even more the value of these educational endeavors. The Mississippi tour certainly set the standard other states tried to exceed. It also benefited members of the Mississippi League who were invited the next year to put on a "Mississippi Day" at the general convention of the NNBL to showcase to the nation what Washington observed during his visit—the progress African Americans were making in the Magnolia State. Flattered by the invitation, Banks orchestrated a very memorable exhibit and presentation at the August 1909 meeting held in Louisville, Kentucky, just a few months before Washington toured Tennessee. At the start of the NNBL program, Washington turned the chair over to Banks, who introduced the Mississippi delegation. They discussed farming, merchandizing, banking, pharmacies, managing a cottonseed oil mill, fraternal insurance, and blacks in the professions. At one point during the program, at least fifty Mississippians "occupied a section facing the rostrum."[1]

This type of fanfare encouraged other state leagues to perform and certainly raised the stakes among the groups. One such league was the Tennessee State Negro Business League (TSNBL). James C. Napier cofounded the Nashville branch of the NNBL in 1902. Napier served as president of the Executive Committee of the NNBL and became perhaps second or third in command behind Washington in the organization. Napier and Washington were close friends and had met in 1891. Napier attended Wilberforce College and Oberlin and later earned a law degree from Howard University. After moving to Nashville, he worked as a lawyer and cofounded the One Cent Savings Bank of Nashville, serving as cashier. He also helped lobby for the creation of Tennessee Agricultural and Industrial State School in Nashville (now Tennessee State University), and served as Register of the United States Treasury beginning in 1911, the highest appointed position held by any African American at that time. Napier became one of the most prominent black leaders in Tennessee, becoming Washington's chief lieutenant for the state, and succeeded Washington as president of the NNBL upon the latter's death.[2]

James Napier, Richard Boyd, and others founded the Nashville chapter of the NNBL to "arouse business interests among Negroes by advocating the support of industries and business houses already established and encouraging the establishment of new ones and such other manufacturing enterprises that will enable the world and ourselves, as well, to know of our possibilities as business men," Bobby Lovett recorded. The next year in 1903, Nashville hosted the NNBL's annual meeting where Washington spoke and interacted with numerous black Tennessee businessmen, along with others, who agreed with his philosophy of racial uplift.[3]

Napier extended an invitation to Washington to visit the Volunteer State some time after the Mississippi trip in 1908. After Washington agreed, members of the TSNBL began making arrangements in the cities he would visit, establishing host committees, arranging transportation, and securing funding for the trip. Just like the Mississippi tour, Washington wanted to make sure a representative number of African Americans along with whites heard his talks. "As you know, I have spoken to the colored people there a good many times," Washington wrote Napier during the early planning of the trip. "What I am especially anxious to accomplish when I speak in the Auditorium is to get before a large and representative class of Nashville white men and white women. I shall expect the colored people to be present also, but the colored people know my views pretty well," he said. "I hope you can get hold of the white institutions of learning in a way to secure the attendance of both the professors and students."[4]

Having whites in attendance at his speeches and "the best whites" participating in programs in some form or fashion became a strategy Washington employed to win the support of not only Southern but also Northern whites. Moreover, the Tuskegee leader understood that by gaining the endorsement of influential whites, he would be able to win over other blacks too, some of whom looked to whites for approval and validation for who their leaders should be. He also recognized the value of displaying to the best whites the progress African Americans were making because that group could help advance progress and fairness in ways that common whites could not. No doubt, Washington clearly calculated the value of having white support and whites in attendance at these venues. Plans were made for the Tuskegean to visit nearly two dozen cities—Bristol, Johnson City, Greenville, Knoxville, Harriman, Chattanooga, South Pittsburg, Winchester, Decherd, Fayetteville, Columbia, Pulaski, Nashville, Springfield, Guthrie and Hopkinsville (Kentucky), Clarksville, Paris, Humboldt, Brownsville, Memphis, Jackson, and Milan.[5]

African Americans in Tennessee suffered awfully at the hands of Jim Crow, although many were defiant. They experienced discrimination in education at all levels, and the state only halfheartedly funded a state agricultural and industrial college for blacks, Tennessee A&I, located in Nashville in 1912. Up to that point, blacks provided for their own higher educational needs through private and church-related schools such as Fisk University in Nashville, Lane College in Jackson, and Knoxville College.[6] With a few exceptions, blacks were forced out of politics throughout Tennessee, especially at the state and national levels. The Tennessee legislature passed a secret-ballot law, a separate ballot-box law, and a registration law in 1889 to curtail black political influence. The group subsequently added a poll tax to further minimize black voting. African Americans were also exploited economically and suffered physical attacks when they deviated from the code of Southern racial etiquette. Tennessee had its share of lynching and race riots, extending from one end of the state to the other. The Memphis race riot of 1866, the lynching of Calvin McDowell, Thomas Moss, and William Stewart in 1892, the lynching of Ell Persons in 1917, and the Knoxville race riot of 1919 illustrate the terrorism blacks experienced throughout the state during this era.[7]

While the vast majority of lynching in Tennessee occurred along the states' western border, one of the most egregious episodes took place in eastern Tennessee in Chattanooga. On January 23, 1906, twenty-one-year-old Nevada Taylor alleged that she had been attacked and raped one night by an African American man on her way home from work. The person allegedly grabbed her from behind, which prevented her from seeing the attacker. Nonetheless, local Chattanooga papers worked vigorously to stir up excitement among whites. Three days later, Hamilton County sheriff, Joseph Shipp, charged twenty-three-year-old Edward Johnson, a carpenter, with the crime.[8]

After being incarcerated for a little over a month, a mob stormed the prison in March, extricated Johnson, and took him to nearby Walnut Street Bridge over the Tennessee River to an excited crowd of around two hundred spectators. To the very end, Johnson denied having anything to do with the crime. Nonetheless, mobsters tied a rope around his neck and fired hundreds of rounds into his motionless body. Black Chattanoogans were so outraged by this event they "stormed into downtown streets, throwing bricks and stones at whites and police," according to Philip Dray. Sheriff Shipp activated the local militia to quell this uprising.[9] Washington was fully aware of the conditions among the blacks and whites in the Volunteer State and said he wanted to bring about better feelings between the two races.

Tennesseans eagerly awaited Washington's visit: "The whole state is alive with enthusiasm, and the tour is sure to be unusually successful," the *Baltimore Afro-American* reported. Washington began his tour in the eastern part of the state in Bristol, right across the Virginia state line. Eastern Tennessee had several prosperous manufacturing towns like Bristol, Johnson City, Knoxville, and Chattanooga. In addition, many Northerners had moved to that part of the state bringing along with them more progressive ideas in terms of race. Compared to other parts of the state, blacks made up only a small proportion of the overall east Tennessee population. Although Tennessee became a dry state, there were saloons that lined the streets across the line in West Virginia, and Bristol's townsmen went there to mix and mingle. Some observers considered Bristol to be an educational center as it had four institutions of learning—Virginian Southwest Institute, King's College, Sullings College, and Bristol Normal Institute, a coeducational African American school operated by the Presbyterians. Blacks made up about half of Bristol's population of eleven thousand.[10]

Washington arrived in Bristol on November 18, 1909 to what one reporter called "a driving flurry of snow."[11] He traveled with an entourage that ranged from twenty-five to fifty persons during his eight-day visit through the state on a special Pullman tourist car. The party included Emmett J. Scott, Washington's personal secretary; William H. Lewis, Assistant United States District Attorney, Boston; Charles Banks, founder and cashier, Bank of Mound Bayou; John E. Bush, Receiver of Public Moneys, Little Rock; Robert E. Park (white), newspaper writer, Boston; Warren Logan, treasurer of Tuskegee Institute; John A. Kenney, physician at Tuskegee; Nathan Hunt, stenographer; Bishop Isaiah B. Scott of Monrovia, Liberia, in charge of the missions of the Methodist Episcopal Church (North) on the west coast of Africa; and Major Robert R. Moton, Commandant, Hampton Institute. All of these distinguished men were placed in Napier's charge, along with many other African American leaders of the state, who joined the entourage.[12]

Following are some of the state and local leaders who accompanied Washington at different points along the tour: Robert R. Church,

Memphis businessman; Josiah T. Settle, prominent Memphis attorney; Richard H. Boyd, Nashville businessman and national church leader; William Haynes, president of the Tennessee State Baptist Convention and pastor, Sylvan Street Baptist Church, Nashville; G. B. Taylor, superintendent, Negro Reformatory and Orphanage; Andrew N. Johnson, Nashville undertaker; Robert E. Clay, barber, Bristol; George W. Franklin, Chattanooga undertaker; Henry T. Noel, physician, Meharry Medical College, Nashville; George W. Hubbard, physician, dean of Meharry Medical College, Nashville; George A. Gates (white), president of Fisk University, Nashville; Robert F. Boyd, nationally recognized surgeon, Nashville; Charles V. Roman, Nashville physician; James F. Lane, president of Lane College, Jackson; and J. J. Lay, official photographer.[13] According to Park, a friend of Washington's, and a reporter covering the trip, Washington invited these men along with him because their presence guaranteed that "the statements made by Mr. Washington who was their spokesman, represented the sentiment of the most influential of the Negro people of the state."[14]

During the trip, someone asked a member of Washington's party why they were using a private train rather than ordinary traveling facilities. "The private train is used in order to cover more towns than could possibly be reached by any other means," the person replied. "They could not...attach a private car to any trains and cover as much territory as they can at present," the man concluded. However, they mainly rented private railcars to avoid the humiliation of Jim Crow travel and all that came along with it. As mentioned previously, many middle-class blacks resented receiving second-class service for the money they paid for first-class accommodations and they waged vigorous battles in the courts against this type of treatment, especially in Tennessee. According to historian Lester Lamon, "more affluent blacks throughout the state avoided using the Jim Crow streetcars and railways whenever possible."[15]

When Washington arrived in Bristol, a crowd of several hundred blacks and whites met him at the train station, vying for the opportunity to see him. A committee of the Bristol Negro Business League, the local affiliate of the TSNBL, escorted the Tuskegee leader through the cheering crowd to carriages and then took Washington and his special guests on a tour of the city.[16]

After the tour, the Tuskegean delivered his first address at the opera house at eleven o'clock that morning. Most of the shops in Bristol closed and "the white population had indeed joined with their black neighbors in making the day a virtual holiday," one person observed.

A standing-room-only crowd of more than five thousand people gathered in the town theater, but the lines of segregation were strictly adhered to on and off the stage. On the "white side" of the theater, a hundred girls from Sullins College in mortarboards and blue uniforms were marshaled in. Seated on the stage were judges, businessmen, city officers, and college presidents. Robert E. Clay, president of the Bristol League, presided over the program. Clay worked as a barber, proprietor of a coal yard, and operated a grocery store. He also actively participated in the Tennessee prohibition movement and served as the guiding force behind the building of Mercy Hospital in the town. In explaining Clay's success, one newspaper reported that he "practices the doctrine of Booker Washington."[17]

Bristol's Mayor, George E. Burbage, gave Washington a strong welcome. Judge John H. Price, a Democratic leader in Western Virginia and son of a former slaveholder, introduced the Tuskegean as "one of the Old Dominion's most distinguished sons." Price conceded that he did not know the text of Washington's address, "but I am willing to endorse anything that he says, before he says it," the judge announced. Although he adjusted his message and added bits and pieces, Washington basically used the same speech throughout his Tennessee tour. He urged blacks to cultivate self-reliance: "Buy your homes and become taxpayers instead of rent-payers. Start a bank account…Make yourselves valued and respected members of the community. Whatever work or business you engage in put your best effort into it. Don't be satisfied with doing anything half-well," he advised the cheering crowd.[18] The meeting closed with the singing of plantation spirituals.

A white person commenting on Washington's speech told a friend: "yo' cayn't tell me that man ain't inspired. Why he's inspired just as surely as Moses was sir; yes, sir, Moses." The friend responded: "Yo' are right, sir, God did cert'nly raise him up to lead his people out of darkness." Another more erudite white educator, Dr. S. R. Preston, commented: "I don't believe you can calculate the amount of good this speech will do, he didn't utter a sentiment that every white man cannot endorse fully."[19]

From the theater, Washington went back to his private train where he held an impromptu reception. At least five hundred people of all races filed through the car to shake his hand and thank him for visiting Bristol. One such person was Reverend Ambrose H. Burroughs, known as Bristol's "marrying clergyman" as he had performed over three thousand weddings. To Washington's surprise Burroughs was a grandson of his former owners, James and Betsy Burroughs. Expressing some excitement Washington exclaimed to his friends: "Why, Dr. Burroughs and I belong to the same family. I was born on the Burroughs plantation over in Franklin County [West Virginia]." Burroughs likewise enjoyed seeing Washington. "Just to think of it," he wondered, "this great man once belonged to our family. I'm proud of him, sir—mighty proud of him." As they continued to romanticize about the good old days, Washington asserted "with some feeling...how he was virtually free long before the [Civil] war in the hands of such a woman as 'Aunt Betsy' Burroughs."[20]

The train proceeded from Bristol to Johnson City, a manufacturing town in eastern Tennessee with a population of around twelve thousand. Johnson City had a Carnegie Library, steel mills, and tanneries, and when Washington arrived at the train station at two thirty in the afternoon, a band from the National Soldiers Home played a welcoming tune. As in the case of Bristol, businesses closed and schools let out early so all could hear the famous leader. Washington spoke at the Hippodrome, a large rink-like hall that looked like a big barn. Close to three thousand people turned out to hear him, of whom about one thousand five hundred were white. This became reportedly the largest crowd that had filled the hall apart from the one that turned out to hear William H. Taft the previous year during his presidential campaign. Mayor W. H. Carriger introduced Washington and the crowd received his words enthusiastically. After he finished, many people shook his hand before he departed.[21]

The third and final stop for the day was at Greenville, a town with around five thousand inhabitants. Although darkness prevailed when he arrived, a crowd of one hundred men and women were at the train station waiting to greet him. The entourage went to Greenville Normal and Industrial College, a black school located about half a mile from town, and had dinner. After eating, the group went back to the town hall where T. C. Irwin, president of the Greenville Normal and Industrial College, introduced Washington; after which, the Tuskegean spoke to more than a thousand people. Washington ended the day having spoken to over six thousand people.[22]

Still in the eastern part of the state, Washington began the second day of his tour in Knoxville on November 19, 1909. Out of Tennessee's four metropolitan cities—Chattanooga, Knoxville, Nashville, and Memphis—Knoxville had the smallest black population, hardly exceeding 15 percent, which may account for the comparatively easy race relations there. Among other things, Knoxville even had five black police officers. Nevertheless, as with the rest of the South, racial violence and oppression still surfaced in this city. For instance, in July 1908, a little over a year before Washington's tour, black miners in the Knoxville area were threatened, assaulted, and forced to quit their jobs. Although most quit, some remained, and on August 17, 1908, about seventy of them were given weapons by the sheriff to protect themselves. Eventually, a shootout ensued and the white aggressors were repelled. The *Knoxville Daily Journal and Tribune* attributed this violence to whites wanting to deny black miners the "privilege of working for a living" and said their "objection lies more in the fact that it is thought that white men should have their places."[23]

After Washington arrived, members of the Knoxville Negro Business League escorted the party to Knoxville College, a Presbyterian-run institution for blacks, where they ate breakfast. Afterward, Washington spoke to students at the college chapel. Then he went back to the city escorted by Knoxville's African American policemen with the accompaniment of a band. An estimated ten thousand people lined the streets to view the procession as it moved to Market Hall. Interestingly, only the black schools in Knoxville closed for his visit.[24]

The mayor of Knoxville, John M. Brooks, presided and gave the welcome address. Reverend A. L. Carter, pastor of Zion Baptist Church, introduced Washington to the evenly numbered segregated audience. Many prominent white businessmen of the city sat on stage as the Tuskegee leader spoke to a crowd of around three thousand. Although he thought Washington's visit provided encouragement, one white banker, blinded by the normalcy of white supremacy in Knoxville, denied that a race problem ever existed there. "The so-called 'race problem' has never been a very serious one here . . . where, we are proud to say, the Negro population has always been honest and industrious." He also felt that if Washington gave the same speech throughout the state, the time will come, "when the relations of the races will be as favorable in every section as they are here among us." While a relatively mild racial climate existed in Knoxville, black suffering and oppression still occurred as evidenced by the attack on the black miners less than a year before. On the whole, Washington enjoyed the reception he received in Knoxville and stated with a bit of hyperbole that "he had never been accorded a more generous reception than was given him here."[25]

Leaving Knoxville, the party made a whistle-stop at Clinton, where the Tuskegean spoke to several hundred people from the rear platform of the train. Next they went to Harriman, a town with a population smaller than five thousand, reputedly dry even before the state prohibited alcohol. In Harriman, Washington and his associates were escorted to a hall "by an old ex-slave on a prancing white horse, resplendent in a sombrero with a cockade, a black velvet coat, a green sash, and a sword," a reporter noted. The Tuskegee leader spoke before a group of mostly working-class white men who listened with interest.[26]

Washington made the last stop for this grueling day at Chattanooga, where blacks comprised roughly 40 percent of the population. The *Chattanooga Daily Times* announced that Washington would be speaking on "the moral and material uplift of his race." The paper also related: "there is no money-making feature in connection with his presence in the city or about the tour in which the negro educator is making." Normally Washington charged $325 for his lectures. Like Nashville, Chattanooga had a progressive black Tennessee community, though they did not have a large class of moderately wealthy African Americans. Nonetheless, according to the Chattanooga city auditor, a "surprisingly large" number of blacks owned homes in Chattanooga. They had their own benefit society worth $12,000 that provided some of their banking and insurance needs. A black grocer on White Street had property and stock totaling $35,000. African Americans also had fifteen churches ranging from $3,000 to $30,000 in value, excluding the land.[27]

There were black contractors, builders, brick masons, and reportedly hundreds of metal workers and carpenters who earned between $2 and $3.50 per day in Chattanooga. Moreover, Chattanooga boasted that it had three grammar schools, one high school, and thirty-five black teachers who earned an average of $12 per month. Three black principals earned salaries of $1,100 per year, and the curriculum at the black grammar schools seemed "identical to those of the white schools." Unlike many Southern schools, the black high school had a two- to three-year requirement.[28] These were all signs of race progress and manliness for African American men.

George W. Franklin, a businessman with "one of the largest undertaking establishments in the South," served as president of the local Chattanooga Negro Business League, second in size only to Nashville's chapter. Franklin also owned some of the best real estate in the city and suburbs, including two beautiful cemeteries, and over one hundred acres in the famous Walden's Ridge. Franklin coordinated the arrangements for Washington's visit to Chattanooga and reported in the *Chattanooga Daily Times* that "a large portion of the best seats in the Auditorium will be reserved for the white people of the city, in accordance with the expressed wish of Washington."[29] Having whites see black progress was one of Washington's major reasons for taking these tours. Such exhibitions countered white notions of black regression.

The Howard High School chorus sang "America" before the sage of Tuskegee gave his speech. The Tuskegean spoke to an estimated six thousand people, approximately half of whom were white. By contrast, William W. Finley, president of the Southern Railway, in town for the opening of a new rail station the same day, spoke to only around one hundred businessmen. After Washington's speech, two hundred prominent African Americans of the city held a banquet at James Hall, a facility adjacent to the auditorium. Dr. H. E. Sims served as toastmaster and short speeches were given by Professors William Jasper Hale and W. H. Singleton, Franklin, Charles V. Roman, Napier, and others. This concluded the eastern portion of the tour with the Tuskegean making some nine addresses.[30]

On November 20, 1909, Washington began lecturing in middle Tennessee, where the environment differed sharply from the east. Washington stopped first at South Pittsburg, located on the Alabama border, where conditions more closely resembled the "old South." Both races had tilled the soil for generations, but blacks comprised the working-class and their employers were largely planters or the sons of planters. Blacks also constituted about 50 percent of the population in the southern tier counties.[31]

Washington spoke to a crowd of mostly white men in South Pittsburg who had traveled from surrounding rural areas. Unfortunately, most of the "mill hands" (presumably blacks) were busy. This stop appeared uneventful and newspapers did not record much about it. From South Pittsburg, the party traveled to Winchester, where they were followed by a "great crowd of Negroes" to the courthouse. As they passed through the square, "hundreds of lanky, scrawny, roughly dressed white men appeared as if by magic from every side," a reporter noted. Both races crowded up the stairs and sat on "worn, wooden benches that had been whittled away by inches." Winchester's environment appeared rather primitive compared to Washington's previous stops. There were no decorations in the building and the only sign present there read: "Gentlemen will please not spit on the walls." According to a reporter, "the stains which decorated the floor demonstrated how well this injunction was observed."[32]

Judge Floyd Estill, described as a "fine type of the old-time Southern lawyer of ante-bellum days" and "the one white man in Winchester that all Negroes swear by," presided over the program. Estill praised blacks in Winchester for being "the best Negroes in the whole state of Tennessee" and introduced Washington as "one of the most distinguished citizens and truest men that has ever spoken from this platform." The Tuskegee leader gave a plain talk, well-received by the audience. "There was not one word of resentment or criticism" after the speech, according to one source, and just as many whites as blacks followed Washington to the train station to bid him good-bye.[33]

Moving on, Washington made a whistle-stop at Decherd and gave a brief talk from the rear of the train. After he finished his talk, the party proceeded to Fayetteville. That venue compared most similarly to the Winchester stop. Dr. Boyd and Charles H. Clark spoke to the audience initially because Washington, for some reason that is not clear, fell behind schedule. In the meantime, Washington arrived at the courthouse to a crowd that had been waiting for more than two hours for his speech, which he finally delivered.[34]

Sources describe the next stop, Columbia, as the "most difficult place" that had been visited up to that point. Townsmen called Columbia "Carmack's town," named after the late Edward W. Carmack, Democratic senator and editor of the *Nashville Tennessean*, who openly espoused white supremacy. Duncan Cooper and his son later assassinated Carmack in Nashville on November 9, 1908 over blistering editorial attacks Carmack had made against Tennessee's governor Malcolm R. Patterson, a friend of Cooper's. Washington did not arrive in Columbia until around seven o'clock that evening. Nonetheless, approximately one thousand African Americans gathered at the station "carrying flaring torches" to escort the party to a lodge hall. Afterward, they went to the Opera House where the Tuskegean spoke to a crowd of three thousand including blacks and whites. Interestingly, no whites in Columbia participated in the program and no African Americans were allowed on the ground floor of the Opera House.[35]

The entourage stopped at Pulaski, a big farming community and birthplace of the Ku Klux Klan, on Sunday, November 21. As Washington's party proceeded to the park in carriages, several floats and more than one hundred and fifty black people in all sorts of vehicles fell in line behind the first carriages. The procession ultimately circled the courthouse square, surrounding the statue of Confederate spy Sam Davis, who had been shot for refusing to provide information about fellow spies. According to the *Nashville Banner*, "In the windows of the negro business houses and on the front doors of their homes hang two pictures decorated in national colors—one of Dr. Washington, the other of Dr. Boyd." Even more amazing were the pictures of "Washington in the banks, drug stores and other establishments run by white people," the paper noted.[36]

More than one thousand African Americans "dressed in their Sunday-go-to-meetin' clothes" attended the event. Dr. Boyd, who was born in Pulaski, spoke just as he had done in Fayetteville. Washington ultimately lectured at the Amusement Park for two hours to a mixed audience of two thousand, and "round after round of applause greeted him from beginning to end of the speech," reported one source. The *Nashville Globe* reported that after the Tuskegean finished his speech, "it could be heard on all sides coming from thousands of throats 'Go on! Go on!'" Time, however, did not permit Washington to speak longer as the committee had scheduled the train to leave Pulaski for Nashville at two o'clock in the afternoon.[37]

Clearly, Nashville became one of the biggest stops on Washington's Tennessee tour. The capital city provided many higher educational opportunities for African Americans. Fisk University, Roger Williams University, and Walden University, connected with Meharry Medical College (Tennessee A & I did not come about until 1912), all provided for the educational needs of black Nashvillians and others. Meharry had reportedly trained half of all the African American doctors practicing medicine by 1909. The educational level of blacks in Nashville led one writer to conclude: "Nowhere in the South is the average of intelligence and literacy among them higher than here."[38]

Nashville certainly had a respectable black business and middle-class population. It had thirty black physicians, four dentists, and four black drug stores. Some African Americans owned property ranging from $100,000 to $500,000, and blacks paid taxes on millions of dollars worth of property in and around the city. Nashville had two black banks, several publishing houses, and a hospital, and "many of the Negro residences are well up to the average of the dwellings in the best white residence districts," one source noted. At least six of Nashville's black businessmen had a net worth of $100,000, a figure that would be worth millions apiece today. The fact that black people's homes were just as good as whites demonstrated black progress and symbolized manliness for the race. The dissemination of this type of information in newspapers throughout the country went a long way in helping the Tuskegee leader undermine white supremacy.[39]

Richard Henry Boyd became one of the leading African American citizens of Nashville. According to Paul Harvey, Boyd "fostered religious independence from white denominations and economic self-sufficiency through black-owned businesses." In 1896, Boyd founded the National Baptist Publishing Board, which supplied Sunday School literature to African American churches. The company became the largest black-owned publishing house in the nation. Clearly ambitious, he also cofounded the One-Cent Savings Bank and Trust Company in 1904; the *Nashville Globe*, the leading black newspaper in the city in 1906; and the National Negro Doll Company in 1911. Boyd used his progressive paper to challenge Jim Crow policies and practices and to stimulate race consciousness. He serves as an example of the accomplished men who traveled with Washington's entourage through the state.[10]

Washington spoke to anywhere from seven thousand to ten thousand people at the Ryman Auditorium in Nashville. In fact, so many people turned out that about one thousand were too late to get inside the building. Reverend Henry Allen Boyd started the program promptly at eight o'clock in the evening. A chorus began to sing "America" and the audience "caught the spirit of the song and were intensely patriotic," the *Nashville Globe* reported. Meanwhile, Washington entered the auditorium and received a thunderous ovation from the crowd that lasted several minutes. In the absence of Governor Patterson (who had taken ill), Hilary Howse, Nashville's mayor and Robert L. Jones, state superintendent of public instruction, welcomed Washington to the city and state. Napier gave the occasion and Charles V. Roman, a physician and president of the National Medical Association, introduced the Tuskegee leader. When Washington rose to speak, "it seemed as though the house could not applaud long enough so profuse was the welcome," one observer noted. During his speech Washington called for "justice on the part of whites, industry and reliability on the part of Negroes, and cooperation on the part of both."[41] Washington asserted:

> I am sure that every white man in Tennessee will agree with me, the Negro should have the same chance of preparing himself for life, so that he may understand the law and know how to obey the law. If he must be put on equality with the white man at the finishing end of life he should also have an equal chance at the preparing end of life, and this can only be brought about by proper methods of education; I mean education of head, heart and hand; that education which will teach every member of our race the dignity of labor and at the same time will teach every member of the race some trade or special occupation by which a living can be obtained.[42]

"Nashville presents an object lesson to the United States," Washington proclaimed. "I have had with me, bankers, business men, school teachers, doctors, lawyers, ministers, farmers, undertakers and other successful men who reside in Nashville or in Davidson County. These colored men could not have reached their present degree of success in your city without the help, encouragement and protection of the best white people in Nashville or Davidson County." Although

Washington had been around these men for several days, he declared that he had "not heard one word of bitterness nor a single word of adverse criticism uttered against the white citizens of Nashville. On the other hand, they have been emphatic and constant in their commendation of how they are treated," he said.[43]

Obviously, Washington's speeches included information that appealed to all races and classes in his audiences and he catered to them. The Tuskegee leader mastered the art of double-talking. Some blacks would hear his call for equality of opportunity; while some whites would hear that blacks needed to learn the "dignity of labor," which they assumed meant working for them or in menial capacities. Washington's statement that every black person should be given the opportunity to learn a trade or "some other occupation" from which to earn a living encouraged not only the carpenters, but also doctors, lawyers, and entrepreneurs. This is how blacks interpreted his call for "education of the *head*, heart and hand" (emphasis mine).[44] In addition, it is difficult to determine Washington's candor in reporting that nothing negative had been said about Nashville whites. The Tuskegean fully understood that even the best whites had the potential to turn bad, join mobs, participate in lynching, and so forth. Thus, his strategy of praising whites was done mostly for white consumption. It presented a win-win situation for whites and the black leadership class. It endeared the black bourgeoisie to the "best whites" and made whites feel good about how they were treating African Americans, even if they did not deserve it. Unfortunately, this strategy encouraged some whites to ignore the ongoing injustices African Americans faced in Nashville and throughout the country.

The *Nashville Globe* had been very critical of whites in the city on numerous occasions over the years. And, the editors of the paper accompanied Washington's entourage so Washington knew of problems that existed in the city and state. The point is, even if he had heard negative things from the people traveling with him, Washington would not have repeated them in that setting. It is interesting how gullible were the many whites who unwittingly accepted these fantastic claims made by Washington. Perhaps they did so because they could not overcome the notion of black inferiority and could not fathom the idea of African Americans outsmarting them.

On Monday, November 22, Washington's party arrived in the tobacco belt of Tennessee at Springfield, to heavy rain. While in Springfield, he encouraged the tilling of the soil as black people's "greatest hope for race advancement." This differed sharply from the emphasis in his speech at Nashville where the population had more classical education. Washington realized that "the problem in one section of the South is not the same as that in another section. It is different in every state and often in every county," he once asserted. Like any good elocutionist, Washington adjusted the tone and focus of his presentation depending on his audience.[15]

Only about three thousand people lived in Springfield, but whites and at least one thousand black farmers came from surrounding areas, some traveling up to 15 miles, to hear the Tuskegean speak. Black and white business owners on Main Street had their buildings decorated and many closed for the occasion. Nearly a thousand people met Washington at the train depot and "led by the band and a cavalcade of mounted Negroes decorated with broad red scarfs and yellow rosettes, a procession of a hundred or more gayly bedecked carts and wagons, proceeded to the hall where the speaking took place," one reporter wrote. Nearly four hundred black school children lined the streets waving American flags as the processional passed. Napier gave a vigorous address before Washington; after which, Mayor W. W. Pepper, a prominent Springfield lawyer introduced the Tuskegee educator. By the time Washington finished his speech, he had inspired at least one white man in the crowd. "We've been so busy raisin' tobacco down here that we ain't given enough thought to raisin' educated young folks," he said. "I guess we're all beginnin' to see the point now, and Washington done a lot of good by droppin' off here."[46]

From Springfield, Washington's train crossed over into Kentucky, where he gave a thirty-minute speech at Guthrie from the rear of the train. Farmers and farm hands constituted most of the Guthrie audience. Next, he stopped at Hopkinsville, a larger town of sixteen thousand known for its tobacco market. There had been a serious terrorist incident involving Kentucky night-riders in Hopkinsville in 1908. That year a group of "masked men rode into the city and practically took possession of the place while they burned tobacco warehouses and shot down all who opposed them," one source reported. This did not deter Washington from going there to speak, however.[47]

Kentucky blacks were said to be "in a class by themselves." Around three thousand five hundred people turned out to hear Washington and were "the most demonstrative in its expression of approval that he has yet addressed," a newspaper claimed. Several excursion trains brought people from nearby towns to Hopkinsville. One proprietor even gave the day off to all his employees who wanted to hear Washington because he thought some good would result from the experience. Peter Postelle, an ex-slave, real estate owner, and successful merchant, had been one of the wealthiest citizens in Hopkinsville with a $300,000 net worth. Unfortunately, he died a few years before Washington's tour, but blacks there still mentioned him and his accomplishments during the Tuskegean's visit.[48]

Before the party arrived at Hopkinsville, they were assigned to carriages by threes. Because of the way the local committee structured it, no delay or confusion occurred in transporting the group from the train, as had occurred at some previous stops. A mammoth parade consisting of nearly every African American "who appeared to be worth while" followed, according to the *Nashville Tennessean*. They escorted Washington through the main streets to the college where they ate lunch. I. A. Henderson, an older, respected citizen of the community, introduced Washington, who then addressed the people.[49]

From Hopkinsville, the train reentered Tennessee for Clarksville on November 23, another big tobacco-producing area. Clarksville abutted Green County, Kentucky, a county that proudly boasted that no blacks lived there because they were all lynched or chased out of the area. African American school children put on an exhibit for the Tuskegean, conducted and arranged personally by the white school superintendent. The president of the Chamber of Commerce, Matthew Sprague, gave the welcome address and T. J. Ford, a lawyer and state senator, introduced Washington. During the introduction, Senator Ford expressed how much he agreed with Washington's belief that the race issue remained a Southern problem, "for Southern men to solve" and he claimed he wanted to join with Washington to accomplish it. The Tuskegee leader gave another rousing speech in Clarksville; after which, "hundreds crowded forward to shake hands with him, and other hundreds followed, cheering, to the train."[50]

One white Clarksville business owner observing this entire spectacle commented:

> Say, I guess those fellows [blacks] do love that man. They're always a-copyin' some one. Seems to me, if they want to do some copyin' that'll do good, they ought to copy him. If they all did that, I 'spose there wouldn't be any race problem. I ain't been much of a nigger lover, but I do believe in givin' them a chance.[51]

From Clarksville, the party went to Paris where Washington spoke to a large crowd at the rail station. Members of Washington's party also descended on an area known as "Big Sandy," where reputedly "no Negro is allowed to remain after sunset," just to say they had been there. Some members of the party also spoke and gave good advice to the blacks in Paris. Next, they visited Humboldt where Washington spoke for an hour at Lane Chapel CME Church. There were so many people in attendance that many "stood up in the windows and peered in from points of vantage on adjacent telegraph poles," a reporter asserted. After he finished his speech at Humboldt, Washington brought on Robert Moton to sing a few plantation songs. He described Moton as looking like a white man, but when Moton got up to the podium "almost as black as coal—a true African in appearance," the crowd along with Moton laughed heartily at the joke Washington had played. Washington made the last address of the day at Brownsville to a crowd of mostly cotton pickers and farmers where many small black farmers applauded the Tuskegean's sentiments about the goodness of country life.[52]

Washington wound up his tour in west Tennessee where the majority of Tennessee's African Americans lived. Seventy-three percent of those blacks resided in rural areas and the vast majority were farmers. Heavily agricultural, the western part of the state and its cities reflected rural values. In terms of the overall black-to-white ratio in west Tennessee, in 1900, blacks comprised roughly 39 percent. In Shelby, Fayette, Dyer, Haywood, and Tipton counties, all old Black Belt plantation counties, Lamon concluded, even though blacks made up a significant portion of the population in west Tennessee, "a combination of economic and racial vulnerability created apathy among [these] rural blacks." Even so, Memphis, with its large urban black population, remained different.[53]

On November 24, 1909 Washington spoke in "the Bluff City" of Memphis, the only city in the state to which he devoted an entire day. Memphis exhibited constant racial unrest as Kenneth Goings and Gerald Smith demonstrate in "'Unhidden' Transcripts: Memphis and African American Agency, 1862–1920," and they called Memphis "a racial battleground." On December 10, 1908, less than a year before Washington's visit, Bill Latura (white) walked into a saloon on Beale Street, and shot and killed four African American customers for no apparent reason. Although Latura admitted to the killings, an all-white jury acquitted him. However, Memphis blacks did not exemplify the kind of passivity found among some blacks in middle and eastern Tennessee, possibly because they made up such a significant portion of the population. On the contrary, they often got out of place. "They talked back. They fought back. They shot back. These were not the submissive and deferential darkies perpetuated by Old South mythology," Goings and Smith explain.[54]

When he arrived in Memphis, Washington toured a black medical school and hospital, several black schools, and black residences in the city. Memphis reportedly had over thirty black doctors and a successful local black medical society. Black Memphians owned and operated successful barber and beauty shops, funeral homes, grocery stores, saloons, and other businesses in their community. In fact, the success of the People's Grocery store owned by three African Americans—Calvin McDowell, manager; William Stewart, clerk; and Thomas Moss, mail carrier—led to their lynching in Memphis. People's Grocery drew customers away from W. H. Barret's white-owned store, across the street. The idea of black competition struck a nerve with some whites and led to horrendous acts of terror. After being in Memphis during this lynching, Ida B. Wells-Barnett lamented that "the South's cardinal principle [is] that no matter what the attainments, character or standing of an Afro-American, the laws of the South will not protect him against a white man." According to Dray, "lynch mobs that sought to punish such strivers were often spurred into action by the idea that successful blacks represented just as keen a threat to Southern life as the black rapist."[55]

While traveling through the city, the Tuskegee leader saw both the blacks who were working steady and those who were idle, which deeply troubled him. Washington attended a banquet before giving his speech later that day. By the evening, some five thousand people had arrived at the Church's Park to hear the Tuskegee educator. Judge J. M. Steen of the Circuit Court offered the welcome address and stated: "We believe that as the patriarchs of old were inspired by God to lead their people out of darkness into light, to [lead] them on the right road to right living and success, so he who is to speak to us tonight is inspired to lead his race to higher, better things."[56]

Robert R. Church, Sr., father of Mary Church Terrell, and one of Memphis's most successful blacks, accompanied Washington. Born in Holly Springs, Mississippi, in 1839, Church established himself in Memphis. He owned a saloon, restaurant, hotel, and invested in real estate. During the Memphis Riot of 1866, rioters shot him as he tried to protect his saloon and left him for dead. Church remained in Memphis during the Yellow Fever epidemics of 1878–1879 and invested heavily in real estate. This investment later paid great dividends as he reportedly paid taxes on $220,000 worth of property, becoming "the wealthiest Negro in this state," according to a contemporary source. Church owned an amusement park located in the center of the city on Beale Street, containing the auditorium at which Washington spoke. The auditorium had modern conveniences, served as a recreational, cultural, and civic center for Memphis blacks, and was reportedly "the only one of its kind in America owned and operated by a man of color for members of his race."[57]

As with Nashville, Washington changed the emphasis of his speech and directed most of his remarks to the teachers, doctors, lawyers, businessmen, and preachers while in Memphis, another urban area. He felt the more accomplished blacks should "make it a part of their duty to reform the criminal loafers or have them move on to some other part of the world." From the Tuskegee leader's remarks, it was obvious that the vagrancy he witnessed while touring the city disturbed him. Washington felt that if Memphis's black leaders did not intervene, the vagrants "will tear down and disgrace our entire race in this city. Loafing brings together the worst elements of whites and the worst elements of blacks," he warned. "Nothing hurts our race more than for one to go through a city and find whole corners and sometimes blocks occupied by a set of loafing men and women who seem to have little or no purpose in life."[58]

Washington tried to encourage African Americans to "cast down their buckets" in the South. "The South is the best country for the industrious man," he told Memphians. "Negroes are best off in the small towns or in the rural districts close to the towns." The Tuskegee educator felt that "our people move around too much." Washington's words were applicable to Tennessee blacks because they moved frequently after 1900. Mostly by choice, some black men and women changed jobs and residences, constantly increasing the state's urban population. An African American lawyer from Nashville explained this phenomenon by asserting that "it is a question of meat and bread ... The negro is just like other men—he will go where he can live best."[59]

During the speech, Washington criticized colonizationists like Georgia's Bishop Henry McNeal Turner of the AME Church. To those people telling blacks they would never receive justice in this country and encouraging them to go back to Africa, Washington said:

> Six hundred negroes sailed from Savannah for Liberia one day and everybody said that the race problem was solved. But before breakfast that morning 600 more negro babies were born in the cotton states.
>
> If you set aside an island in the sea upon which to colonize all the negroes, it would require a wall to keep the negroes in there and it would require five walls to keep the white man out.[60]

An article in the *Boston Transcript* on December 10, 1909 later concluded that the Tuskegean's words boded "ill for the colonization schemes of Bishop Turner and all others who have been urging a hegira of the colored race to Africa." Nevertheless, while Washington spoke of the strengths and weaknesses of the race during his message, he told the Memphis crowd that "nothing but a love for my race has prompted me to do so."[61]

On November 25, Thanksgiving Day, the "Sage of Tuskegee" closed his eight-day tour by speaking at Royal Street Park in Jackson, the fifth largest town in Tennessee, and then Milan. While in Jackson, progressive blacks arranged lavish entertainment for the distinguished guests. Beyond these points, very little is known about these last two stops.[62]

After the tour finally ended, newspapers praised Washington and the coordinators of the affair, especially Napier. "To J. C. Napier and other prominent negro citizens of the race in Tennessee the race generally is indebted for this visit of Dr. Washington," the *Johnson City Comet* reported. "It was upon their express invitation that he consented to make the trip, and all the details have been largely in Mr. Napier's hands."[63]

Those who attended Washington's lectures enjoyed them and thought that good would result from his visit. "I consider that his speech...was his masterpiece and the best he has delivered in twelve years," said Squire J. B. Burge, a black leader from Chattanooga. Professor W. H. Singleton, principal of the Main Street School, opined: "We are all satisfied with the address and think it was timely and to the point and will undoubtedly result in much good." H. E. Sims, reflecting on his address concluded: "Prof. Washington inspired us all. His address was what we needed." What is more, "I have talked with many people today and all are pleased with what they heard and agree that it can do us good."[64]

Influential Northerners also followed Washington's tours very closely. For instance, Robert C. Ogden fondly read about Washington's trip in the *New York Evening Post*. "As your campaigns progress through the various states," Ogden wrote Washington, "I think they rise constantly in influence and power."[65] Washington himself even felt good about the success of his trip for he told Sarah Newlin, a contributor to both Tuskegee and Hampton Institute for many years, that he had "never felt more encouraged regarding the future of our people and their relations toward the Southern white people than at the present time as a result of this trip."[66]

Following a grueling schedule, Washington spoke to an estimated fifty thousand people in twenty-six different audiences over an eight-day period, nearly half of whom were white, according to the

New York Evening Post.[67] Having these stories reported in the mainstream white media as well as leading black newspapers worked well for Washington especially since the NAACP began the same year as this tour. The trip provided Washington with the forum he needed to show blacks and whites that he reigned as the "head Negro in charge." Once again, Washington took reporters along with him, camera men, and a host of black leaders. He also made sure that participation and attendance by blacks and whites prevailed at each major venue. Moreover, Washington received endorsements from many papers covering his tour. The Tuskegean calculated very well how to maintain his status and power in the country, and these tours became a vehicle for doing so, guaranteeing him that his ideas, philosophy, and solutions to the race problem would be plastered in newspapers throughout the country, North and South.

The tours brought great visibility and recognition to the men traveling with Washington, serving an added benefit. Napier told Washington that people had been constantly stopping him to talk about the trip through Tennessee and "to commend in the most flattering terms all that you said and did." Judge John W. Judd, a professor of law at Vanderbilt, followed stories of Washington's tour and concluded that the Tuskegean "seems simply to be a wonderful man. The effect of his tour through this State will be far reaching and will work an incalculable amount of good among all the people." Then the judge told Napier: "I want to talk at length with you about these matters." This is just one example of how relationships and connections were made by Washington's supporters after these trips.[68]

This type of self-promotion helped the Tuskegean in a number of ways to maintain his control over black America. One newspaper concluded that anyone who heard Washington's address would know "that he is by every right the proper man to lead his race out of the darkness of ignorance into the light of education."[69] "More than any other prominent man of the race," another newspaper asserted, "Booker Washington is the acknowledged leader of his people." That article went on to say, seemingly in direct response to his critics and the newly formed NAACP, that "to be sure, he has some opposition, and some vehement disagreement is often expressed to his views, but the reports of these various trips will show that every man in the community which he visits, every man of worth and standing, who has accomplished something, and who holds the respect of his fellow citizens in the community, regardless of race, holds the idea that Dr. Washington is the *real leader* of the people, and to some extent enjoys his confidence and esteem"[70] (emphasis mine).

Ultimately, on these tours Washington furthered his efforts to counter white propaganda about black degeneration by displaying the very accomplishments whites so deeply wanted to deny. By showing the houses, schools, and businesses owned by African Americans, and by exposing the country to professional black doctors, lawyers, teachers, and so on, Washington worked to counter racial stereotypes about African Americans so prevalent at the time. What is more, Lamon examined the long-term impact of Washington on blacks in the Volunteer State and concluded that he "greatly influenced the racial attitudes of the state." African Americans "drew comfort from the 'Tuskegee ideal' of steady economic advance and hard work," Lamon continued, "while whites appreciated the conservative preachments of 'common sense' and the rejection of specific social and political goals."[71] The same could be said for blacks and whites in North Carolina.

CHAPTER 6

Tour of the Tar Heel State, October–November 1910

Public opinion can prove a fickle mistress and, as Washington's actions in late 1910 illustrated, required continuing attention and more than a little courting. One year earlier, his tour of Tennessee and portions of Kentucky had served to remind the nation's leaders, black and white, that he stood supreme as leader of his race in the United States. Washington had taken the tours in part to counter attention that was being afforded to the nascent association soon to be known as the NAACP. The following May the second National Negro Conference resulted in the NAACP's formal creation with Washington's most capable African American critic Du Bois emerging as its director of publicity and research, and serving as the only black officer of the group. By mid-September, Du Bois had issued a prospectus for a monthly publication to be known as *The Crisis: A Record of the Darker Races*. The editor scheduled its first issue for November. Considering his insistence that the *Crisis* traced its lineage to William Lloyd Garrison's abolitionist *Liberator* and Frederick Douglass's famed *North Star*, Du Bois desired to claim the mantle of race leadership despite print media's seeming attachment to the sage of Tuskegee.[1]

The challenge clearly required Washington to respond, and he chose to do so through a tour of the state that, arguably, evidenced proof most clearly of the value of his philosophy. At that time, North Carolina, at least when compared to other Southern states examined in this study, enjoyed in the minds of many the easiest and most flexible patterns of race relations. The Tar Heel State differed from other Southern states in that, while the others began their campaigns of redemption through disfranchisement at or soon after the close of Reconstruction, North Carolina blacks—especially those in the eastern part of the state—continued to vote in large numbers and to hold state and national office throughout the late 1870s, the 1880s, and into the 1890s. According to Frenise Logan, "even the physical separation and segregation of the races which were so prominent in the first decades of the twentieth century were not legalized or codified and were often ignored by whites and Negroes alike."[2] Nonetheless, "racial civility, for which North Carolina was widely known," Raymond Gavins says, "prevailed only so long as African Americans abided by the legal and extralegal rules of Jim Crow." When blacks stepped out of bounds, they met with swift and severe punishment.[3]

The case of Wilmington corroborates this point. H. Leon Prather Sr. asserts that from the 1860s to the late 1890s, Wilmington evolved into one of the best Southern cities for African Americans. By the century's final decade, the city boasted the largest and most important seaport in North Carolina. Blacks comprised 56 percent of Wilmington's population in 1890. Indeed, blacks and whites lived at times in integrated neighborhoods, purchased goods from the same shops, and commonly walked the same streets. Wilmington's African Americans also exercised considerable political clout, comprising 30 percent of the Board of Aldermen, the city's most important elected body. At Wilmington, blacks also served as coroner, justice of the peace, superintendent of streets, and deputy clerk of court. Black policemen, firemen, and mail carriers were present as well. To the chagrin of whites and some local blacks, in 1897, President William McKinley even appointed John Campbell Dancy as collector of customs at the Port of Wilmington, replacing a white Democrat. In that job he earned roughly $4,000 per year while the governor made only around $3,000.[4]

African Americans in Wilmington also succeeded in business. They enjoyed an almost complete monopoly in the barber trade (91 percent) and operation of the city's restaurants (91 percent). Of the butchers, 33 percent were black. They outnumbered whites as shoe and boot makers. Many of Wilmington's artisans were African American including painters, brickmasons, wheelwrights, mechanics, plumbers, furniture makers, jewelers, and watchmakers. Black grocers, pharmacists, and realtors made a good living, and the city produced the first black daily newspaper in the state. Edited by Alexander Manly, an acknowledged grandson of former North Carolina Whig governor, Charles Manly, the *Wilmington Daily Record* earned respect and a wide readership.[5]

Politically, blacks and some whites discovered that they shared common political ground. Disenchanted with the policies of the Democratic Party, thousands of white farmers defected to the Populist or Peoples Party. In order to break Democratic control of the state's political apparatus, these Populists placed class before race and fused with the state's Republicans, most of whom were black. The successful fusion of Republicans and Populists in the 1890s demonstrated an aberrant peculiarity among this group of Southerners, albeit a short-lived one. In 1894, this interracial ticket took control of the state legislature and began the job of dismantling the Democrats' election machinery. They enacted new registration procedures and electoral laws that encouraged African Americans to vote. Two years later, the Fusionists won every statewide race in the Old North State, resulting largely from black voting. They increased their majority in the General Assembly and elected Wilmington Republican Daniel L. Russell as governor.[6]

North Carolina Democrats, as was expected, determined to redeem the state by any means necessary, and this fact tarnished, even though it did not destroy, the state's reputation for African American opportunity. Organizers from the state's Democratic leadership traveled to Wilmington, among other places, to incite a white supremacy campaign and organize white supremacy clubs. Simultaneously, a racist labor movement endorsed by the Wilmington Chamber of Commerce moved to oppose African Americans who competed with whites for jobs.[7]

Manly added fuel to the fire when he published an editorial in the *Daily Record* reacting to a call by Rebecca Latimer Felton for white men to "lynch a thousand times a week if necessary" to protect white women from assaults by black men. While the editor could have ignored such inflammatory rhetoric on most occasions, this time he felt compelled to act because of the stature of the person issuing the call. Felton stood out as one of Georgia's leading female activists. The wife of one-time Congressman, William H. Felton, she served as a white temperance crusader, suffragist, journalist, and in 1922, became the first woman to sit in the U.S. Senate.[8]

Manly wrote that, were the facts on her side, Felton's plea would be worth considering. But he insisted that not every white woman who cried rape told the truth, and consensual sex between black men and white women did not constitute an act of rape. Moreover, he asserted that many black men were attractive enough "for white girls of culture and refinement to fall in love with them, as is well known to all." When Democratic newspapers republished his comments, some conveniently edited out the second half where he argued that "white men also seduced and raped black women, and 'carping hypocrites…cry aloud for the virtue of your women while you seek to destroy the morality of ours.'" Manly continued: "Poor white men are careless in the matter of protecting their women, especially on the farms.... Tell your men that it is no worse for a black man to be intimate with a white woman than for a white man to be intimate with a colored woman." At his own peril he warned, "Don't think ever that your women will remain pure while you are debauching ours." With this strong but true editorial, Manly had immersed himself in the deep pool of the South's most serious racial taboo. Public calls resounded that Manly be whipped, run out of town, and worse. "Why didn't you kill that damn nigger editor who wrote that?" South Carolina Senator, "Pitchfork Ben" Tillman asked North Carolina whites.[9]

A terrorist wing of the Democratic Party, the Red Shirts, also made their first appearance in the state around this time. The group began holding rallies and terrorizing blacks and their white allies especially across the eastern part of the state. In November 1898, a white mob comprising Wilmington's professional and business leaders, including a former congressman, destroyed the office of the *Daily Record*. Although the black officials resigned from their posts in an effort to head off any further violence, more was to come.[10] The Reverend Charles S. Morris, an eyewitness, recorded what happened next. There were, he wrote:

> Nine Negroes massacred outright; a score wounded and hunted like partridges on the mountain; one man, brave enough to fight against such odds would be hailed as a hero anywhere else, was given the privilege of running the gauntlet up a broad street, where he sank ankle deep in the sand, while crowds of men lined the sidewalks and riddled him with a pint of bullets as he ran bleeding past their doors; another Negro [was] shot twenty times in the back as he scrambled empty handed over a fence; thousands of women and children fleeing in terror from their humble homes in the darkness of night.... All this happened, not in Turkey, nor in Russia, nor in Spain, not in the gardens of Nero, nor in the dungeons of Torquemada, but within three hundred miles of the White House, in the best State in the South, within a year of the twentieth century, while the nation was on its knees thanking God for having enabled it to break the Spanish yoke from the neck of Cuba.[11]

Recent scholarship suggests that the riot saw at least twelve black men murdered, with some one thousand five hundred black residents of Wilmington fleeing the city. In its aftermath, whites quickly commenced purchasing black property and homes at bargain rates. A leader of the mob soon presided as mayor. George H. White, the African American congressman who represented the second district of North Carolina that included Wilmington, finished the remainder of his term in 1901 and then moved to the North. "I can no longer live in North Carolina and be a man and be treated as a man," he lamented. White remained the last African American to serve in the U.S. House of Representatives until Andrew Young won the election from Atlanta in 1972.[12] Ultimately, blacks learned that even in the Tar Heel State, violations of the Southern code of racial etiquette could bring about devastating consequences as was typical throughout the South.

A dozen years had passed and tensions had eased somewhat when Washington visited North Carolina at the end of October and into early November 1910. Only one week earlier he had returned from a two-month trip to Europe visiting over ten countries. He had visited, among other places, London, Scotland, Berlin, Budapest, Sicily, Naples, Austrian and Russian Poland, and Hungary. He even had dined with notable personages such as the king and queen of Denmark, an occasion that he called the biggest surprise of his life next to receiving an honorary degree from Harvard. Washington had received numerous prestigious invitations while in Europe, most of which he had turned down. However, he did speak in London, Prague, and Berlin.[13]

What the Tuskegean witnessed overseas deeply influenced his ideas and broadened his perspective on the possibilities for African Americans back home. While in Poland, he was taken aback when he saw filth, dirt floors, and six European men in a farm house eating from the same bowl. The large landowning Hungarians awed Washington by the technological advances they had made in agriculture; however, he was distressed to see the Hungarian farm workers living in mud houses, the soldiers forcing barefoot Slavs to work, and by the widespread farm strikes. In Naples, around fifty beggars followed him through the streets, and he even "found a blacksmith shop in one bedroom and a poultry yard in another and filth everywhere." In Catania, he observed some families working for as little as 17 cents per day.[14]

These observations deeply touched the Tuskegee leader, challenging the myths of European supremacy that had bombarded him since birth. Moreover, whites in the United States had degraded Africans and African Americans regularly as dirty, backward, and uncivilized. Scientific racists, journalists, clergymen, and others had consistently used "science" and "religion" to explain these "black traits," and they circulated this sort of racist propaganda throughout the country. But Washington now perceived firsthand a different story, one that led him to a different conclusion. The Tuskegean realized that contrary to the beliefs and teachings of many white Americans, the blacks in America were more refined than were many of the white Americans' cousins in Europe. In fact, Robert Park, a white American sociologist and friend who accompanied Washington on the trip believed that the Wizard started focusing too much on the shortcomings of Europeans. "Park became rather disillusioned by Washington's [racial] chauvinism," Harlan observed. "He was not interested in the common people as I thought he would be. They were just foreigners," Park later wrote. "He was an American and thought everything in America surpassed anything in Europe," Park added. "He just wanted to get the dirt on them that was all, to discover for himself that the man farthest down in Europe had nothing on the man farthest down in the U.S." In 1912, Washington even published a book on the subject titled *The Man Farthest Down: A Record of Observation and Study in Europe* to further publicize his perspective.[15]

Pleased with the success of his trip, Washington contacted Park shortly after they returned to the United States so they could plan another trip to Europe. Unfortunately, World War I began before he could return so he had to put his plans on hold. The war even reinforced Washington's newfound beliefs of the moral inferiority predominant among Europeans. "I suppose we will now have to wait until the majority of Europeans have succeeded in killing themselves off," Washington wrote Park cynically. "The more I see of the actions of these white people of Europe, the more I am inclined to be proud of the Negro race. I do not know of a group of Negroes in this country or in any other country who would have acted in the silly manner that *these highly civilized, and cultured people of your race have acted*" (emphasis mine), Washington concluded with even more cynicism. The Tuskegean's words here are noteworthy for two reasons: first, because they show that Washington lumped American whites into the same category with whites in Europe. Second, because they illustrate Washington's pride in his race, not just in America.[16]

As might be expected, the Tuskegee leader incorporated many of the lessons he learned in Europe into his speeches throughout North Carolina and on other educational tours he subsequently took through the South. He also echoed many of these sentiments through his writings and in other speeches he made for the remainder of his life. Filled with new perspectives, exhilarated by his reception in Europe, and anxious to reassert his position in the United States,

Washington at that point turned his personal attention to North Carolina.[17]

The North Carolina State Negro Business League (NCSNBL) had agreed to sponsor his tour there. Leading businessmen John Merrick and Aaron McDuffie Moore, M.D., had known the Tuskegean for at least a decade. Both men had attended the inaugural meeting of the NNBL in Boston in 1900, and Merrick regularly accompanied Washington on his tours of the South. African Americans in New Bern chartered the state's first local NNBL chapter, and by 1908 chapters had been added at Charlotte, Wilson, Wilmington, Greensboro, Statesville, and Asheville. The statewide chapter of the national association had commenced its work in 1909 with Merrick as its founder. Charles Clinton Spaulding, a business partner of Merrick and Moore, served as secretary of the state league and became a life member of the national organization in 1914. He even encouraged agents of the North Carolina Mutual Life Insurance Company to organize local chapters of the league in their respective communities. By the 1920s, Spaulding, who outlived both Merrick and Moore by three decades, would be secretary-treasurer of the NNBL and serve as chairman of its executive committee.[18]

Bishop George Wylie Clinton of the African Methodist Episcopal Zion (AMEZ) Church, who doubled as a journalist, coordinated the tour. Merrick, Spaulding, James E. Shephard, president of the National Chautauqua and Religious Training School at Durham, and the Reverend George C. Clement, editor of the AMEZ Church's *Star of Zion*, assisted. The AMEZ involvement reflected clearly the denomination's leading role in North Carolina African Methodism. Other prominent citizens joined the party at different points including Professor James B. Dudley, president of the Agricultural and Mechanical College at Greensboro; Dr. Silas A. Peeler, President, Bennett College, Greensboro; Dr. Henry L. McCrorey, President, Biddle University, Charlotte; and W. S. Young, of the *Durham Reformer*. Over twenty towns applied to be included on the itinerary, but the steering committee only scheduled thirteen because of time constraints. Charlotte, Concord, Salisbury, High Point, Winston-Salem, Greensboro, Reidsville, Durham, Wilson, Rocky Mount, Washington, New Bern, and Wilmington made the list. The touring party traveled to each point on a special Pullman railcar as had become traditional in the past. Strangely, records do not indicate that Dr. Moore traveled with the entourage or had anything to do with planning the trip, although he supported Washington's belief of economic self-sufficiency.[19]

Available records also fail to reveal why the organizers did not include Raleigh, the state's capital on Washington's itinerary. It could have been because of time constraints, its close location to Durham, Wilson, and Rocky Mount (all stops on the tour), or other unknown logistical reasons. However, by 1900, Raleigh's black community comprised 42 percent of its population. A small, but successful, business class including lawyers, teachers, undertakers, caterers, grocers, and contractors had coalesced. One livery business owner named John O. Kelley even employed whites. Another black resident, Berry O'Kelly, became postmaster in 1890 and later emerged as a successful merchant and educator in Method, a black community in west Raleigh. In fact, Berry became one of the wealthiest African Americans in the state. The activist also led efforts to consolidate three rural African American schools in Wake County in 1914, and in their stead, formed the Berry O'Kelly Training Center in Method. Raleigh, home to Shaw University and Leonard Medical School, trained scores of successful black physicians beginning in 1882. Nonetheless, the majority of African Americans in the city were mired in the lowest-paying jobs, which could have driven the decision not to include Raleigh on the itinerary. Black women worked almost entirely as washerwomen and domestics, while black men labored primarily as servants and laborers. Moreover, due to local opposition from whites, many black artisans in Raleigh struggled to find work as plumbers, cabinetmakers, or machinists.[20] Beyond speculation, the fact of the matter may never be known.

In any event, the tour commenced on October 28 and ran till November 4, 1910. In promoting the excursion, the white-run *Charlotte Daily Observer* asked for "a great outpouring of the representative citizenship of the community." The paper observed: "There are few gatherings of a political nature which merit more attention than this non-political event." It added, "the keynote of it all, we think, has been an effort to renew sympathetic relations, strained by the crimes and blunders of Reconstruction, between the two races whose destiny is cast together here in the South." The *Observer* also published an article titled "White People Invited," noting that special provisions had been made for whites. But Washington's friends took care that the black, as well as the white press, covered the event. "The North Carolina 'educational pilgrimage' of Dr. Booker T. Washington will be up to the standard set by Mississippi, South Carolina, Tennessee, Delaware and Arkansas," the *Indianapolis Freeman* observed. "Leaders like Bishop G. W. Clinton, John Merrick, C. C. Spaulding...know how to 'do things' and they never do things by halves."[21] Surely these three men were among the most prominent African Americans in the state.

Entering the state from the south, Washington arrived in Charlotte, home of Clinton, on Friday, October 28. Born a slave in Lancaster County, South Carolina, Clinton attended the University of South Carolina from 1874 until 1877 when Reconstruction ended and the doors of the university were closed to African Americans. He then matriculated at Brainard Institute in Chester, South Carolina, and Livingstone College in Salisbury, North Carolina, where he studied theology and received ordination in 1879. In 1889, he founded the *A.M.E. Zion Quarterly Review* and edited the denomination's weekly publication, the *Star of Zion*, from 1902 to 1906. Clinton accumulated some wealth during his lifetime possessing between $18,000 and $25,000 in property holdings alone. He remained a staunch supporter of Washington, defending him against growing attacks by his adversaries whom Clinton once called "would be leaders." He also traveled with the Wizard's entourage through five other states. Although Clinton did not advocate interracial mingling, he later became active with the Southern Interracial Commission and the Southern Sociological Congress.[22]

In Charlotte, Washington spoke to the Baptist Convention at Friendship Baptist Church the afternoon of October 28, and told the audience that he made all his addresses "with the object of helping poorer people, the common people of the race." Then he "showed the importance of lifting up the masses as the only means of elevating the race," according to the *Observer*. After which, he participated in laying a cornerstone at the new Varick Memorial building, the publishing house of the AMEZ Church. Then Washington visited Biddle University (now Johnson C. Smith University), a Presbyterian school that was headed by Reverend Henry Lawrence McCrorey and attended by children of Charlotte's black "better-class."[23] Born on March 2, 1863 in Fairfield County, South Carolina, McCrorey worked on a farm as a youth and attended the Richardson School in Winnsboro, South Carolina. In 1886, he enrolled in Biddle University where he graduated from the high school, collegiate, and theological departments, and later studied Semitic languages at the University of Chicago. On returning to Biddle, he worked as a teacher and principal of the high school, became head Latin teacher in the collegiate department, chaired the Hebrew and Greek Department in Theology, and became president of the entire university in 1907. During his tenure, the school grew tremendously and among other things received a Carnegie Library that cost $15,000. McCrorey took an active part in church and community uplift, served as a delegate at the Pan-Presbyterian Alliance in New York City in 1909, and became a member of the American Academy of Political and Social Science. He was also president of Charlotte's black chamber of commerce.[24]

Biddle opened its doors on September 16, 1867 to forty-three students and by 1919 it had enrolled over ten thousand students, had eighteen professors, and had grown from eight to over eighty acres with fourteen buildings valued at $225,000. After Mrs. Henry Biddle of Philadelphia made a donation to the school in honor of her late husband (Major Henry J. Biddle who died in the Civil War), officials named the school after him. The university consisted of four main departments: preparatory, collegiate, industrial, and theological. The preparatory department trained students for teaching, business, and college. Taking four years to complete, the college department had two tracks: the scientific and classical. The industrial department offered training in trades such as plastering, carpentry, bricklaying, shoemaking, blacksmithing, printing, and agriculture. The theology department followed the standard seminary curriculum of the Presbyterian Church, and took three years to complete.[25] By describing the assets owned by the school and its curriculum offerings, Washington illustrated, once again, that Southern blacks were progressing. No matter how much racist whites argued to the contrary, these visible signs of progress turned their claims upside down.

After the cornerstone laying and the Biddle visit, Washington made short addresses at the Saint Michael's School and then at the colored missionary and educational convention. After which, Washington gave his first formal lecture in the Old North State, with hopes of "bringing about a better understanding and . . . mutual interdependence between the races."[26] People crowded into the largest auditorium in Charlotte to hear the leader from Tuskegee, paying 15 cents for one person and 25 cents for two. Conforming to the requirements of Jim Crow, Thad Tate, secretary of the Charlotte league, arranged for whites to enter the building from the Fifth Street side of the hall and blacks from the College Street side. It came as no surprise that Washington received a warm reception. As early as October 1902, John W. Smith, editor of the *Star of Zion*, noted that Charlotte's African American better class had embraced Washington's philosophy, calling for blacks to devote themselves to business and spurn politics totally. "Some of our Negro leaders since the enactment of the disfranchisement law and the turning down of the Negroes by lilly [*sic*] white Republicans are advising the Negroes to get out of politics and enter business," Smith observed.[27]

Clinton presided and introduced prominent businessman J. T. Sanders, president of Charlotte's local Negro business league. In 1896, Sanders had opened a bank, he partnered with W. F. Thompson and opened the Charlotte Clothing Cleaning Company in 1899, and he owned over forty acres of land in Western Heights, a Charlotte suburb. Sanders agreed wholeheartedly with Washington's philosophy of racial uplift and thought that blacks should emphasize economic development over politics. "You may talk about the Negro problem and say all sorts of things about him," Sanders once wrote in a letter to the *Star of Zion*, "but his condition will remain just as it is now until we shall master the principle of business as other business men have done. No race in the world has ever succeeded without first learning business and how to do business economically," he asserted. Of course, some North Carolina blacks disagreed. Editor John Smith denounced this position saying "It is bad advice for it means giving up on our rights as citizens." Furthermore, if African Americans "give up the fifteenth amendment to the Constitution of the United States, which gives us the ballot, our political enemies will attempt to force us to give up the thirteenth amendment which sets us free, and the fourteenth amendment which makes us citizens." Smith urged blacks to "agitate in the newspapers, on the platform, in the pulpit, in the legislative and congressional halls and, if necessary, contend for them in the highest courts of the land until they are granted."[28]

Sanders presented Mayor T. W. Hawkins, who introduced the Tuskegean. Washington spoke to about three thousand people in Charlotte, half of whom were white, for nearly two hours. "While I have not been very much in the State of North Carolina, I have kept in close touch with the progress which our race is making in this state," Washington said early on. "I have noted with interest the friendly relations that exist for the most part between black citizens and white citizens in North Carolina, and I know of few, if any, States where the relations are more friendly than they are in this State," he opined.[29]

Reflecting on lessons he learned while overseas, Washington told the audience that he had spent two months in Europe, and while there he observed "the condition of the poor classes, and because of what I have seen in Europe I return to this country more encouraged, more hopeful concerning the condition of the Negro and his future than I have ever been before." He continued: "As compared with the condition and the outlook of the working classes in Southern Europe especially, the Negro has a chance in the South that is from 50 to 100 per cent more hopeful than is true of the working classes in Southern Europe."[30]

The Wizard spoke on opportunities for blacks to buy land, although some whites felt threatened by this aspect of his philosophy.

Fundamentally in practically every part of the South, the Negro has a chance of purchasing land, of buying his own farm and town lot. It is almost impossible for a poor man in Europe to get land. In many cases, if he has money, the land is held in such large tracts that it cannot be bought. Here we are urged to buy land, often at prices that seem ridiculously small as compared with the price of ordinary land in Southern Europe where the price ranges in some cases from $800 to $1,000 an acre for farming land no better than ours.

And, wherever I go in the South, despite what may be said to the contrary regarding the relations of the white man and the black man, I find white men urging Negroes to buy land, and willing to lend him money, to give him advice and encouragement in the direction of securing a home. The man who will help us in that direction is not our worst enemy, but our best friend.[31]

The Tuskegee leader felt that when it came to labor, African Americans had a great advantage over Europeans. "The Negro in the South for the main part does not have to seek labor. Work seeks him," he said. "In England where I was recently I found three and four men looking for one job. In this country, in the South, so far as the Negro is concerned, you will find conditions turned around and instead of three or four men looking for a job, the job is in search of the man." Washington went on to assert that African American laborers in the South did not face the same restrictions faced by blacks in many parts of the north and west. "Here the Negro cannot only be a farmer, but a skilled laborer," said he. "The wage which the ordinary Negro workman receives in the South is from three to four times as high as the wage received by the working man in Europe doing the same kind of work."[32]

One person commented that Washington's speech "teemed with ripe philosophy, rare wit, and for an hour and a half he held his hearers literally spellbound." Clearly impressed with Washington's message, a white observer forced to stand because of overcrowded conditions concluded: "I know of no white man that I could have listened to [for] so long on my feet." The *Observer* noted that "everything he uttered was digestible to white and black alike." After the address, a "magnificent banquet" took place at Clinton's "palatial home." The bishop's home, valued at $10,000, sat in the First Ward on North Myers Street, where many other prominent blacks associated with the AMEZ Publishing House lived. Indeed, members of the black "better class" invested in stylish and expensive homes. Publicizing this fact showed that these African Americans were "men" and were progressive.[33]

Following the usual pattern, about twenty-five distinguished men from diverse professions accompanied Washington on his tour, "men who stand for achievement, for things worth while…" a newspaper reported. In addition to the normal cast was John Henry Washington, the Wizard's older half-brother who worked as business agent, farm manager, and director of industries at Tuskegee; Charles W. Greene, head of the Poultry Division at Tuskegee (born in North Carolina); Professor William Taylor Burwell Williams, field director at Hampton Institute and field agent for the John F. Slater fund; William Sidney Pittman, architect and Washington's son-in-law, Washington, D.C.; Reverend Richard Carroll, President, Negro State Fair, Columbia, SC; Robert E. Jones, editor of the *Southwestern Christian Advocate*, New Orleans, LA; Professor Charles H. Moore, first black graduate of Amherst (1878) and national organizer for the NNBL; Edward H. Clement, former editor-in-chief of the *Boston Transcript*; and Horace D. Slatter, newspaper correspondent. Boston's William H. Lewis was perhaps the most accomplished member of the entourage. A graduate of Amherst College and the Harvard Law School, Lewis served as Assistant United States District Attorney of Massachusetts, and with Washington's help became Assistant Attorney General of the United States in 1911, the highest federal office ever held by an African American up to that point.[34]

Early Saturday morning, October 29, the party reached Concord and was met by John Fuller who headed the local committee. They traveled to Scotia Seminary, reportedly "one of the best schools for girls in the country," attended by Charlotte's black elite, where the party had breakfast. After which, the Tuskegee leader spoke to about 265 students. Later that morning, Washington lectured at the opera house to a much larger audience where Mayor Charles Wagoner welcomed him as "one of the ablest and most distinguished educators of the South."[35] The mayor went on to say that

> By sheer force of manhood and strength of character he has risen from humble conditions, overcoming obstacles and almost insurmountable limitations of environment, until today he is recognized not only in this country but the world over as one of the men who has accomplished great things for his day and generation. At the head of one of the great institutions of learning of the South, he has used his influence toward bringing about better social and industrial conditions for his people; and he is a man whom the South does honor and is delighted to honor because he is a great factor in solving the problems that confront it.

> When the final day of reckoning is come, [*sic*] no greater laurels shall rest upon any man than upon him who has spent his life in the service of his fellow man.[36]

One reporter observed that "many whites were in the audience and all gave the closest attention" to the Tuskegean's rousing speech. The party left Concord for Salisbury.[37]

Interestingly, vice president of the United States James Schoolcraft Sherman, who had been traveling the state for three days making political speeches, arrived in Salisbury and requested to meet Washington when he got there. At noon, Washington's railcar backed up against Sherman's and "the two distinguished Americans chatted cordially for a few minutes, while the immense crowd cheered vociferously," the *New York Age* reported. Sherman told Washington that he too was "down here converting sinners." The encounter projected racial equality. Together, the men visited Livingston College and both delivered addresses. Dr. William Harvey Goler, the school's president, showcased the new $20,000 Hood Theological Seminary building and a $12,500 Carnegie Library. Livingston had about two hundred students and the young men performed a military exhibition. These facts went a long way in Washington's efforts to undermine white supremacy. The cordiality extended between Washington and the vice president of the United States clearly illustrated civilized behavior, as opposed to barbarism, the image most often used to depict blacks. Goler then took Washington's party on a tour of the city where they visited the National Cemetery and had dinner at his home.[38]

Washington spoke later that day at Meroney's Theater, a first for an African American function. Mayor A. L. Smoot welcomed the Tuskegean along with ex-mayor Archibald H. Boyden, who gave remarks at the end of Washington's speech. A nostalgic Boyden praised African Americans for carefully watching over his loved ones during the Civil War and adjured the audience to give them fair play. Boyden praised Washington's remarks and thought the lessons taught by the latter would not only help black people in working out their part of the problem, but would help white people also. After this, Major Moton and a local quartette sang folk songs and plantation melodies. "Every race has its own songs and the Negro should be proud of his ability to bring out the *true meaning* (emphasis mine) and pathos of the songs that cheered his fathers and mothers in the dark days when these melodies gave them spiritual solace," Moton declared before he started to sing. As explained in chapter 3, this "true meaning" refers to the coded message blacks interpreted from these songs. The *Observer* reported that Washington told wholesome truths about the races in the South. Indeed, the Tuskegee leader knew how to convey his ideas, sometimes seemingly giving two speeches in one. He "gave the members of his race some good advice [and] at the same time he pointed out to the white people in the audience many ways by which they might be helpful to the negroes in their efforts at race betterment," the *Observer* recorded.[39]

The last stop for the day was High Point. J. A. Garan had charge of the local committee and escorted the party in carriages to the High Point Normal and Industrial Institute, led by Professor Alfred James Griffin. The young ladies of the school, led by Mrs. Griffin, served a "royal feast" for the visitors; after which, the Wizard received an enthusiastic reception when he spoke at the Rink Auditorium to one thousand people, a third of whom was white. High Point Normal's hundred fifty–person choir sang and the African Americans in the audience joined Moton in singing a number of plantation tunes. This stop ended the second day of the tour.[40]

On Sunday morning, October 30, Washington arrived at Winston-Salem to an immense crowd waiting to receive the party. Winston-Salem reportedly had "a progressive and industrious colored population" with "many beautiful homes." The party had breakfast at the home of J. W. Jones, where Mrs. R. J. Reynolds, wife of the tobacco magnate and one of the wealthiest white women in the town, sent over her linen, silver, and two servants to assist in entertaining the party. S. G. Atkins, secretary of education for the AMEZ Church who headed the local committee, took the party to inspect Slater Normal and Industrial Institute until around noon when Washington spoke at the Elks' Auditorium to approximately three thousand people. These school inspections also serve as examples of how Washington used black progress to thwart white supremacist arguments of degeneration. Mayor Oscar B. Eaton introduced the speaker declaring that the Tuskegee sage "possessed in the most wonderful degree the qualifications of common sense, sound character and diligence." After this successful speech the party left for Greensboro.[41]

Between 1870 and 1900, African Americans in Greensboro comprised the overwhelming majority of semiskilled and unskilled workers. Working as carpenters, brick-makers, foundry workers, stone-masons, and skilled railway employees, they also made up nearly half of all the skilled workers in Greensboro. During that time, homes in the city even showed some patterns of integration. Yet by 1900, as William Chafe tells us, "Greensboro had rejected these potentially egalitarian patterns and had moved sharply toward a system of rigid racial and economic discrimination." When Washington arrived in 1910, the percentage of black skilled workers in Greensboro had fallen drastically from 30 percent in 1870 to a mere 8 percent with 80 percent of blacks working as unskilled and semiskilled laborers. Nevertheless, blacks and whites in Greensboro were excited about Washington's visit. The Board of Aldermen for the town took the unusual step of passing a resolution on October 24, empowering the mayor to appoint a committee of whites to join in welcoming the Tuskegean when he arrived. Mayor Stafford in turn appointed some of the most respected whites in Greensboro to carry out the task. They included judges James E. Boyd and N. L. Eure and ex-judges W. P. Bynum, Jr., T. J. Shaw, S. B. Adams, R. M. Douglas, and Dr. J. I. Foust. A reporter noted that "the citizens of Greensboro have left no stone unturned to make the visit of Dr. Washington memorable."[42]

When Washington's train arrived at Greensboro a huge crowd of three thousand African Americans and whites greeted them at the station. Black churches suspended Sunday services and the white churches held early services so everybody could hear the Tuskegee leader. Approximately six thousand to eight thousand people turned out to hear the South's most popular figure at the Hippodrome, reportedly the largest auditorium in the state. At least one thousand five hundred of those were whites and despite the chilliness of the evening, the crowd remained throughout the program. The Honorable E. J. Justice, ex-Speaker of the North Carolina legislature, gave the welcome address. "In the final analysis all labor is honorable and education is a prime necessity in making labor efficient," said Justice. "The best way to get away from drudgery is to become intelligent enough to use the most scientific methods of performing the service the world needs. Along his own line and in his own way, assisted by broad-minded whites, the two races will work out their destiny in this, the best country on earth."[43]

After the welcome address, the choir, led by Professor W. H. Howze, played several classical selections like the "Inflammatus" with obligato, accompanied by Mrs. Annie Nelson. Then Major Moton came up and sang plantation songs "which evoked enthusiastic applause, especially in the boxes occupied by the white visitors," one observer noted. Robert E. Jones, a former resident of Greensboro touring the state with Washington, introduced the Tuskegee leader. Washington then spoke for two hours and reportedly held the audience's attention throughout his oration. "His wit and humor serving to drive home the great truths that, in less skillful hands might not have been palatable in the midst of a political campaign in a Southern community," one person opined. This observation illuminates Washington's ability to double-talk and effectively utilize metalanguage in his lectures.[44]

While in Greensboro, the Washington party visited the North Carolina Agricultural and Mechanical College (a state-supported school for blacks) headed by James Benson Dudley from 1896 to 1925, a member of Washington's entourage. Born in Wilmington in 1859, Dudley received his first schooling through a private tutor. From Wilmington he moved to Philadelphia and attended the Philadelphia Institute for Colored Youths. Later, he earned a Master of Arts degree from Livingston College in Salisbury, and the Doctor of Laws degree from Wilberforce University, Wilberforce, Ohio. After completing his schooling, Dudley returned to Wilmington where he worked as a teacher and later principal of the Peabody Graded School for sixteen years. He also served as Register of Deeds for New Hanover County in 1891, the same year the Agricultural and Mechanical College began. A business-minded person, he created the Metropolitan Trust Company of Wilmington to combine and stimulate black business, and established the Pioneer Building and Loan Association of Greensboro, the oldest such group in the city. He also owned property in Wilmington and Greensboro. In addition, he served as a delegate to the Republican National Convention in Saint Louis, Missouri, in 1896, worked as president of the North Carolina Teachers' Association, and was the chairman of the Negro Railroad Commission, among other things. In 1896, the state board of trustees chose Dudley to lead the Agricultural and Mechanical College. Under his guidance, new courses were added to the curriculum, farms were cultivated, old buildings were renovated, and new ones were erected.[45]

The party also visited Bennett College in Greensboro (an AMEZ institution), and Emanuel Lutheran College, a black-attended school with white teachers supported by the Lutheran denomination. Washington made short addresses at each of these locations that were "appropriate, helpful, practical and to the point."[46] On Monday morning, October 31, the group arrived at Reidsville, where school children showed up waving flags, as a brass band played "Hail to the Chief." People lined the pathway and roses were strewn for the guests to parade on. Three prominent white citizens came to the hall and had breakfast with the entourage and welcomed Washington to the town. The mayor introduced the speaker to about three thousand people who filled the old tobacco warehouse where he spoke. Reidsville's mayor boasted that black children in their town attended school for nine months, and while only one hundred and fifty of the city's African Americans were registered to vote, the mayor won by only nine votes, giving blacks a balance of power, the mayor said. More than one thousand admirers followed the party back to the train station to see Washington off for Durham where they arrived at nightfall.[47]

The Tuskegee leader had been impressed by the "general prosperity" of black people throughout his stops in North Carolina. He had witnessed black-owned farms, truck farms, well-maintained businesses, successful schools, and nice homes among other things. When he talked about his elation at these encouraging signs of black progress, each time the men with him responded: "Wait till you get to Durham, Dr. Washington. Wait until you get to Durham." Durham, one of the richest cities in the state, was the home of Washington and James Duke (the former, a hair client of Merrick) founders of the American Tobacco Company. The city consisted of 18,241 people by 1910, of which nearly 40 percent were black. A number of elite African Americans living in Durham had beautiful and luxurious homes and were relatively well off. Even Du Bois wondered in 1912, just two years after Washington's visit, what "made white Durham willing to see black Durham rise without organizing mobs or secret societies to 'keep the niggers down.'" Easily the leading black businessmen of this community were Merrick, Moore, and Spaulding.[48]

Born into slavery on September 7, 1859 to a black mother named Martha and a white father he never knew, Merrick became the most successful barber in Durham, one time owning as many as nine barbershops. Merrick eventually ventured into real estate where he owned sixty rental properties. He cofounded the North Carolina Mutual and Provident Insurance Company in 1898 (later the North Carolina Mutual Life Insurance Company) that netted $1.7 million in income by 1919, the year of Merrick's death. Along with his other business endeavors, Merrick cofounded the Mechanics and Farmers Bank where he served as vice president. Like Washington and many of his close supporters, when dealing with whites, Merrick practiced black survivalism, being full of calculation and purpose. "He knew perfectly how to play the role, how to wear the mask," Walter Weare wrote. "Laughing at darkey stories and telling his own, Merrick pleased his white patrons; yet he knew how to navigate between affability and buffoonery." But as previously stated African Americans knew that with "great poise" Merrick could "tip his hat to the white man and at the same time call him a son-of-a-bitch under his breath."[49]

Dr. Moore served as the secretary-treasurer and medical examiner for the North Carolina Mutual Life Insurance Company. Born on

September 6, 1863 near Whiteville in Columbus County, Moore attended the Columbus County public school. In 1885, he enrolled in Shaw University and eventually graduated from the University's Leonard Medical School, completing a four-year program in just three years. Moore placed second out of forty-two on the North Carolina medical board examination and became the first black physician in Durham in 1888. He was Durham's only black physician for years. Among his many endeavors, Moore cofounded the North Carolina Mutual, cofounded the Mechanics and Farmers Bank serving as a director, founded the Lincoln Hospital in 1901, and the Colored Library in 1913. Moreover, he became Director of the Oxford Orphan Asylum and by the time of his death in 1923 had become a noted philanthropist. Unlike Merrick and Washington, Moore was less apt to "wear the mask" when dealing with whites. Perhaps because he could almost pass for white and/or because of his reputation as a successful physician, he "spoke straight from the shoulder" and approached whites on a level of equality, according to Weare.[50]

The third member of this triumvirate was Spaulding, nephew of Moore. Born near Whiteville like his uncle in 1874, Spaulding attended the public schools of Columbus County, graduating from the Whitted High School at Durham. After working several jobs, he became manager of a cooperative black grocery store. He so impressed Merrick and Moore with his energy and zeal that they brought him into the Mutual as a salesman and later general manager, where he eventually helped transform the company into the largest African American business in the country. Moore also served as vice president and later president of the North Carolina Mutual for decades. Over the years, the Mutual became an incubator for other black businesses. It produced a drugstore, a cotton mill, a savings and loan association, the Mortgage Company of Durham, the National Negro Finance Corporation, a real estate company, two newspapers, and the Mechanics and Farmers Bank. Spaulding became a director and cashier of the bank. He clearly identified with Washington's economic philosophy during the first half of his career, and according to one writer, believed that "if his generation literally tended to business, the race problem would give way to the structural weight of a society that worshiped business enterprise, especially the underdogs who won success."[51]

There were a number of black-owned businesses in Durham— two drugstores, one shoe store, one textile mill, one iron foundry, one millinery store, a mattress factory, twenty-five groceries, two tailoring establishments, three insurance companies, one bank, eight barbershops, a dry goods store, and one of the largest brick manufacturing plants in the country. Blacks in Durham owned an estimated $125,000 in business property. However, the North Carolina Mutual and Provident Association, called the "World's Largest Negro Life Insurance Company," served as the biggest attraction in Durham. Indeed, the Mutual became the nation's largest black-owned business in the United States until World War II. Durham quickly gained the reputation of "The Black Wall Street of America," the "Capital of the Black Middle Class," and "The Magic City" and Washington deeply influenced Durham's black leadership class. Weare concluded that "the story of black Durham and the North Carolina Mutual belong to the New South, to the age of Booker T. Washington and his gospel of self-help."[52]

On October 31, Washington spoke at one of the largest black churches in Durham and deviating from previous Tar Heel stops, allowed a local black leader (instead of a white one), Dr. James E. Shepard, head of the National Religious Training School (now North Carolina Central University), to introduce him. Born in Raleigh in 1875, Shepard graduated from Shaw University at age nineteen. He worked in the Recorder of Deeds office in Washington, DC, for one year and then became deputy collector of internal revenue at Raleigh from 1900 to 1906. His interest in training black ministers led him to found the National Religious Training School in 1910, and he served as its leader until 1947.[53]

After Shepard's introduction, Washington moved to center stage. "Both races of the South suffer at the hands of public opinion in one respect, and that is by reason of the fact that the outside world hears of our difficulties; hears of our crimes, hears of mobs and lynchings," Washington told the Durham audience. "But the outside world does not hear of, neither does it know about, the evidence of racial friendship and good will which exists in the majority of communities in North Carolina and other Southern States where blacks and whites live together." Washington proffered that of all the places in the world he had visited, there were none where "the white and colored races living side by side dwell in such satisfactory relationship as they do in the South." Doubtless, Washington wanted his words to become a self-fulfilled prophecy. The Wizard also spoke at the training school and the graded school where he "showed his versatility by being able to entertain and instruct little ones between six and twelve years of age." Black citizens of Durham boasted that their public schools had ten-month terms. Ultimately, Durham, like the rest of the state, was no utopia for its black residents. "Too frequently black leaders viewed the effects of caste through the filter of their own favorable experience," Weare concluded, "others, however, painted a more sober picture."[54] Nevertheless, Washington publicized his stop at Durham to show the world the remarkable progress of his race, and it served his purpose in his efforts to undermine white supremacy.

The party left Durham for Wilson, but en route Washington made a whistle-stop at Selma, speaking from the rear platform of the train to roughly three hundred people. At Wilson, he spoke in the auditorium at a large African American school where whites constituted more than half of the audience. Frederick A. Woodard, a lawyer from Wilson and ex-Democratic U. S. Representative, introduced the Tuskegee leader and Washington spoke movingly. Afterward, Charles L. Coon, a white local superintendent of schools, commended Washington for his efforts at racial uplift and spoke on some of his research findings regarding how blacks were being unfairly taxed throughout the South, especially when it came to education. "With figures to back it up," one observer noted, Coon said "the Negroes are not only paying their proportion of the school tax, but in some instances educating white children." Indeed, Coon found that all over the South, contrary to white beliefs, African Americans were not recipients of white tax funds and did not even receive all the taxes they paid directly or indirectly. After 1907, Coon became one of the most persuasive proponents of racial justice and educational reform in the South. In a 1905–1906 state school report, Coon had shown statistically that blacks paid more in taxes than was spent on their schools and in 1909, he expounded on these findings with statistics from other states in a paper titled "Public Taxation and Negro Schools," presented at the Twelfth Conference for Education in the South in Atlanta.[55]

Leaving Wilson, the party visited Rocky Mount, described as "a Southern town to delight the eye." Rocky Mount reportedly had electric lights, running water, modern sewage systems, and new buildings. About twelve thousand people lived there, half black and half white. A uniformed brass band met the party when they arrived and the local committee led the entourage to carriages and paraded them through the city. At midday, they attended a banquet, and later that afternoon six thousand people gathered in a cotton warehouse to hear the Tuskegean. Several businesses and schools closed for the occasion and Thomas Battle, former mayor (1886–1896) and president of the Bank of Rocky Mount, introduced Washington echoing the same sentiments as many other Southern whites. "He is a man to be proud of," Battle said, "we who have watched him and read his speeches and his writings feel that he is best fitted to settle the greatest question of our time, on the proper solution of which depends the welfare of our entire Southland." Washington spoke for two hours moving the audience to laughter and then to more sober and serious things.[56]

The Wizard made whistle-stops at Tarboro and Parmelee and then stopped in Washington, where, Nathaniel Harding, the white ex-superintendent of schools and rector of the Episcopal Church, introduced the Doctor to a huge crowd at Brown's Opera House. "His speech was a fine one and full of good advice for both colored and white people and every day philosophy without a discordant note or word out of tune with either race's characteristic," the *Observer* noted. This again highlights Washington's success at double-talk. After his address, Washington received a gold-decorated fountain pen and flowers. The next stop was New Bern where the Tuskegean and his associates were met by a brass band and carriages that transported them to the local opera house. As with most of his other stops in North Carolina, a former mayor of New Bern introduced Washington to the audience that included the Board of County Commissioners, the Board of Education, and many other distinguished citizens. A newspaper called the stop "an epoch in the history of the colored citizenship of New [Bern]" and said the visit would "cause the colored citizens to throw off faults as far as possible, and meet as men and women the issues that shall advance the race." After a successful presentation, the party headed to Wilmington, the final stop on the itinerary.[57]

Members of the entourage experienced some anxiety in terms of how the reception would be in Wilmington because they remembered the horrendous racial massacre that engulfed the city, twelve years earlier. However, over three thousand people packed the streets leading to the train station, and so many people turned out that the local police were called for crowd control so the party could reach the carriages awaiting them. On November 4, the Tuskegean spoke at the spacious and beautiful Academy of Music, "the best auditorium in the city." Following Southern customs, the "whites occupied one side of the orchestra and one tier of boxes; the colored people the other side and boxes and both galleries" to a standing-room-only crowd. One observer mused that on stage, leading white citizens "sat cheek by jowl with leading colored citizens" with the mayor introducing the speaker. The symbolism of this integrated panel showed that blacks were just as advanced and human as the whites participating with them. This type of racial cooperation helped to marginalize, to some extent, white racist arguments that demeaned blacks. Washington spoke for close to two hours and during his address he boldly mentioned that the last time he visited Wilmington was in 1898 just before the riot. He asserted that the problem had changed; now they are "having a political campaign with the Negro left out." According to Lewis, a guest of the Tuskegean, this subject "was a delicate one and the situation rather tense, but, as usual, the speaker got away with it by one of his inimitable stories:"

> He said the situation reminded him of an old colored man down in Alabama who had a pig and sold it to a white man for three dollars. The pig came back, and he sold it to a second white man for three dollars. The first white man, going back to the old colored man to look for his pig, found the second man coming out with his pig, and said to him: "That is my pig; I paid Uncle Jim three dollars for it." The second man said: "It is my pig; I paid Uncle Jim three dollars for it." So they decided to go back to Uncle Jim and put it up to him. So in a few moments they met him and the first man said: "Uncle Jim, didn't I pay you three dollars for this pig?" "You certainly did, boss." The second white man said: "Uncle Jim, didn't I pay you three dollars for this pig?" "Yes, boss, you gave me three dollars, too." "Well, Uncle Jim, whose pig is it?" Whereupon the old man said: "Fo' de Lord, can't you white folk settle your own troubles without bothering a poor colored man?"[58]

Washington's words were well-received for after the address black and white citizens flocked to the stage to shake his hand, a clear violation of the Southern code of racial etiquette. Others followed Washington back to his railcar in an effort to meet the Tuskegee Wizard before he departed.[59]

Prominent white businessmen and planters from Robeson and Scotland counties wanted Washington to speak to the black farmers in Maxton and Laurinburg so badly, they paid for a special coach to stop in the towns for two hours. At Maxton, former Congressman George B. Patterson introduced the Tuskegean and at Laurinburg, Mayor Maxey L. John introduced him. Washington adjusted his remarks to fit the rural audience, simultaneously giving one address to blacks and another to whites. He made "special emphasis on that portion of his addresses advising people of his race to remain in the country. He likewise appealed in a very strong manner to the white people to see to it that negroes had ample educational facilities and that they were protected in their lives and property," a newspaper reported.[60]

On the whole, the trip proved to be a smashing success with the Tuskegee Wizard speaking to an estimated fifty-five thousand to one hundred thousand people. One paper even suggested that through the press and other sources, he may have reached as many as five hundred thousand people. The party dined so well throughout the visit that one person in Washington's group commented that "we have been eating our way through North Carolina, digging our graves with our teeth."[61] Newspapers covering the trip continuously referred to Washington as the representative leader of black America. The *New York Age* called him "the acknowledged leader of the Negro race," and the *Indianapolis Freeman* described him as "the world's most famous advocate of 'common sense education.'" "The speaker made a great impression not only upon the large crowd of negroes who heard him," noted the *Observer*, "but the large audience of white people from whom he elicited nearly as much applause as from the colored portion." That white-owned paper also called Washington "the genius of the Moses of the colored race and the brainiest representative of his people." The *Baltimore Afro-American Ledger* asserted that "the hold which Mr. Washington has upon the people of the South was shown by the felicitous addresses of welcome delivered by prominent white and colored citizens at the various places at which Dr. Washington spoke."[62]

By contrast, the December edition of the *Crisis* edited by Du Bois gave only a sparse mention of the trip saying in its entirety: "Mr. Booker T. Washington with a number of companions has been making a tour of the State of North Carolina."[63] It is worth noting that Du Bois remained guarded in his criticism of Washington's tour because he keenly understood that while the trips promoted Washington's agenda and Washington personally as a leader, they also helped to vindicate the race and undermine white supremacy by placing black achievement and progress on display. Perhaps he realized that the fight against white supremacy took primacy over the other matters.

Most black newspapers heaped praise on Washington for the success of his tour. Richard W. Thompson, who ran the National Negro Press Association until 1903 and served as editor of the *Indianapolis Freeman*, published several blurbs from people who had attended at least one of Washington's presentations. One person wrote that "'the Wizard' was never in better voice nor in better humor throughout." Another observer noted: "there were banquets galore, the party literally 'ate its way through North Carolina.'" Others were impressed by Washington's meeting with Sherman: "The meeting between Dr. Washington and Vice President Sherman, at Salisbury, was one of the delightful events of the itinerary." Similarly another person opined that "the meeting with Vice President Sherman at Salisbury was a happy incident."[64]

Although these tours taxed Washington's health, he did not falter. "Dr. Washington's powers of endurance are simply wonderful," an observer recorded. The writer praised Washington for delivering "from three to five and sometimes seven speeches of varying lengths per day, and never showed the slightest sign of fatigue or hoarseness, despite the fact that he frequently addressed crowds in the open air, amid a chilly breeze." Washington spoke with the same energy and zeal at small and large venues. "His last speech...was delivered with as much vim and in as happy a vein as his first utterance at Charlotte, eight days earlier," another observer wrote.[65]

The trip helped Washington receive endorsements from prominent white politicians and praises from all over the political spectrum in North Carolina. As a case in point, former U.S. senator and ex-governor Thomas J. Jarvis, a Democrat, wrote the Tuskegean a letter of praise that said in part: "the colored people are a part of the citizenship of the State...and I heartily welcome and indorse any movement and influence to make them better citizens." Then the clincher: "I believe the teachings contained in your address will be helpful to those who hear them." Similarly, as noted above, Battle, former mayor of Rocky Mount, concluded that Washington "is best fitted to settle the greatest question of our time."[66]

These clippings show not only the general sentiment about Washington's visit, but also how his educational pilgrimages helped to bolster his position as *the* leader of the black race. Even though the newly formed NAACP provided meager competition for the Tuskegean, Washington used these tours as a means of not only publicizing black progress, but also to illustrate to blacks and especially whites in the North and South that his philosophy and approach to the race problem was the most palatable and pragmatic, and that most people inside and outside of his race supported him. Repeated newspaper reports that "immense crowds greeted the 'Wizard' at many points not down on the schedule...to the end that the people might hear the Tuskegeean's message of hope and cheer," lent credence to his status as *the* legitimate black leader. The tours also countered white propaganda that promoted myths of black degeneration. By now these trips had become a fixed part of the orbit of Washington's Tuskegee Machine.[67]

Moreover, the fact that Washington traveled with such a distinguished entourage showed outsiders again that a substantial portion of the Talented Tenth supported his agenda. As a case in point, about a month after the tour, the *Indianapolis Freeman* reported that "in personnel the party was an 'all-star' aggregation. It embraced eminent churchmen, physicians, lawyers, capitalists, journalists, farmers, educators, mechanics, architects, federal office-holders, business-men, fraternity directors, artists, and musicians." Further, "all had earned a reputation that could not be gainsaid—every man was educated and qualified for leadership. It was a group of high-toned gentlemen, whose coming was an inspiration to the people of both races in the State."[68]

Clinton, Merrick, Spaulding, Dudley, and other leading African Americans presented Washington with the following resolution at the end of the tour:

> The undersigned representatives of 50,000 loyal North Carolinians upon whose ears fell the message of cheer, hope and amity which you brought to us during your recent tour of our beloved State together with those of our fellow-citizens who, through the press and from the lips of those who shall herald the tidings of this great commonwealth, salute you.
>
> We would hereby make known to you our full appreciation of your sojourn in our midst, our hearty gratitude for the magnificent work you have already accomplished, our faith in the achievements which a practical application of your wise policies to the solution of our problem will make possible and our purpose to apply them as that they may bear their appropriate fruit in the future life of our people in this State.
>
> May the All-Wise and All-Powerful One continue to guide you and prosper the labors of your hands wherever His spirit leads you is our prayer; and when in His providence the fruition of your hope and ours shall have been realized, may they be many who shall rise up and call you blessed.[69]

It seems that these words were not just for Washington's edification, but for white readers of the *Observer* as well. The leaders conveyed the idea that they were going to follow Washington's proscription to the race problem, but they certainly hoped that whites would follow the Tuskegean's advice and fulfill his prophecy too.

"The trip was all that could be desired," asserted Clinton, the tour's main organizer. "The reception accorded Dr. Washington is conclusive evidence that his work is next [to] the hearts of the people, and I am quite sure that his coming to our state will be productive of much good." Lewis, another Washington supporter, asserted that he could not "recall any occasion in this country where a mere private citizen who has not held high public office has been received with greater general acclaim, by both white and colored citizens, because of his services to his fellows, than was Dr. Washington upon his trip

through the Old North State." "Those who came out of curiosity...,"
Lewis continued, "went away with praise upon their lips and giving
hearty expressions of good will and approval and support, and
absolutely sure that Dr. Washington was pointing the true and the
only way."[70]

Last, members of the party praised the railroad officials for the
courteous treatment they received throughout the tour, especially
officials from the Southern Railway located in Charlotte. By the
time this tour ended, plans were already underway for Washington
to visit Texas.[71]

Charles Banks

Booker T. Washington

George Clinton

Robert L. Smith

James C. Napier

Matthew M. Lewey

Figure 1 Washington and the coordinators of his five tours. Center: Washington, president and founder of the National Negro Business League. From William N. Hartshorn, *An Era of Progress and Promise, 1863–1910* (Boston: Priscilla Publishing, 1910). Top left: Charles Banks of Mound Bayou, Mississippi, coordinated Washington's Mississippi tour. From Green P. Hamilton, *Beacon Lights of the Race* (Memphis, TN: E. H. Clarke and Brother, 1911). Top right: Bishop George Wylie Clinton of Charlotte, North Carolina, coordinated Washington's North Carolina tour. From Washington, *My Larger Education* (New York: Doubleday, 1911). Bottom left: Robert L. Smith of Waco, Texas, coordinated Washington's tour of Texas. Courtesy of Will Guzman. Bottom middle: James C. Napier of Nashville, Tennessee, coordinated Washington's tour of Tennessee. From Clement Richardson, *The National Cyclopedia of the Colored Race* (Montgomery, AL: National Publishing, 1919). Bottom right: Matthew M. Lewey of Pensacola, Florida, coordinated Washington's Florida tour. From William N. Hartshorn, *An Era of Progress and Promise, 1863–1910* (Boston: Priscilla Publishing, 1910).

Washington at desk.

Washington speaking.

After Ulrich beating.

Washington in Denmark.

Washington in 1912 speaking in Jacksonville, FL.

Figure 2 Top left: Washington working at his desk at Tuskegee Institute. Courtesy of Titus Brown. Top right: Washington speaking. From Frederick E. Drinker, *Booker T. Washington: The Master Mind of a Child of Slavery* (Chicago: Howard and Chandler, 1915). Center: Washington with bandaged head after the Henry Ulrich assault in New York, March 1911. From *Dayton Herald*, March 23, 1911. Bottom left: Washington speaking in Jacksonville, Florida. Author's collection. Bottom right: Washington in Copenhagen, Denmark. From Frederic E. Drinker, *Booker T. Washington: The Master Mind of a Child of Slavery* (Chicago: Howard and Chandler 1915)

Booker T. Washington   Robert Russa Moton   Emmett Scott

John Merrick   Charles Banks

Charles Spaulding

Figure 3 Top left: Washington, president of Tuskegee Institute. From Frederick E. Drinker, *Booker T. Washington: The Master Mind of a Child of Slavery* (Chicago: Howard and Chandler, 1915). Top center: Robert R. Moton led many of the "plantation songs" on Washington's tours and became his successor at Tuskegee Institute. From Clement Richardson, *The National Cyclopedia of the Colored Race* (Montgomery, AL: National Publishing, 1919). Top right: Emmett J. Scott, Washington's loyal secretary. William Allison Sweeney, *History of the American Negro in the Great World War, His Splendid Record in the Battle Zones of Europe* (Chicago: G. G. Sapp, 1919). Bottom left: John Merrick, business leader in North Carolina and Washington supporter. From Clement Richardson, *The National Cyclopedia of the Colored Race* (Montgomery, AL: National Publishing, 1919). Bottom center: Charles Banks, Washington's "Chief Lieutenant" for Mississippi. Washington, "Charles Banks," *American Magazine* 81 (March 1911): 732. Bottom right: Charles Spaulding, a business leader in Charlotte, North Carolina, and Washington supporter. Author's collection.

Joseph Blodgett

Elias Cottrell

Abraham Lewis

Charles Harry Anderson

W. E. B. Du Bois

Matthew W. Dogan

Figure 4 Top left: Joseph Blodgett, businessman in Jacksonville, Florida, and Washington supporter. Author's collection. Top center: Elias Cottrell, Bishop of the CME Church and Washington supporter. Isaac Lane, *Autobiography of Bishop Isaac Lane, L.L.D.: With a Short History of the C.M.E. Church in America and of Methodism* (Nashville, TN: Publishing House of the M.E. Church, South, 1916). Top right: Abraham Lincoln Lewis of Jacksonville, Florida. Business leader and supporter of Washington. From Clement Richardson, *The National Cyclopedia of the Colored Race* (Montgomery, AL: National Publishing, 1919). Bottom left: Charles H. Anderson, businessman in Jacksonville, Florida, and Washington supporter. From Clement Richardson, *The National Cyclopedia of the Colored Race* (Montgomery, AL: National Publishing, 1919). Bottom center: Distinguished scholar-activist W. E. B. Du Bois. Courtesy of Titus Brown. Bottom right: Matthew W. Dogan, president of Wiley College in Marshall, Texas. From Clement Richardson, *The National Cyclopedia of the Colored Race* (Montgomery, AL: National Publishing, 1919).

Home of Charles Banks

Washington's team on an educational tour of Mississippi in 1908

Figure 5 Top: Charles Banks's home in Mound Bayou, Mississippi, at the time of Washington's tour in 1908. Washington is standing in the front and center of the porch with Banks to his right. From William N. Hartshorn, *An Era of Progress and Promise, 1863–1910* (Boston: Priscilla Publishing, 1910). Bottom: Washington and associates at Bishop Elias Cottrell's home in Mississippi during his tour of the state in 1908. (Seated, left to right): Emmett Scott, Robert Moton, Washington, and (far right) Bishop Elias Cottrell. (Standing): William H. Holtzclaw (second from left) and Charles Banks (fifth from left). From Emmett J. Scott and Lyman B. Stowe, *Booker T. Washington: Builder of a Civilization* (Garden City, NJ: Doubleday, 1916).

Washington and entourage visiting Florida in 1912

Washington and entourage visiting North Carolina in 1910

Figure 6 Top: Washington and associates in Florida during his tour of the state in 1912. From left to right (Back Row): Sumner A. Furniss, Emmett J. Scott, William T. Andrews, Matthew M. Lewey, and J. C. Thomas. (Front Row): James C. Napier, Booker T. Washington, Samuel E. Courtney, John B. Bell, and Gilbert C. Harris. From Frederic E. Drinker, *Booker T. Washington: The Master Mind of a Child of Slavery* (Chicago: Howard and Chandler, 1915). Bottom: Washington and associates in North Carolina during his tour of the state in 1910. From left to right (Back Row): J. T. Saunders, George C. Clement, J. A. Dellinger, Nathan Hunt, C. S. Brown, R. W. Thompson, Silas A. Peeler, James B. Dudley, Henry L. McCrorey. (Middle Row): William S. Pittman, John H. Washington, James E. Shepard, Emmett J. Scott, William H. Lewis, Booker T. Washington, John Merrick, George W. Clinton, Charles W. Greene, R. B. McRary, G. W. Powell. (Front Row): Horace D. Slatter, D. A. Winslow, George F. King, Charles C. Spaulding, John A. Kenney, Charles H. Moore. From *Indianapolis Freeman*, November 19, 1910.

Home of John Bell

Home of Elias Cottrell

Home of Washington

Home of John Merrick

Figure 7 Top left: John Brown Bell's home in Houston, Texas. From Clement Richardson, *The National Cyclopedia of the Colored Race* (Montgomery, AL: National Publishing, 1919). Top right: Elias Cottrell's home in Holly Springs, Mississippi. From "Negro Homes," in *Century* (May 1908). Bottom left: "The Oaks," Washington's home. From Frederick E. Drinker, *Booker T. Washington: The Master Mind of a Child of Slavery* (Chicago: Howard and Chandler, 1915). Bottom right: John Merrick's home in Durham, North Carolina. Author's collection.

Masonic Temple Building
Jacksonville, FL

FAMC Mechanics Arts Building at
Tallahassee, FL

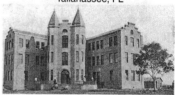

Girls Dormitory at Paul Quinn
College in Waco, TX

FAMC Carnegie Building at
Tallahassee, FL

Rust University at Holly Springs, MS

Figure 8 Top left: Masonic Temple in Jacksonville, Florida. From J. L. Nichols and William H. Crogman. *Progress of a Race* (Naperville, IL: J. L. Nichols, 1920). Top right: Florida A&M College's Mechanics Arts Building. From Clement Richardson, *The National Cyclopedia of the Colored Race* (Montgomery, AL: National Publishing Company, 1919). Middle right: Girl's Dormitory at Paul Quinn College, Waco, Texas. From Clement Richardson, *The National Cyclopedia of the Colored Race* (Montgomery, AL: National Publishing, 1919). Bottom left: Florida A&M College's Carnegie Building. From Clement Richardson, *The National Cyclopedia of the Colored Race* (Montgomery, AL: National Publishing, 1919). Bottom right: Rust University in Holly Springs, Mississippi, was attended by Charles Banks and Ida B. Wells-Barnett. From J. L. Nichols and William H. Crogman, *Progress of a Race* (Naperville, IL: J. L. Nichols, 1920).

Figure 9 Top left: Original caption under photo reads: "Christ—The Son of God. Man was created in the image of God. Is the negro in the image of God's son—Christ?" From Charles Carroll, *The Negro a Beast or in the Image of God* (Miami, FL: Mnemosyne Publishing, 1900). Top right: Beastly depiction of black man with white woman. Caption under photo reads: "The Beast and the Virgin. Can you find a white preacher who would unite in holy wedlock, a burly negro to a white lady? Ah! Parents, you would rather see your daughter burned, and her ashes scattered to the winds of heaven." From Charles Carroll, *The Negro a Beast or in the Image of God* (Miami, FL: Mnemosyne Publishing, 1900). Center: Negative depiction of black infant. Caption under photo reads: "The Virgin Mary and the Child Christ. Could the Child Christ possibly be of the same flesh as the Negro?" From Charles Carroll, *The Negro a Beast or in the Image of God* (Miami, FL: Mnemosyne Publishing, 1900). Bottom left: Negative depiction of black child. Caption under photo reads: "Adam and Eve in the Garden of Eden. Is the negro an offspring of Adam and Eve? Can the rose produce a thistle?" From Charles Carroll, *The Negro a Beast or in the Image of God* (Miami, FL: Mnemosyne Publishing, 1900). Bottom right: Black "brute" ravishes white woman. Caption under photo reads: "Natural Results. The screams of the ravished daughters of the 'Sunny South' have placed the Negro in the lowest rank of the Beast Kingdom." From Charles Carroll, *The Negro a Beast or in the Image of God* (Miami, FL: Mnemosyne Publishing, 1900).

CHAPTER 7

Tour of the Lone Star State, September–October 1911

Blacks in Texas suffered because of their race, just as much as blacks in Mississippi, Tennessee, and North Carolina did. In fact, Texas gained a dubious reputation throughout the nation among African Americans after the Brownsville Affair. In 1906 (just five years before Washington's tour), black army troops stationed in Brownsville, Texas experienced severe hostility. These soldiers stationed at Fort Brown encountered racism and discrimination from both Mexicans and whites along the Rio Grande. Although they were putting their lives on the line for the country, white businesses would not serve them, and they were restricted from public parks. Worse still, on several occasions, civilians taunted and even attacked individual black soldiers.[1]

On August 14, 1906, shortly after twelve noon, shooting erupted in Brownsville and approximately hundred fifty shots rang out. In the melee, a white civilian and a white policeman were injured. Of course, black troops were blamed for the violence especially after cartridges and clips from their army rifles were found in the street. Although two military investigations concluded that African American soldiers had participated in the shooting, they could not identify the perpetrators. After none of the soldiers would confess or name any of the alleged shooters, President Theodore Roosevelt, without a hearing or trial, dishonorably discharged three companies of black men, a total of 176 soldiers, from the military. They were barred from rejoining the military, could not work for the government, and were ineligible for veterans' pensions and other benefits. Roosevelt did this against the strong advice of Washington. Joseph B. Foraker, a Republican senator from Ohio, called the president's actions an "executive lynching." African Americans throughout the country were outraged at the treatment the soldiers were given by Texans and the president. This became a major reason blacks turned against President Roosevelt and William Howard Taft, his secretary of war who would later become president. Future investigations determined that the cartridges and clips used as evidence against the black troops were deliberately planted in a setup.[2]

By 1908, few African Americans participated in national and state politics in Texas. William "Gooseneck Bill" McDonald, Texas Republican Party leader; N. Q. Henderson, a deputy collector of internal revenue; and Mack Matthew Rodgers, another deputy collector of internal revenue for the Third District of Texas who received his appointment through his friendship with Washington, continued a futile struggle against lily-white Republican opposition to keep their jobs, but were forced out by March, 1910. That same year, disaffected African Americans in Texas organized a National Democratic League, claiming six hundred members in its first two years; however, the move provided blacks no viable alternative. In 1910, Democrats, who overwhelmingly controlled the state house of representatives, passed a resolution calling for the repeal of the Fifteenth Amendment and a modification of the Fourteenth Amendment. On the whole, Texas blacks, just like others throughout the country, found themselves losing ground with the Republican Party, but still found no viable alternative in the Democratic Party or the Populist movement.[3]

However, black Texans made strides in areas other than politics. Jack Johnson, born in Galveston, Texas in 1878, lived in the Lone Star State during this era and worked as a dock hand before becoming a professional boxer in 1897. He severely defeated Tommy Burns in Australia in 1908 and became heavyweight champion of the world. After defeating several challengers, he knocked out the "great white hope," Jim Jeffries, on July 4, 1910. The former heavyweight champion, Jeffries, had come out of retirement just to take on Johnson. Lerone Bennett observed that Johnson's practice of beating white men in the ring during that era amounted to "a political act of far-reaching dimensions." Indeed, whites feared Johnson's victories would shatter myths about white supremacy and show blacks they could beat whites when competing on equal terms. Although this event gave African Americans a psychological lift, it created cognitive dissonance among whites, who responded by attacking blacks all over the country. The Texas state legislature, fearing riots among blacks, banned the showing of Jack Johnson's boxing victories over whites. Even Congress outlawed interstate transporting of films representing prizefights. In reference to Johnson's fights, one congressman even declared that "No man descended from the old Saxon race can look upon that kind of contest without abhorrence and disgust."[4]

However, white Texans did not mind using violence to maintain white supremacy. "No one should try to stop a nigger from being mobbed that had killed a white man," one unsuccessful Texas lyncher argued, "because mobbing Negro[e]s put fear in Negro[e]s that keeps them in their places. A nigger isn't a citerzen [sic] any way." Indeed, between 1900 and 1910, Texas ranked third in the country for lynching. Over one hundred people were lynched during that ten-year period, peaking with twenty-four in 1908. A year later, fears of labor competition caused a white mob to beat an African American janitor and force other blacks out of San Angelo. In 1910, Anderson County whites became fearful when rumors began to circulate that blacks were allegedly meeting to organize attacks on whites. These rumors enraged a white mob leading them to kill eighteen African Americans in a series of raids in that county. Moreover, "whitecaps," particularly in east Texas, threatened and whipped blacks and destroyed their property in an effort to stifle economic competition and to keep down wages. In sum, Texas totally aligned herself with the traditions, values, and mores of the rest of the South, especially when it came to how she treated African Americans.[5]

Washington and his supporters realized the dangers that confronted blacks daily in the South and North. On March 19, 1911, just a few months before his trip to Texas, a white man in New York assaulted the world famous Tuskegean. Henry Ulrich claimed he caught Washington trying to steal and that he saw him peeping through a key hole at the front door of a white woman's apartment. Ulrich, a carpenter by trade, took a walking stick and beat Washington severely striking him almost twenty times. Washington pleaded for the man to stop: "If I'm breaking the law call an officer and have him arrest me if I'm doing anything wrong," he begged. Luckily, a plainclothes policeman saw Washington and intervened. By that time, the Tuskegee leader had blood gushing from his head, requiring sixteen stitches. He wound up getting a bandage wrapped around the entire top of his head except the crown, and a skull cap to cover the gauze. The officer arrested the black man first; however, when he learned that the victim was Washington, he dropped all charges against him and then charged Ulrich with felonious assault.[6]

About three weeks before his trip to Texas, the *Washington Bee* quoted Washington condemning lynchings in Pennsylvania and Oklahoma in very strong terms. On August 12, 1911, Zachariah Walker emerged drunk from a saloon in Coatesville, Pennsylvania and began firing a pistol into the air. This led to a confrontation with Edgar Rice, a law enforcement officer, who began tussling with Walker in an attempt to subdue him. Somehow, Rice lost his nightstick and then drew his gun, but Walker shot him first, three times, killing him almost instantly. Walker then fled and hid in a barn all night. The next morning, he attempted suicide by shooting himself in the head but when the gun discharged, it only fractured his jaw. The sheriff eventually captured Walker and took him to jail and then to the hospital. A Pennsylvania mob later extricated him. "I killed Rice in self-defense," Walker pleaded, "Don't give me a crooked death because I'm not white." An estimated five thousand men, women, and children watched the proceedings in Coatesville "as though it were a ball game or another variety of outdoor sport," one source noted. The mob stacked wood and other flammable materials around Walker and poured oil all over him. Someone then set him on fire. As he tried to escape the flames, mob members pushed him back with fence rails and pitchforks. Just as in the South, they waited for his body parts to cool, then took his charred fingers and toes as souvenirs.[7]

"The lynching and burning of human bodies, whether occurring in the North or in the South, is an injury and a disgrace to our civilization," Washington said in utter disgust. "The recent lynching of a man in Coatesville, Pa., and of another in Oklahoma, especially puts us in a bad light before the people of Europe," he argued. The Tuskegee leader went on to say that to remedy such crimes the law should be enforced everywhere regardless of race or color and as Northern and Southern sentiment turned against lynching, "such outrages will be fewer in the future than in the past." Moreover, "the better element of my own race thoroughly condemn and deplore crimes committed by individuals, *but the punishment should be administered by the court and not by the mob*" (emphasis mine), he asserted. Interestingly, the last part of that statement sounds eerily reminiscent of Washington's pleas to convince Ulrich to stop assaulting him. It could be that Washington became more outspoken because he had been personally victimized by white violence just a few months earlier. Nevertheless, these major events set the backdrop for Washington's educational pilgrimage through the Lone Star State.[8]

Members of the Texas State Negro Business League (TXSNBL) invited Washington to visit their state. African American businessmen in Texas founded local chapters of the NNBL in Galveston and Dallas during 1904 and at Fort Worth in 1905. They organized a state league in 1907, electing Washington's friend Robert Lloyd

Smith as president. Smith served in that capacity for ten years. Well over 50 percent of the black businesses in Texas consisted of barbershops, saloons, restaurants, boarding houses, drug stores, and grocery stores. Corporate businesses were unknown. In larger urban areas like Houston, African American businessmen capitalized on segregation by advocating self-sufficiency within the black community and by appealing to racial pride. Some blacks became wealthy like Houston's Hobart Taylor, Sr., who opened an insurance company and later expanded into the taxicab business—becoming a millionaire by the early 1930s. By selling stocks to mostly white investors, an African American Masonic Lodge in Dallas founded the New Century Cotton Mills in 1901. The mill employed sixty workers and produced three thousand yards of yarn per day. The Penny Savings Bank opened in Dallas in 1909 but closed in just three years. African Americans in Dallas were not alone in starting banks. During the early 1900s, black Texans also opened banks at Fort Worth, Palestine, Waco, Tyler, Galveston, and Houston.[9]

In early September, the *Indianapolis Freeman* began publicizing the arrival of Washington. The *Dallas Express*, another black paper, advised that standing room will be at a premium at the Tuskegean's speeches.[10] The group's schedule included visits to eleven Texas cities over eight days. The tour began in El Paso on September 25 and ended in Texarkana, on October 5, 1911, with stops at Juarez, San Antonio, Houston, Prairie View, Austin, Waco, Fort Worth, Dallas, and Marshall in between. As in the past, there were distinguished men from around the country accompanying Washington through Texas. Among them were his son Washington, Jr., Emmett J. Scott, John A. Kenney, a physician; Bishop Isaiah B. Scott, the only black bishop in the Methodist Episcopal Church; Hightower T. Kealing, president, Western University, Quindaro, Kansas; W. T. B. Williams, agent for the John F. Slater and Jeanes Fund Boards; Elias Camp Morris, president of the National Baptist Convention, Helena, Arkansas; Robert E. Park, magazine writer; and Walter L. Cohen, former register of the United States land office, New Orleans, Louisiana. A number of well-known African American leaders from Texas joined the entourage as well, including Emanuel Matthew Griggs, president, Farmers Bank and Trust Company, Palestine, Texas; Lee Lewis Campbell, pastor of the Ebenezer Baptist Church in Austin, and a prohibition leader; Matthew Winfred Dogan, president, Wiley University; Edward L. Blackshear, president, Prairie View State Normal School; John Brown Bell, businessman, Houston; and R. C. Houston, banker, Fort Worth.[11]

Washington entered El Paso from Phoenix, Arizona, on September 25, 1911, arriving at five thirty in the evening. The Tuskegee leader and his entourage were immediately ushered to the home of prominent black barber Charles W. Bradley. Approximately one hour later, they attended a dinner prepared by the "colored women of El Paso" at the home of Exel T. Perrett, a black railroad switchman. After dinner, Washington spoke to a standing-room-only crowd at the El Paso Theater, two-thirds of whom were white. Whites also covered 85 percent of the expenses needed to rent the theater. A number of prominent El Paso blacks joined Washington on the platform including Bradley, E. D. Williams, barber from Las Cruces, New Mexico; Leroy White, barber; Amos Williams, janitor at the El Paso City Hall; Frederick D. Clopton, teacher at Douglass High School; Jasper Williams, black messenger employed by the United States Immigration Service; and Henry R. Wilson, pastor of Second Baptist Church. William Coleman also participated.[12]

Born in Georgia five years after the Civil War, Coleman studied at Valdosta Academy for eight years, Howard University for another five, and then Brown University where he earned an AB degree in 1897. About three years later, he became assistant principal of the all-black high school in Fort Worth. In 1907, he became principal of Douglass High School in El Paso. Coleman also helped organize the Fraternal Bank and Trust Company, reportedly the first black bank in Texas. Coleman introduced Washington as the savior of his people, the man who, "[w]hen everything seemed dark for the future of the Negro race and progress seemed an idle dream," he said, "appeared upon the scene and by the power of his personality, the wisdom of his advice, and the light of his example, pointed the way to the happy condition in which now 'both races are living under the same flag, side by side, in peace and harmony.'" The last part of Coleman's remarks were clearly said for white consumption, as he fully understood the arduous times members of his race experienced in Texas and those days did not amount to "peace and harmony."[13]

However, by using this kind of metalanguage, Coleman wanted whites *to behave* in the manner he described, to live up to the expectation of peace and harmony. He wanted it to become a self-fulfilled prophecy. As stated earlier, Rosenthal and Jacobson called this phenomenon the self-fulfilled prophecy, "because a prophecy about behavior is often fulfilled." Indeed, Coleman gave a suggestive message filled with "prophecy." He, like Washington and other Bookerites, spoke in the past tense about things they wanted whites to do and see in the future. Thus, this type of speech remained a coded, but tactful way of placing demands on whites without crossing the line of racial etiquette. This simply became another method of black survivalism used by African Americans to navigate the perils of Jim Crow, a way of trying to get whites to live up to higher moral standards. As we have seen, this approach explains why Washington's speeches went over so well with mixed audiences.[14]

The sage of Tuskegee began his speech as he had many times before. "I have but one object in coming into this state," he said, "that of seeing for myself what progress our race is making with its opportunities, and to note also the relations existing between black men and white men and to say a word wherever I can that will encourage further progress among our people, and that will further promote friendly relations between black man and white man." As an icebreaker, the Tuskegean recalled how during his childhood he observed the eight-hour day faithfully—working eight hours in the morning and eight in the evenings. He told how he would spread molasses all over his plate by tilting it in different directions, to make it appear that he had more than was really there. He also related stories about his labor on the farm, in hotels, coal and salt mines, and in other occupations. From there, he moved on to the more substantive part of his address.[15]

Washington asserted that about seven-hundred thousand African Americans and three million whites lived in Texas. And since the blacks were there to stay, he reasoned, it should be the duty of black and white leaders to promote rational and friendly relations between the two races. "Is it possible for these two races unlike in color, unlike in tradition, to live together in peace and harmony for all time?" he asked. The speaker felt the races could, but warned that "there is no greater enemy today to a state than the man, whether he be black or white who will spend his time stirring up racial strife." At the same time "there is no greater friend today to a state than the man, whether he be black or white, who uses his talents and influence to promote the progress of both races and to see to it that peace and goodwill are maintained." Blacks in the audience heard in this Washington calling for an end to wanton racial violence against them, even though he directed his words to both races. After the Tuskegean finished his talk at the theater, he gave two more addresses: one at the Second Baptist Church headed by Henry R. Wilson, and the other at the First Methodist Church.[16]

At nine o'clock the next morning, September 26, 1911, Washington crossed the border into Juarez where he met Mayor Gutllermo [sic] Alvares and the city councilmen. This turned out to be the Tuskegee lecturer's first trip to Mexico, and he noted the courtesy the people showed him. After a brief stay in Juarez, Washington and his party had trouble securing sleeping car accommodations to San Antonio because Texas law remained very strict with respect to Jim Crow travel. According to the *El Paso Herald*, the person responsible for arranging Washington's Pullman berth learned that "the only way a negro could get Pullman accommodations in the state of Texas was to buy the entire car space. This would necessitate buying 18 full tickets and 18 Pullman ticket[s]." In 1909, the state legislature had added a law requiring "separate-but-equal" waiting rooms at train stations. In 1911, the year Washington made the visit, the Texas legislature passed another transportation law calling for separate-but-equal employee compartments. Yet the facilities were not equal, and some trains had no colored cars or diners, and Pullman cars were totally off limits. Washington's group eventually worked out these difficulties, and secured "a special train" to San Antonio, but transportation difficulties in the Lone Star State resurfaced later.[17] These experiences inevitably reminded the party of the humiliating restrictions imposed by Jim Crow travel and the vicissitudes that came along with being African American.

Dr. James Tart Walton headed the local welcoming committee in San Antonio. Born in 1875, Walton graduated from Meharry Medical College and had worked in the Alamo City as an obstetrician and surgeon since 1896. He also became a wealthy real estate developer, building more than four hundred affordable homes for San Antonio blacks. In addition, he had investments in several businesses including banking and a drug store.[18] Walton took the party to Second Baptist Church where Washington spoke for about fifteen minutes to around two thousand school children and their parents, advising them to make the most of their education and to share their learning with their parents. "Don't let people discourage you. Do not listen to such talk that will make you despondent or dissatisfied," the Tuskegee leader said. "People will tell you that you are poor, that you are black and members of a despised race." However, Washington advised them not to be dismayed: "take lessons after the foreigners who come here in the direct poverty, peddle bananas on the streets, then rise to owners of small stores and afterwards to directors of banks. Begin now to save your pennies and help your mothers and fathers in your own support."[19]

After this brief talk, the group went to Dr. Walton's home for a reception. Next, they proceeded to City Hall where the Tuskegean met San Antonio's Mayor Bryan Callaghan, who served from 1905 to 1913. "I am pleased to meet you. Your name is known throughout the world and I have great respect for your great work at Tuskegee," Callaghan said. John Wickeland, a white alderman-at-large, and Bernard J. Mauermann, a white realtor, exchanged similar greetings with Washington. Dr. Walton extended an invitation to these men to join the party later that day for the Wizard's main address. Meanwhile, Mayor Callaghan told Washington of his satisfaction with race relations in the Alamo City, adding that "when away from here San Antonio Negroes were loud in singing the praise of the city." The popular mayor declared, "We are fair to our colored citizens."[20]

Undoubtedly, Callaghan had forgotten about or turned a blind eye to the mob violence blacks in the city endured. The horrendous execution of a black woman by a San Antonio mob a few years earlier illustrates the point. The mob placed the woman inside of a barrel, drove long, sharp nails into the sides, and then rolled the barrel up and down a hill until the victim became a bloody corpse. Ida B. Wells-Barnett learned of the incident while far away at a meeting in Manchester, England. She recalled that tears began to roll down her cheeks as she just "sat there as if turned to stone" on hearing this "evidence of outrage upon my people, and apathy of the American white people."[21]

Next, Washington's party went to Douglass High School for lunch. The students lined the stairs, and as Washington approached they began to sing "Our Leader." Just before they sat down for lunch, they sung another song called "We Welcome You," written for the occasion by S. J. Sutton, principal of the school. The domestic science class prepared the meal. Later that afternoon, three thousand people, a third of whom were white, occupied every available seat at Beethoven Hall to hear the renowned educator speak. Dr. Walton gave the welcome address during which he criticized black efforts to pursue political power immediately after slavery. "The Negro race, shot like a catapult into a civilization all new, and for which it was all too little prepared, has gone for half a century, misguided, buffeted about by designing politicians and over ambitious would-be Negro leaders, until Booker T. Washington arose to point the right way."[22]

Further, endorsing the Wizard's philosophy over his critics', Walton asked rhetorically: "Who is it among us of clear mind, unprejudiced heart and right habits will say that Booker T. Washington is not right, in counseling his people in the way of industry, enlightenment and morality, and in soliciting the aid and sympathy of the white man in his uplift movement?" Dr. W. M. Drake introduced Washington and echoed many of Walton's sentiments, asserting that "few Americans had made such an impression upon public opinion, removed so many prejudices and awakened greater helpfulness in relation to the solution of a problem" as had the featured speaker. These remarks, too, were geared toward Washington's critics and helped make the Tuskegean's approach to racial uplift seem the sanest.[23]

Washington rose to speak to deafening applause. According to one source, "not since the day when Prof. Booker T. Washington made the opening speech of his life at the Atlanta Exposition, many years ago, has he received such a royal welcome...as was witnessed by him during his recent visit to the Alamo City." In the absence of Robert Moton, Washington asked the audience to sing two "old-time Negro plantation songs with him: 'Lord, I'm Climbing Up Jacob's Ladder' and 'The Old Time Religion.'" Drawing on a technique he used on his Mississippi tour, the Tuskegee leader cited several prominent white citizens of San Antonio during his speech, such as George W. Brackenridge, a Harvard graduate and president of the San Antonio National Bank, and Albert Steves, head of a large lumber company in the city. He also acknowledged Southern whites who aided and encouraged black progress. Washington received constant rounds of applause and one observer believed that the San Antonio stop set the standard for all other Texas cities. Reflecting on the success and impact of his visit, a newspaper asserted that the Wizard's "influential and timely lecture inspired new life in the Negro Business League here, which means continued birth of Negro enterprises among us."[24] Surely the stimulation of black businesses became one of the consequences of these tours.

Leaving San Antonio, the party headed to Houston. However, a train wreck on the Southern Pacific Railroad caused the party to be delayed by seven hours so they missed many of the scheduled activities that had been arranged for them. Nonetheless, Houston served as a very important stop for Washington's party because Scott grew up there. Two thousand black and white people crowded the station, lining the sidewalks from the Southern Pacific station to the office of the Orgen Company, a banking institution headed by F. L. Lights, a black Baptist clergyman. Washington gave a short speech to the African American businessmen of Houston, congratulating them on their accomplishments and urging them to cultivate friendly relations with white businessmen. After this, he went to Trinity Methodist Episcopal Church and spoke to a group of black school children. Both the city and county school superintendents had made arrangements for all the African American teachers and children to hear the distinguished educator. The hosts canceled the local tour of the city because they were already behind schedule, so the party went to John Brown Bell's home for dinner. Born in 1858, Bell worked as a successful real estate dealer and owned a grocery store in Houston. He later opened a black hospital and clinic in the city. The female students of the Langston School's domestic science department prepared the meal.[25]

Next, the committee organized a reception in honor of Scott and Washington, hosted by the trustees of the Carnegie Library at Dr. Benjamin J. Covington's home, a black surgeon in Houston. Although Houston's mayor and other city officials supported the effort, Washington and Scott "more than any other individuals" were responsible for securing the library for Houston's black population, according to one source. Most county and city libraries in Texas discriminated against or excluded African Americans. In 1904, Galveston created one of the first branch libraries for blacks in the South, followed by Houston in 1909. "If a library is necessary to save and keep the people of the white race," Washington told citizens of Houston, "it is equally necessary for a race that is behind the other race in many respects."[26] This was the Tuskegean's way of presenting a point that made it difficult for whites to disagree with. After all, they were the ones espousing notions of black inferiority.

As early as six o'clock in the evening, throngs of people began to file into the city auditorium and by the time the program began, a large number of people were standing. Over seven thousand Texans, two thousand of whom were white, turned out to hear the Wizard of Tuskegee and as Washington stepped up on the platform the crowd went wild. A number of Tuskegee alumni, seated on the side of the platform greeted their former president with the Tuskegee Institute college yell. As usual, many distinguished black and white preachers, school officials, judges, and businessmen were on stage with him.[27]

During the program, the crowd began to call on its native son, Scott, to give remarks. Scott, admittedly not a great speaker and known for being modest, moved to the podium and demurred:

It is the common-place, the trite, the quite bromidic thing to say that I am glad to be here tonight with Dr. Washington in this matchless city, the place of my birth, the Queen City of the Lone Star State. The years have not flown too fast to dim my memory of the greatness of Texas, nor have the duties and responsibilities of the advancing years served to make me forget the radiant glory of the golden crown which encircles her imperial brow. No matter where I find myself, I am first of all a Texan!

These minutes, however, are too precious to be used except for the purpose which has brought you here; I must use but few of them. We have made educational pilgrimages similar to this one through the states of Oklahoma, Mississippi, Tennessee, North Carolina, South Carolina, Delaware and Virginia. I have constantly said to Dr. Washington, "wait till we get to Texas; wait until you have seen something of the progress of the Negroes of Texas and of the more than friendly relations that here exist between the races." I have said to him over and over again that in this state the Negroes and the whites have literally seized upon the pregnant passages of his epoch-making Atlanta address and are working out the destiny of both races, side by side, "separate as the fingers," as he has phrased it, "in all matters purely social and yet one as the hand in all matters that concern the moral and material well-being of this our common section."[28]

Scott went on to assert that "in Texas we practically have no race problem for there can be no problem in any section where blacks and whites alike acknowledge and appreciate the fact that races and men not only have duties toward each other, but responsibilities as well."[29] Again, this is an example of black survival metalanguage from this Bookerite. Scott's remarks about white cooperation and there being "no race problem" were said for white consumption. Scott knew fully well of the Brownsville Affair and how it shattered any notion of egalitarian treatment of Texas blacks along with other racial problems that plagued the state. But these suggestive comments were things to be hoped for from Southern whites. Scott used psychology by describing the kind of behavior he wanted whites to live up to, a self-fulfilled prophecy. Just as important was how well Scott and other blacks "on display" with Washington articulated themselves and utilized the King's English during the programs. As these stories were disseminated throughout the country, it became more and more difficult to argue that blacks were inferior and regressing since slavery. The examples of so many successful African Americans and African American agency became a compelling force for white supremacist ideologues to reckon with.

When Washington finally moved to the podium, the crowd greeted him with vigorous applause again. "I have been surprised and delighted ever since I came into the state of Texas to note the evidences of progress on the part of my race," he began. The Wizard paid tribute to three black Texans early on during his talk, declaring them as examples of what African Americans throughout the country could become. First, he discussed John B. Bell, real estate dealer and grocer in Houston. "What Mr. Bell has done others can do," Washington exclaimed. He then praised Robert Lloyd Smith for "devoting himself most unselfishly, wisely and generously in the direction of helping the Negro in Texas to get homes, become farmers, save their money and lead useful lives."[30]

Born free in Charleston, South Carolina, on January 6, 1861, Smith attended Avery Institute, a private black institution, from 1871 to 1875, then the University of South Carolina from 1875 to 1877 when blacks were forced out. He transferred to Atlanta University, graduating in 1879; after which, he taught in both Georgia and South Carolina public schools for five years before moving to Oakland, Texas, as principal of Oakland Normal School. In 1891, Smith organized the Farmers' Improvement Society to help black farmers improve their business and farming methods and to strengthen their political voice. Smith became an active member of the NNBL, serving as president of the TXSNBL for a decade. He also started an overall factory in 1914. An active politician, Smith served in the Texas legislature from 1895 to 1899 and became the last African American legislator in Texas until 1966. Smith spoke out against separate waiting rooms and lynching, and although lily-white Republicans in Texas opposed him, President Theodore Roosevelt, at Washington's urging, appointed him Deputy U.S. Marshal for the Eastern District of Texas from 1902 to 1909. Smith also served as a trustee of the Anna T. Jeanes Foundation.[31]

Washington saved remarks about Scott for last. "The Tuskegee Institute in Alabama owes a great debt of gratitude to Houston which it can never repay," Washington continued. "Here it was some years ago when I was seeking throughout the country for a man of high character and common sense, combined with intelligence, who could serve as my right hand in the capacity of a secretary. I found a man for the place in the person of Emmett J. Scott, who was reared in this city and trained in your public schools."[32] Scott, born on February 13, 1873, attended Wiley College in Marshall, Texas, from 1887 to 1890. Some considered Wiley the best black college in the state. Scott then left the school and became a journalist, working as a reporter for the white-owned *Houston Post* for three years. In 1894, he became associate editor of the *Texas Freeman*, a newly created black paper. Soon afterward, Scott became editor of the periodical and built it into one of the region's leading black papers. The Tuskegean offered Scott a position as his private secretary a few days later, after he successfully managed the promotion and publicity for his visit to Houston in June 1897. Scott, with some hesitation, accepted the offer and began working at Tuskegee on September 10, 1897. He quickly became Washington's friend, confidant, and agent. Scott helped run Tuskegee when Washington was away, and he constantly served as the latter's eyes and ears throughout the country. Scott also developed close ties with other leaders like Charles Banks of Mississippi from all over the country. He served as secretary of the NNBL for twenty-two years and according to Edgar Toppin, even though Washington served as president of the League, Scott actually ran it. An active Republican, Scott also believed in black business, and invested in black-run real estate, insurance, and banking enterprises.[33]

Of Scott, Washington said that "from the first day that he came to Tuskegee in this capacity until the present he has not only performed his duty, but is always ready and anxious to do more than his duty, and in this has set a rare example to the rest of the young men in the country." He went on to say that "Houston, unlike some other cities, sees the wisdom of treating the Negro fairly and justly in the public schools. There are few places in the country, if any, where the Negro has better provisions made for his public school education than is true of Houston."[34]

The Tuskegean's remarks were true, for in 1900 Texas blacks had one of the lowest illiteracy rates in the South at 39 percent, and they led the country with nineteen black high schools. Nonetheless, black schools and teachers received less funding and pay, respectively, during this time. For example, in 1910 Texas school districts on average spent $10 per year on each white student, but only $5.74 on each black student. White teachers received an average of $62 per month, while black teachers received only $46. The average school term for African Americans in Texas from 1909 to 1910 was 135 days just 4 days below the average white school term of 139 days, yet black Texans on average still had the longest school terms among blacks in the South, according to one scholar on the subject. For this reason, "some white Texans continued to express fears that education would stimulate black opposition to their restricted economic, social, and political status," Alwyn Barr perceptively wrote, while "other whites, who believed Negro education would advance the interests of the state, successfully urged larger state appropriations to provide improvements. Yet, the emphasis remained heavily on industrial, mechanical, and agricultural education, which would raise the level of black skills within the occupational areas already acceptable to whites."[35]

Washington perfected the metalanguage of race. An observer wrote that he essentially gave one message to blacks and another one to whites. Speaking mainly to whites, he encouraged *the races* to live peacefully together, a veiled way of speaking out against lynching and other forms of violence against blacks. Then he advised blacks to be hard workers in many different fields so that "they would become indispensable to the white man." In the vein of self-help, he also encouraged them to be good fathers and mothers, husbands and wives, to accumulate property, save their money, and above all, to "be good citizens." Black and white members of the audience alike applauded his sentiments.[36]

The Tuskegee leader's call for home ownership resonated throughout black Texas. Working-class African Americans, forming the vast majority of black families in the state, tended to live in small, dilapidated houses on dirt roads that had no plumbing. There was variance in home ownership rates between different Texas cities. For instance, 45 percent of blacks in Denison owned their own homes, but only 14 percent in Dallas owned theirs. Overall, by 1910 less than 30 percent of blacks in Texas owned their own homes.[37]

White citizens had a way of seizing upon the Tuskegee leader's message to blacks while virtually ignoring the advice he had for them. The *Houston Chronicle*, a white newspaper, makes the point. The paper editorialized that Washington had "wrought a *great work for the people of his race*, and has by both precept and example, sought *to lead them* into the paths of nobler and more useful living" (emphasis mine). This editorial is very revealing because at no time does it suggest that whites should follow Washington's advice or even that his work would benefit the white race or even that his teachings would lead whites to nobler paths. No matter how well-intentioned, white supremacy so contaminated the lives and psyches of even "good whites" that they could not even see their own faults, immorality, and bigotry.[38] By contrast, blacks walked away with a different message, one that placed major demands on whites.

The next morning, the party left Houston for Prairie View where they received a "royal welcome" from eight hundred students at Prairie View Normal and Industrial Institute. The only state-supported black college, Prairie View offered courses ranging from the elementary to the university level, accommodating various interests and backgrounds of its students. "Yet the emphasis remained on agricultural, industrial, and teacher education, to fit black people for their 'place' in society," wrote Barr. The students lined up in two rows and sang an original song dedicated to Washington as his party approached the school grounds. "What's the matter with Washington, he is our leader loved and true; he, large of heart and broad of view. Then Rah, Rah, Rah, for Booker T.; he is the man for me," they sang. College yells for Prairie View and Tuskegee began to fill the air. As soon as the party left the frenzied young people, they visited the homes of faculty members and then went to a luncheon back at Prairie

View. Washington and his guests later toured the school and inspected its industrial program. The Tuskegee leader spoke later that afternoon to a mixed audience of roughly five thousand people. Interestingly, more whites than blacks were present at this venue.[39]

In his address, Washington discussed the dawning of democracy in education, asserting that the time would come "when the ignorant man and not the learned man would be the curiosity of a community." He then encouraged the students to apply their education to their home conditions and commit to moving back to the rural communities from which they had come. However, Washington lamented "that all too often the educated boy or girl left for the city after graduation, being too proud to stay on the farm," but asserted that "the country communities and homes should be made attractive enough to hold the educated young person." Indeed, because of better economic and social opportunities, most educated blacks in Texas lived in urban rather than rural areas. This became a growing trend among African Americans in general. For example, in 1900, only 19 percent of the black Texans lived in urban areas but by 1930 the number had grown to 39 percent.[40]

The Tuskegean went on to say that "the Negro race has made greater progress in the last twenty years than in all the previous history. The chance in Texas for the Negro is as good, if not better, than any other place in the South." This was a direct attack on white arguments of black regression. He then described some of the progress black Texans had made. They paid taxes on $30 million dollars worth of property. By 1910 they owned nearly seventy-five thousand farms, and black farmers there raised about four hundred sixty-five million bales of cotton valued at roughly $32 million dollars. By Washington's count African Americans in Texas had amassed total earnings of nearly $50 million dollars.[41] The Wizard then revealed what he called the secret of the race problem.

> To a very large extent, the problem of the Negro in the Southern States is a labor problem. In order to secure effective and satisfactory labor from any race, two things have got to be borne in mind: First, people must be taught a love for labor, must be taught the dignity of labor, and at the same time given proper methods in direction of skill. Secondly, they must have their minds and ambitions awakened, so that their wants will be increased. No individual labors except as he has a motive for doing so. The ignorant, untrained Negro in South Africa works only one or two days in each week. He quits and returns to his little hut at the end of that time. The white man in South Africa wonders why this is true, grows impatient and angry for this kind of conduct.

The white man in South Africa forgets that he ought to do the same thing with the Negro there, that has been done with the Negro in the Southern States—that he ought to educate the Negro so that he will want more. The Southern Negro wants land, wants a house with two or three rooms in it, wants some furniture, books, newspapers, education for his children; wants to support the minister and the Sunday school, and in proportion as those wants are increased, he is led to work an increasing number of days each week, in order to satisfy them.[42]

Washington went on to assert that in addition to desiring education for his children, blacks have "ambition to improve the life of his family." If African Americans found better school facilities in the city they would move there to educate their children. However, if they could find comparable school terms and facilities in rural areas, more would live there, Washington argued. "Our white friends can help the Negro and help themselves at the same time by seeing to it that the Negro's family is provided with just as good accommodations in the country as in the city."[43] In wrapping up this point, the Tuskegean opined:

It would pay in the matter of dollars and cents for every white man who owns a large plantation in this state to see to it that on that plantation a good teacher and upright minister are encouraged in that community. This will mean that labor will come to that plantation, will be satisfied there; that the individual who owns such a plantation and makes provisions for school and church, will not have to seek labor, but labor will seek him.[44]

Sprinkled throughout Washington's address were demands for better educational facilities and opportunities for blacks. Although he presented these propositions in terms of benefits they would bring white plantation owners, he realized that ultimately, black people needed adequate education.

The next scheduled stop was Austin, the capital, but on September 30 travel complications resurfaced. This time Washington learned that officials of the Missouri, Kansas & Texas Railway had demanded that he either ride in a compartment reserved for blacks only or purchase a special railcar to transport him about two hundred miles from Austin to Temple. According to a newspaper report, "the Texas Jim Crow law is firmly enforced and the railroad officials could not afford to be accommodating." Nevertheless, Washington demurred and "notified the railroad passenger agent that he wanted a sleeper anyhow and chartered a special Pullman for the trip."[45]

When the party finally arrived they had breakfast at the St. John Orphan's Home located just a few miles north of the capitol. While the state maintained segregated juvenile rehabilitation schools, insane asylums, and schools for the deaf, dumb, and blind, it did not fund its first state-supported orphanage until 1929. Thus, including St. John's, blacks founded a total of six orphanages in Texas. The Washington party had lunch at Tillotson College and then dinner at Samuel Houston College. A newspaper reported that the local committees were all "bustle and hurry" in trying to make the trip a perfect success for the Tuskegee leader. Washington gave short speeches to students at each school before giving his main address. Once again, the Tuskegean received a blow to his prestige when the Texas legislature refused to allow him to speak at the state capitol. Nevertheless, he spoke later that night at Wooldridge Park in a natural amphitheater to five thousand people. Mayor A. P. Wooldridge, after whom the park was named, had many laudatory things to say about the Tuskegee educator. "To the white people here, I wish to say that I do not bestow too much praise in saying that his life is consecrated to making his race better understood by the white people and bringing about more harmonious relations between the races," he informed. "Our people are a liberal minded people, they want to see your race prosper, they want to see them become more contented and happy." The mayor went even further asserting, "I am glad to bear testimony to their good character and their worth. I am glad to say that for the most part the colored people around here are a law-abiding and self-respecting class of citizens. They are not by any means a burden upon their white friends and neighbors."[46]

The mayor, who served from 1909 to 1919, concluded by saying: "I welcome him here because of his personal worth, his service to his race, and *I also welcome him here because of that vast constituency, of which he is pre-eminently representative*"[47] (emphasis mine). People like Wooldridge served a critical role for Washington on these tours. Remarks of this nature helped legitimize Washington's leadership to African Americans and just as importantly, to whites in the North and South. People could read and hear this white Southerner's perspective on Washington and be won over to the latter's point of view. His comments also helped counter rising anti-Washington sentiment emanating from his detractors. Last, but not least, these remarks helped undermine white supremacist arguments about black degeneration.

The group left Austin and went to Waco, home of Robert L. Smith. Many people waited at the train station to greet the party even though the train arrived several hours late. According to Horace Slatter, a newspaper correspondent traveling with the entourage, "young people, old people, people of all ages and conditions [began] shouting themselves hoarse when Dr. Washington came into view." The people were waiving American flags, while a band played "Dixie." One man walked up to Washington and gave him a shiny silver dollar as he shook his hand, while a woman grabbed his hand and shouted "praise the Lord." Still another man walked away declaring, "Now I's seed him and shuk his han'; I's satisfied."[48]

Students from Paul Quinn and Central Texas Colleges gave Washington a warm reception. J. C. Lattimore, city superintendent of schools, introduced him. During the introduction, the entire student body from Baylor University, a well-known school for whites, came in and took seats. Samuel Palmer Brooks, president of Baylor, and Samuel Sanger, a Texas merchant prince, along with other well-known white men of Waco, also gave Washington warm greetings.[49]

Although Washington received a warm welcome from Waco whites, he understood that whites still had a proscribed place for blacks. He also understood that Waco whites could be just as violence-prone as other whites when African Americans stepped out of their "place." No doubt, the sage of Tuskegee understood the general environment in Texas and throughout the South and the prevalence of violence against blacks during this era.[50]

Leaving Waco, the train once again delayed the arrival of Washington's party at their next stop at Fort Worth, reputedly "one of the most important towns from a Negro standpoint in the state." Washington was scheduled to arrive in Fort Worth in the early afternoon and give his lecture at three o'clock. However, he did not reach the theater until nine o'clock in the night. Nevertheless, an audience of five thousand people anxiously kept their seats until he finally arrived. R. C. Houston, Jr., president of the Provident Savings Bank at Fort Worth, headed the local committee. After Washington finished his speech, he still visited some of the more prominent African American businesses that stayed open for inspection. Fort Worth blacks boasted a $50,000 Masonic Temple and the Negro High School, "considered the best in the South."[51]

Structures like the Masonic Temple were symbols of manhood. According to historian Martin Summers, "Masons continued to view entrepreneurship, and the ability to support entrepreneurial efforts, as one of the integral factors in the achievement of individual and collective male identity." Moreover, "this equation of manhood and entrepreneurship was particularly prevalent in the Masonic efforts to build temples [because they] embodied notions of commerce, property ownership, race progress and manhood."[52]

On Monday, Washington spoke in Dallas at the State Fair grounds. The Dallas Business Men's League hosted the event. However, just days before Washington's arrival, Dallas organizers were soliciting money from local teachers, lawyers, bankers, clerks, porters, waiters, preachers, and butchers among others. "Pay whatever the cost is and let the speculation part disappear and the whole people hear Dr. Washington untrampled, same as other places have done, and are doing," one newspaper article pleaded. It seems that local coordinators in Dallas had to take extra measures to encourage representative participation in the event. Another newspaper published a rather elitist call to "help the struggling members of the race to better their condition." It continued: "There is no better way to do this than to have them come out to hear the good men and women of the race who are touring the country, meeting the masses in the plain and common walks of life. A contact with these good people will help to elevate them to live better lives and do better work." The article also said that "an invitation is presented to them when a lecturer is here and they are requested to attend." Interestingly, little else is recorded about the Dallas stop, even by those reporters traveling with the entourage.[53]

However, more is known about the stop at Marshall. The Marshall Negro Business League took charge of the arrangements and in an effort to outshine other cities already visited, they dispatched Matthew W. Dogan, president of Wiley College (the school Scott attended), to accompany the party until just a few days before the Dallas stop. Whatever Dogan saw at other places, he intended to have Marshall do even better. At Marshall, there was a mile-long parade consisting of various "tastily decorated" floats from Wiley University, Bishop College, and the Central High School. Boys from the carpentry department built the floats, while girls from the sewing, printing, and domestic science departments decorated them. These things illustrated Washington's doctrine of industrial education in action. The Wiley University brass band headed the parade, followed by members of the local business league, and then boys from the carpentry department, who were dressed in overalls carrying their tools.[54]

When Washington finally gave the featured address, the "meeting seemed to be of the very best element, well-dressed, well-behaved," one observer commented. Songs by the Wiley college Glee Club became a feature of the occasion. Chesley Adams, former county superintendent of public schools, introduced the guest of honor saying: "I know of no great public leader whose advice to his people has been more helpful, more hopeful, and of greater influence than that of Dr. Booker T. Washington." Adams went on to call Washington "the one great leader of his people. I present him as the greatest living character the Negro race has yet produced, in this or any other clime." Adams also had nothing but praise for African Americans in Marshall. He told Washington that "in presenting you to Harrison County, I present to you the best element of Negroes in the world. They are intelligent, peaceful and law-abiding, largely because of the influence of these two schools." The former superintendent said he believed that education would make blacks better citizens and thus "Harrison County rightfully claims the best Negro citizenship in the state of Texas."[55] Washington and his party made their final stop in Texarkana. Similar to Dallas, there are even fewer details available on this stop. None of the reporters accompanying Washington even discussed that visit.

Norman M. Walker, a white man, attended one of Washington's addresses and made reflections. He described the Tuskegean as being "yellow in color, with a nose of the typical flat, broad nose of the African and hair that has a tendency to kink. Dr. Washington is just what he is—a Negro," Walker said. "The high forehead indicates the presence of the massive brain behind it." Walker went on to praise the Tuskegee leader for being an eloquent public speaker asserting that he "talks as a college professor in a modern eastern university would talk to a class in advanced English literature." To him, Washington had become "a man who has forgotten himself in thinking of others. This is the lasting impression of the great negro educator," he said. Walker felt that Washington "is so busy thinking what is best for his people and the best way of obtaining this that he has no time for thoughts about himself." Consequently, "he has forgotten everything else about himself, he has also forgotten the low art of dressing well, the glittering jewel of the average negro. Life has been a serious business for the kinky haired picaninny who applied to the Hampton Institute for an education," he concluded.[56]

This white writer's reaction to Washington is a good example of what psychologists call cognitive dissonance. In describing this behavior, Biehler and Snowman assert that if people are "exposed to evidence that might lead to incongruities or inconsistencies in our perceptions, we make an effort to reduce this 'dissonance' either by perceiving selectively or by supplying an explanation." After people attached characteristics and labels to people, good or bad, "there is a tendency to pick out the things that fit under it and ignore those that don't," they concluded. Obviously, Walker felt conflicted over how to react to Washington. Perhaps, he did not feel comfortable with just complimenting the speaker outright. Thus, for the positive things he said about Washington, he countered them with negatives. For instance, in a breach in the Southern code of racial etiquette, he called the visitor "Dr. Washington" on the one hand, but came back later and called him a "picaninny" on the other. After crediting Washington with being a polished speaker, he criticized his appearance. Perhaps this is the dilemma many whites faced when trying to deal with the race question, stereotypes, whiteness, and the maintenance of white supremacy, especially when they met African Americans who defied all their prejudices and preconceptions.[57]

It is interesting that Washington and his supporters could find so many Southern white people from around the country to proclaim their desire for black progress. The unfortunate thing is that many times their behavior did not match their rhetoric or their rhetoric did not match the feelings of the majority of whites in their communities. Out of all of the tours examined in this study, it appears that Washington experienced the most logistical glitches in Texas. Due to wrecks and delays, Washington did not have an opportunity to visit Houston or Fort Worth during the daytime. In one case, he arrived more than six hours behind schedule. This limited what his party witnessed in terms of the progress local blacks were making. The Texas tour is also the only trip where Jim Crow rail transportation issues became a barrier. That may be why there were no reported whistle-stops given by Washington from the rear platform of the train in Texas.

On the whole, Washington's tour proved successful with him speaking to over fifty thousand people. However, these efforts were not enough to satisfy a growing number of disenchanted African Americans. Nearly a year after Washington's visit, black Houstonians formed the first Texas chapter of the NAACP in 1912. Before the close of the decade, over thirty-one chapters with seven thousand members—one thousand in Dallas and another thousand in San Antonio—had been founded. Nevertheless, even though a minority of Texas blacks began affiliating with the NAACP, the overwhelming majority of them throughout the state believed in and supported the Tuskegean's philosophy of racial uplift. "In response to disfranchisement, segregation, and violence," Barr concluded in his study *Black Texans*, "most black Texans chose accommodation and self-help within the caste system as the safest methods of advancement in the early twentieth century." Moreover, "the prominence of Booker T. Washington and the development of partially self-sustaining black ghettoes in Texas urban areas strengthened that philosophy."[58]

The small shift developing away from Washington's philosophy by this time coincided with the trend throughout the country. African Americans had been following Washington's advice, but they received little reprieve from white violence and oppression. Nonetheless, black Floridians, like the blacks in Texas, were elated to have the Tuskegean visit their state because they too recognized the significance of placing their progress on display for the rest of the country to witness.[59]

CHAPTER 8

Tour of the Sunshine State, March 1912

Although race leader Bishop Henry McNeal Turner called Florida a "paradise" for blacks and a place where they could make a lot of money, race relations in Florida in the early twentieth century were not good.[1] In fact, race relations were worse for Florida blacks in many ways than for blacks in other Southern states such as Mississippi, Tennessee, North Carolina, and Texas. Although Florida is not usually thought of as a Deep South state, white Floridians carried the same attitudes and assumptions of superiority as other Southern whites. Florida had its share of lynching and mob violence, residential segregation, black codes, discrimination, and even the total destruction of one of its all-black towns, Rosewood.[2] The Democratic Party controlled the political system in Florida and functioned on the tenet of white supremacy. Florida led the nation with eleven lynchings in 1920, and between 1880 and 1930, blacks were more likely to be lynched in Florida than any other state; for every hundred thousand blacks, 79.8 were lynched. Mississippi followed with a relatively distant second with 52.8 per hundred thousand.[3]

Prior to his Florida trip in 1912, Washington caused a great stir in the Sunshine State on at least two occasions—once in 1901 when he had dinner with President Theodore Roosevelt at the White House and again in 1903 when he spoke in Gainesville. After white Floridians learned of Washington's dinner with Roosevelt, the vast majority lambasted both men throughout Florida's newspapers for violating the code of racial etiquette. White newspaper editors, along with concerned citizens, voiced their displeasure with this affair. "Eating at the same table means social equality. Social equality means free right of inter-marriage, and inter-marriage means the degradation of the white race," E. Y. Harvey wrote to the *Jacksonville Evening Metropolis*.

"When the white race yields social equality with the negro it has defied the laws of God, and he will sweep them from the earth," he said. According to Harvey, this social mingling could move from the dinner table to the bedroom, which would spell the genetic annihilation of the white race.[4]

Although white Floridians were more acerbic with comments toward Roosevelt than Washington, they still let the Tuskegee leader know he had stepped out of his "place" by accepting the dinner invitation from Roosevelt. The *Evening Metropolis* noted that "Booker Washington lost the golden opportunity of his life in not declining the invitation to dine with President Roosevelt. Booker rather went back on his own advice to his race by accepting." As illustrated above, this dinner engagement and other acts by the Tuskegee leader, created dissonance on the part of whites because they often were blatantly confronted with the fact that Washington's rhetoric did not match his actions. They erred in interpreting the Tuskegean's words literally and not as a strategy of black survivalism. Roosevelt never invited Washington to a White House dinner again, and over time fury over this affair diminished. Ultimately, African Americans, Washington's main constituents, praised him for the dinner and his prestige suffered very little among most Floridians over the long term.[5]

Controversy over Washington erupted again in Florida a little over a year later, early in 1903. Washington received an invitation to speak at the joint meeting of the General Education Board and county superintendents of education at Gainesville. Intense controversy emerged because he was invited to lecture to white educators at a white school. This invitation stirred up so much commotion that the speech had to be moved to the courthouse in Gainesville. Washington even considered withdrawing his acceptance of the invitation. William N. Sheats, the state superintendent of education and one of the South's most renowned educators, among others, extended the invitation to Washington.[6]

Highlighting this controversy, the *New York Times* on January 30, 1903, headlined a story: "Race Prejudice in Florida, Citizens of Gainesville Refuse to Allow Booker T. Washington to Speak in Auditorium." Jefferson B. Browne, chairman of Florida's railroad commission, summed up the sentiment of many Florida whites when he cautioned that Washington was "a threat to the preservation and purity of the white race." He felt that if blacks followed Washington's lead, they would think that by industrial education "they too can dine with the white president in the North and sit on the rostrum with the white educators of the South."[7]

Ultimately, Washington spoke in Gainesville on February 5, 1903, to a racially mixed, standing-room-only crowd of two thousand. Blacks sat on one side of the courthouse and whites on the other. Washington's lecture lasted for two hours and he frequently received applause. After he finished, many people in the audience rushed up to shake his hand. People generally supported his talk in both national and Southern newspapers, and Washington's white associates felt he had disarmed his critics in Florida. Nevertheless, in 1904, Sheats lost the Democratic race for state superintendent, his first major election defeat, largely because he extended to Washington this invitation. Sheats's friends suffered politically as well because of their affiliation with the Washington incident. White Floridians did not forgive them for breaching the code of racial etiquette. These two affairs set the backdrop for Washington's tour of the state in 1912.[8]

The Florida State Negro Business League (FSNBL) sponsored Washington's Florida tour. Some leading Florida African American businessmen and women called for the organizing of the FSNBL in May 1906, in Jacksonville. Businessmen from all over the state were invited to attend and organizers believed they could form a "good strong organization" that would "benefit and upbuild the colored race" if everyone cooperated. Although few details are known of the first meeting, the second annual session of the FSNBL took place in Tallahassee beginning on June 26, 1907 at the Monroe Opera House. Among those in attendance were Matthew M. Lewey, publisher of the *Florida Sentinel*; Napier, delegate from the executive committee of the NNBL; Nathan B. Young, President of the Florida A&M College; and Professor John G. Riley, educator and businessman in Tallahassee.[9]

W. Thompson, president of the Tallahassee local league, presided over the meeting where twenty-minute long speeches and papers were delivered on various business topics. Napier of Nashville gave the featured address. He spoke for more than an hour and discussed all phases of black life and the opportunities available to blacks for racial uplift. "He preached the doctrine of Booker T. Washington and was warmly applauded by the audience," according to the *Weekly True Democrat*. Lewey became president of the FSNBL; J. D. McDuffy of Ocala, first vice president; B. J. Jones of Lake City, secretary; Dr. A. W. Smith of Jacksonville, treasurer; and J. N. Dukes, state organizer. Although Lewey gave limited remarks, his address "set out the actual purposes and reasons for such an organization among his race." FSNBL members also elected a nine-member executive committee and scheduled their third annual meeting for Ocala.[10]

The invitation to Washington grew out of a 1911 FSNBL meeting in Live Oak. Lewey ultimately organized and conducted Washington's party through the state.[11] Members of the FSNBL adhered to Washington's philosophy of racial uplift through economics and education. His tours were essential in promoting his agenda throughout the South and in his usual pattern, Washington traveled with a coterie of distinguished black leaders demonstrating to his detractors he had support for his agenda, even among the Talented Tenth.

When Washington visited Florida, twenty to thirty-five distinguished African Americans accompanied him at different points. Among them were Banks, race leader from Mississippi; Napier of Nashville, Register of the U. S. Treasury; Dr. George C. Hall, Washington's personal physician and head of Provident Hospital in Chicago; Dr. John A. Kenney, head of the John A. Andrew Hospital at Tuskegee; Scott, Washington's personal secretary; Major Robert R. Moton, commandant at Hampton Institute; Dr. Matthew W. Gilbert, president of Selma University; John B. Bell, a wealthy real estate man from Houston; Honorable Robert Lloyd Smith of Texas, former House member of the Texas legislature, educator, and president of the Farmer's Improvement Society of Texas; and Alain Leroy Locke, a Phi Beta Kappa graduate of Harvard University and English Professor at Howard University. The party visited Pensacola, Tallahassee, Lake City, Ocala, Tampa, Lakeland, Eatonville, Palatka, Daytona Beach, and Jacksonville and made a number of whistle-stops along the way. The tour lasted from March 1 to March 7, and one newspaper predicted that Washington's Florida tour would be "the most important educational trip that he has made."[12]

The Florida legislature passed a series of measures between 1905 and 1909 that outlawed miscegenation, interracial cohabitation, and racial integration in jails, higher education, electric street cars, common carriers, public waiting rooms, and at public ticket windows.[13] To avoid the humiliation of Jim Crow travel and problems similar to those encountered in Texas, Washington and his entourage paid for their own special railcar just as they had on other trips. Indeed, a breach in Florida's Jim Crow travel code could easily lead to assault or murder. For instance, two angry Florida mobs almost killed Smith Wendell Green, an African American Supreme Chancellor of the Knights of Pythias, on his way to a session of the Grand Lodge at Ocala, just for riding first class and having breakfast in a Pullman railcar, although he had paid for first class accommodations.[14]

Green hailed from Louisiana and had risen through the ranks of the Knights of Pythias, holding several offices. He joined the order in July, 1883 as a charter member of Pride of Tensos Lodge No. 21 in Saint Joseph, Louisiana. A year later, lodge members elected him to restore stability to the organization's finances that were in shambles. One writer commented that "under his direction, the organization took on new life; the membership increased to 9,000; a new temple was erected at New Orleans, La., at a cost of approximately $200,000 and the finances of the organization increased to $100,000." These accomplishments caused other black Pythians throughout the country to have great respect for Green. They ultimately rewarded him in 1908 by electing him as Supreme Chancellor of the organization and he served in that capacity for several years. Under his administration, not only did the black Pythians erect a $200,000 temple in New Orleans, they also built a $450,000 bath house and sanitarium in Hot Springs, Arkansas, and a $1.4 million Supreme Temple in Chicago. As stated earlier, these structures stood as manifestations of black manhood. Green also served as president and organizer of the Liberty Ind[ependent?] Life Insurance Company, was elected a delegate to the National Republican Convention, and worked as a member of the Republican State Central Committee for many years. In a 1912 case that went before the Supreme Court, Green defeated white Pythians who sued to prevent blacks from operating under the name, Knights of Pythias. These are only a few of his achievements and they won him wide respect and national recognition.[15]

Nonetheless, Green's status or accomplishments did not preclude him from white envy and violence. By riding first class, Green greatly offended State Representative T. J. Fenn of Santa Rosa County, a passenger on the train. After Fenn (who was not as well educated as Green) spotted the latter, he protested "that the presence of the colored man on the Pullman made conditions unbearable; that a white woman was likely to swoon any minute," the *New York Age* reported. The train conductor told Fenn that "the colored man had both Pullman and railroad tickets to Jacksonville from New Orleans, and that he was afraid to evict him from the Pullman, as a damage suit might be instituted against the company," the paper continued. The conductor stated that if Green left the Pullman and went to the Negro coach on his own, conditions would be "less chaotic."[16]

This response, however, did not satisfy Fenn, who then went into the parlor car and told several "colonels" about this "uppish" black man. Fenn and the others plotted to evict him, but "Fenn did not try to do it alone," the *Age* noted, because ".... it always takes from six to a dozen white men to show their manhood when one Negro is concerned." Fortunately for Green, the conductor overheard the men and advised him to go to the railcar designated for black riders. Interestingly, when the train reached De Funiak Springs another mob gathered after hearing that an "impudent darkey was traveling in style." Fearing trouble, the conductor instructed the engineer to leave "De Funiak at high speed" for even the white women on the train had become "excited at the mob."[17]

A strong-willed and defiant leader, Green, on his return trip, almost became the victim of two other Florida mobs, one at River Junction and the other at Milton. The Supreme Chancellor remained mindful of the unpleasant experience he had on his way to Ocala, so he secured an entire section of a railcar and was reportedly "living in ease and luxury." On the return trip, he did not mingle with the whites so he went unnoticed at first. However, before he reached River Junction, the train conductor asked him to "go into the 'Jim Crow' car, as a mob was bent on lynching him for having the nerve to ride on a Pullman. When the train reached River Junction a crowd of poor whites boarded the train in search of him, but he was not identified in the 'Jim Crow' coach," a newspaper related. At Milton, word had been sent ahead "of the stylish manner in which the negro was traveling and occupying the same coach as white people." This time a crowd formed, identified Green at the depot, and "handled the negro pretty roughly." The sheriff eventually appeared, charged Green with violating the Jim Crow law, placed him under arrest, and fined him $25. To avoid another mob assault, Green "left Milton on a boat for Pensacola" and this time, when he finally resumed his journey by train, he stayed in the "negro coach."[18]

Although the outcome of the case is unknown, Green later sued the Louisville and Nashville Railroad Company in federal court for $25,000 for failing to protect him.[19] Besides the violence they faced, this example underscores the cognitive dissonance whites experienced when they saw blacks who did not conform to their stereotypical notions. They considered African Americans to be deferential, uneducated, poorly dressed, and economically deprived, so when they saw images to the contrary, it drew their ire.[20]

African American riders in Florida were not always as fortunate as Green to live to tell their stories after confrontations on Jim Crow trains. In another incident, an unidentified black porter working on the Atlantic Coast Line train number 82, allegedly "insulted" a white woman on the train. When the woman arrived in Bartow, she sent Chief Deputy Sheriff Clyde Olive to arrest the porter for this infraction. Olive arrested and handcuffed the man, but on his way to the jail three carloads of men overtook the sheriff and wrested the porter from him. Officers later found the man's body on the side of a road outside of Lakeland riddled with around fifty bullets. As a warning to other blacks, a card placed beside the corpse read: "This is what you get for insulting a white woman." So Washington and his entourage were very deliberate in arranging their own private travel to avoid any problems.[21]

The first stop for Washington's party on the tour was Pensacola, home of Lewey. Lewey served on the Executive Committee of the NNBL and published one of the first black newspapers in the Sunshine State, the *Florida Sentinel* in 1887. Lewey boasted that his paper had the second largest advertising patronage of any black paper in the South. Before starting the paper, he worked as a teacher, postmaster, Mayor of Newnansville, Florida, served in the Florida House of Representatives, and was among the earliest licensed African American lawyers in the state. Dr. C. V. Smith, Dr. H. C. Williams, and Mr. S. W. Jefferson headed the local committee that arranged Washington's Pensacola stop.[22]

In 1907, Washington referred to Lewey's city, Pensacola, as "a typical Negro business community" that illustrated how blacks had progressed economically since the Civil War. Demographically, Pensacola had around twenty-eight thousand people equally divided by race. Although Lewey informed Washington of the economic plight of blacks in his city, Washington said Pensacola represented "that healthy progressive communal spirit, so necessary to our people..."[23] One-half of the African Americans in Pensacola owned their homes and paid about $450,000 in property taxes. Unfortunately, this prosperity did not last long. An April 1912 article in the *Southern Workman* surmised that in the western part of Florida "with its poorer soil the people lag far behind the active, progressive inhabitants of the eastern section with its fine soil, beautiful orange groves, and thriving cities... In west Florida the colored people in general do not succeed nearly so well as among the more intelligent, progressive, and liberal white people of the eastern section."[24] According to another essay, "it would appear that the early promise of Pensacola as an area for black progress and success had by 1910 become an illusion." The rise of white supremacy along with general economic decline in the area led to the deterioration of black prosperity in the city.[25]

Nonetheless, when Washington visited Pensacola in 1912, Mayor Frank Reilly introduced him to the audience. Washington began his address by asking Moton to lead the audience in a few old-time plantation songs. They sang "Until I Reach My Home" and "In Bright Mansions Above" in a way "only negroes can sing," a newspaper reported. Washington spoke at the Opera House in Pensacola on March 1, 1912, to an audience of over two thousand, of whom eight hundred were white. He made basically the same speech at every other city he visited. While in Pensacola, he encouraged those in attendance and gave them moral advice. "We not only have the advantage in a state like Florida of securing land, but the further advantages of finding plenty of work," he said. "There are few if any members of our race who have spent any considerable length of time in seeking labor. Instead of having to seek labor, labor seeks them. Our condition is different from laboring people in many parts of the old world where they have to spend days and sometimes months in seeking labor and then are not able to find it." Even after those people found employment, Washington later asserted, their earnings were "much smaller than the wage paid to the average negro man or woman in the State of Florida."[26] As mentioned earlier, these sentiments were a direct reference to Washington's experiences in Europe and the difficult conditions he witnessed among whites.

While blacks faced many disadvantages throughout the South, Washington asserted that "the soil in Florida draws no color line; its soil will yield as much of her riches to the touch of the blackest hand in Florida as to the touch of the whitest hand in Florida." Moreover, "the rain draws no color line. The sun draws no color line," he said. Thus, in all these ways blacks were placed on the same footing as whites. Washington went on to encourage African Americans to stop viewing certain types of work as disgraceful. Some blacks, only a few generations after emancipation from slavery, refused to perform "nigger work," rebuffing any jobs that approximated the times of slavery. Nonetheless, the Tuskegee leader said "we must impress upon our people everywhere that it is just as dignified to work in a field or in a shop or in a kitchen or laundry as it is to teach school, preach the gospel or write poetry."[27] During his lecture, Washington also encouraged Florida blacks not to waste time.

"Everywhere we must impress upon our people the fact that the idle man or woman must be gotten rid of, that an influence must be brought to bear on them that will make them go work and earn an honest living and cease disgracing our race with their idleness." He surely thought that this type of behavior lent credence to stereotypes about black laziness and shiftlessness. Washington also admonished whites to do their part by setting a good example, because he felt blacks would follow their lead. If whites followed the law, Washington believed that African Americans would follow the law. A few days later, a writer commenting on Washington's Pensacola address asserted that "if the members of his race would follow his advice they would improve their condition morally and financially." Like other white journalists, this person only noted the advice the Tuskegean had for blacks, making no mention of his advice to whites. Of course, the racial code prohibited white men from taking advice from blacks anyway, so this was not much of a thought, especially in terms of publishing that information. Even so, Pensacola blacks needed this kind of encouragement from the sage of Tuskegee considering their deteriorating economic situation.[28]

Along the 250-mile route from Pensacola to Tallahassee, Washington waved at admirers from the rear platform of the train and made a number of whistle-stops. For instance, he made a twenty-minute stop at Quincy, where the entire student body at the Dunbar Graded School met the Tuskegee Wizard, singing "America" and waving flags. W. A. King, principal of the Quincy Dunbar School, led the delegation that greeted Washington, and ten-year-old student, Altia Hart, presented him with a bouquet of flowers.[29]

His next major stop was Tallahassee, Leon County, on March 2. Out of 19,427 people there, in 1910, whites made up 4,697 and blacks comprised 14,726 or 76 percent. Leon and Jefferson County (a neighboring county), were the only two Florida counties that had black populations exceeding 75 percent of the total. Of the 170 lynchings that occurred in Florida between 1889 and 1918, only 2 happened in Leon County. One of those took place in 1909, just three years prior to Washington's Florida tour.[30]

While blacks in Tallahassee were conscious of their precarious situation in the racial caste in the state, they were still excited to be on the Tuskegee Wizard's itinerary. When Washington arrived in Tallahassee, a parade consisting of black artisans, professional men, and farmers, headed by the brass band of FAMC (now Florida A&M University) led the crowd to Fish's Green. He spoke to five thousand people, about two hundred of whom were white. The Tuskegean spoke for an hour and a half on "Some of the Essential Things in Race Development." Later that evening, the Tuskegee leader and his party went to FAMC. A formal reception was given at the chapel, led by President Nathan B. Young, where "for thirty minutes or longer all enjoyed the college songs and yells, interspersed occasionally with plantation melodies."[31]

As the party moved onto the rostrum led by President Young, the audience arose and "gave a chautauqua salute" (a high honor and process whereby white handkerchiefs are profusely waved). Washington delivered a very stirring address at FAMC, noting that although he had seen almost all the state institutions of the South, "the State of Florida...has provided for the Negroes in this state the best plant with the best equipment of any state in the Union." Furthermore, "I am glad to add that it is the best kept up plant, the cleanest, and the most systematically arranged of any that I have seen." After his speech, an informal reception took place in the chapel. One person commenting on the visit wrote: "it was a rare treat to have so many distinguished visitors on our campus at one time." At the reception, short addresses were made by Napier, Gilbert, Hall, Locke, and others. Napier gave details on how the Treasury Department made money and Hall told the crowd to understand that "we do not need more opportunities, but the sense to know opportunity when we see it. Not how much is within our reach but capacity to use it efficiently should be the slogan of every young man and woman," he said. The *Weekly True Democrat* asserted that Washington "is setting a good example and his learning has made him extremely conservative and his advice is along the most salutary lines." Washington later told a reporter that he "paid a high compliment to the management of the state school for negroes in Tallahassee."[32]

Leaving Tallahassee, Washington and his entourage stopped at Lake City. According to a newspaper report, Lake City had a notorious reputation for keeping African Americans in their "place." Less than a year before Washington arrived, six black men taken there for safekeeping were lynched. The black men had allegedly shot and killed B. B. Smith and slightly wounded B. Register, both white men, near Tallahassee. Smith and Register had testified against suspect Jerry Guster the day before in court. Guster and Charlie Norris, identified as leaders of the group, were accompanied by Edgar Knox, Paul Norris, Mack Norris, and Jake Norris. When Guster and the others saw the two white men on the road, they "began firing on them almost without warning. Register fled from the fusillade, and received a slight wound as he ran," a newspaper reported.[33] Even with the prevalence of stereotyping, acts such as these dispelled Old South mythology about black timidity, passiveness, and docility.

When several Tallahassee deputies arrived on the scene, they found Guster and the others standing around Smith's body with shotguns. The men surrendered to the officers without resistance and were taken to the Leon County jail. Fearing a lynching in the capital city,

Governor Albert W. Gilchrist had the men moved to Lake City for protection on Saturday night. "The public will demand a speedy and exhaustive trial of these men," the *Weekly True Democrat* reported, "and if the evidence shows willful and premeditated murder nothing short of a hanging will atone for the crime." The very next morning, three members of a mob went to the Lake City jail and gave the jailer a note supposedly from the Leon County sheriff stating he "had received intimations that a mob was being formed in Tallahassee to take the negroes from the Lake City jail. The message ordered that the men be carried further south to frustrate the suspected mob," the paper reported. The telegram appeared authentic, as the six negroes had been moved to Lake City for a similar reason. The Columbia County sheriff was out of the city and had left his sixteen-year-old son in charge of the jail, and this unsuspecting young man possibly did not realize the sinister purpose of the men and turned the prisoners over to them.[34]

According to one source, the mob initially planned to lynch the black men, but after the suspects resisted, they were taken to the outskirts of the city and "literally shot to pieces." Four other black men implicated in the crime and confined to the Leon County jail were released after the Lake City murders because no incriminating evidence existed against them. However, officials still warned the men to leave Leon County for their own safety. Governor Gilchrist offered a $250 reward for each of the three white men who went to the Lake City jail with the phony note. Also, as a result of this egregious act, a state senator introduced a bill in the Florida legislature appropriating a reward of $5,000 for evidence leading to the conviction of the men involved in the murder.[35]

Washington toured Lake City and then attended a dinner held at the home of Professor L. A. Jones, principal of the colored schools; after which, he spoke at the city courthouse filled with white and black residents. At the beginning of Washington's speech, many whites in the audience showed signs of disapproval on their faces. "Gri[m]-visaged, [and] stoic looking, they were a hard set to move," one newspaper noted, "and of course they had a corresponding effect upon the colored people in the audience." But Washington moved the crowd along and won hearty praises from them after the affair. Astounded by this fact, one person wrote: "he completely mastered that set of men."[36]

In Lake City, Washington spoke on the importance of peace, good will, and mutual helpfulness between the races. He also urged black people to be frugal and seek economic stability. He called for better schools for blacks and insisted upon equality of treatment for them. Then to disarm whites in the crowd he said:

> I know there are those outside of the South who do not understand conditions, who say that the negro has no friends in the South; but for the fact that in every community in the South where colored people live in large numbers there are white friends who stand by us, who help us, who guide us, who sympathize with us, who lend us money, who give us work, it would have been impossible for us to have made as much progress as we have made.[37]

Once again, this is a poignant example of black survivalism and how Washington would say things for white consumption even if he really did not believe all of them. On other occasions when Washington and his key lieutenants made similar remarks, they would joke in private about how they only said them to manipulate white people for their own purposes.[38]

Washington conspicuously passed Gainesville and went to Ocala where the situation differed entirely from Lake City. In Ocala, two blacks served on the Board of Aldermen, blacks owned large farms, grocery stores, drug stores, had fine carriages, automobiles, and numerous nice homes. The black-owned Ocala Bazaar and Commercial Company became one of the leading businesses in the city. Managed by Frank P. Gadson, the Bazaar housed three large stores under one roof, with a shoe department, crockery and tinware department, clothing department, and grocery department. The 175x200 two-story brick building, owned by Gadson, sat on the corner and held inventory worth at least $1,000. Gadson rented the upstairs offices to white brokers and lawyers.[39] Judge William S. Bullock, a Southern white judge from the Ocala circuit, emphatically stated:

> I testify to you with knowledge of the fact that the Negro receives a fair trial in the courts of this section. In this community the Negro is given an equal show in the race of life. He enters into industrial contests, exhibits the fruits from his industry, and is awarded the first prizes at the county fair. As a merchant he is liberally patronized by the white people and when his wares and merchandise entitle him to it he is given the preference in trade. As a mechanic and contractor, witness what he is doing in our city. In educational and industrial lines we are not ashamed.[40]

People from nearby towns as well as in the city began arriving in Ocala on horseback and in buggies and wagons early in the morning long before the program began. Some had arrived at the park at seven o'clock in the morning, but Washington did not arrive in the city until eleven o'clock. A number of prominent citizens including Mayor John Robinson, Editor F. E. Harris of the *Ocala Banner*, and Judge Bullock, a circuit court judge in Florida's fifth judicial district since 1908, were on the platform with Washington. Dr. W. P. Wilson, the master of ceremonies, introduced Bullock, who in turn introduced Washington. During his introduction, Bullock described Washington as "an inspiration to every negro in this land and benefactor to this nation." In addition, "he is taking the benighted, vicious, ignorant and superstitious negro from ... [his] condition and clothing him in the garments of industry, intelligence and morality. In short, he is qualifying the negro for citizenship," he noted.[41]

Before Washington began his talk, he said that although whites had beat blacks at most things, there is one thing in which blacks have excelled, and that is at "making his own songs and singing them better than anybody else." After this, he introduced Moton, "who sang a number of plantation melodies, to the delight of all, many in the audience joining in."[42] Moton never forgot that experience. In his autobiography *Finding a Way Out*, Moton recalled how he led the singing of "In Bright Mansions Above" at Ocala:

> The white people unconsciously [began] joining in, a woman of an East Indian cast of features, but coal black and wearing a shawl of oriental colours, rose in the audience and with an exceedingly melodious voice sang with great fervour above all the rest, at the same time waving her red shawl with the rhythm of music. The entire audience, even [two] dignified judges, began swaying with the motion of this wonderful singing – and everyone sang. As we say in our more primitive churches, everybody was truly "happy." Certainly I never heard such singing in all of my experience. It seemed that everyone was swept along with the emotional current of the moment. I had to stop the singing for fear the swaying bodies and patting of feet by the thousands of people on the grand stand would break it down, perhaps with injury to many and great loss of life.[43]

Apparently, Washington was moved by the scene as well, and he carried the enthusiasm over into his lecture. "I had heard him deliver hundreds of addresses and had listened to him a score or more times on this trip," Moton asserted, "but for an hour and a half he held the audience absolutely within his grasp and he kept the same rapt attention that had been inspired by the music from the beginning of his address to the end."[44]

While African Americans and whites enjoyed listening to these songs and Washington's speech, portions of it still meant one thing to blacks and another to whites. Moton, Washington's confidant explained how the Tuskegean engaged in double-talk at Ocala. At one point during his speech, Washington "told the coloured people in his very effective way of the duty they owed to their white neighbors as well as to their own race, touching upon the importance of industry, thrift, and morality as was his custom." Next, "he turned to the thousand or more white people and told of their duty toward the coloured people, producing such an effect on the audience as is altogether impossible to describe." This affirms how Washington, at times, effectively gave one speech to blacks and another one to whites. It also illuminates why his addresses went over so well. The blacks in the audience left with one message and the whites oftentimes left with another, but all were intended to help improve the condition of the black race.[45]

As with his other lectures, Washington's words in Ocala were met with frequent applause. One white woman remained clearly entranced by his speech, noting that "he spoke with such force and vigour that she thought he might be stricken with apoplexy at any moment, and that his *sincerity* and *earnestness* were irresistible" (emphasis mine). The lady also stated "she had never experienced such sensations in all her life." "Suppose he had died? What difference would it have made? For he could never hope to deliver a better address, or do it more effectively than he did this one, nor could he ever create a stronger or deeper impression on any audience," she opined. These remarks demonstrate how some whites interpreted Washington's speeches as "sincere" and "earnest." They could never imagine that he would be manipulating them and saying things strictly for white consumption. Another observer felt that he had given "volumes of safe advice . . . and a great message of hope." As in Tallahassee, five thousand black and white people turned out to hear the Tuskegean speak, and he received a standing invitation to visit Ocala again.[46]

Washington also spoke at Fessenden Academy and Industrial School at Martin, a black school around seven miles away, headed by Professor Joseph L. Wiley. Members of the Marion County Board of Public Instruction who visited Fessenden in 1908 believed that "it was the best colored school" in Florida. Blacks in and around Ocala took "righteous pride" in entertaining the Tuskegee leader and his party. After his talks, business league members took Washington to see the black businesses and best black homes in the city as well as the public school for blacks. These activities were coordinated by the

Ocala chapter of the FSNBL headed by President L. I. Alexander. They were an essential part of his tours because they gave tangible proof of the progress of the race.[47]

Inspired by Washington's visit and meetings of the NNBL, FSNBL members in Ocala opened the Metropolitan Savings Bank on September 9, 1913, which was "visited by large numbers of both white and colored people of the best classes." George Giles served as president of the bank; Joseph Wiley, first vice president; and Frank Gadson, cashier. At previous NNBL meetings, Ocala businessmen learned of other blacks successfully operating banks, and concluded that if others could do it, they could too. Their bank opened with paid-in capital of $25,000 and rapidly growing deposits. During the first five weeks of operation, the bank conducted $50,000 in business and had the well-wishes of the three white banks in Ocala. Savings accounts paid interest of 5 percent during the first year of operation.[48]

Washington's party traveled from Ocala to Tampa where they arrived on the evening of March 4, 1912. Like many other Florida cities, Tampa remained characteristically Southern at the time and showed little interest in black education or black employment outside of menial jobs. After the 1910 election of Mayor Donald Brenham McKay, Tampa politicians implemented a "white municipal primary," which effectively eliminated blacks from having any meaningful voice in selecting local officials. The white primary continued in Tampa until the 1940s.[49] Black Tampans were also subjected to vigilantism. In commenting on the lynching of a black man accused of attacking a white child in Tampa, one writer concluded that white Tampans, like other whites in the Sunshine State, "showed that they would maintain traditional caste arrangements and white supremacy with violence when they felt the use of deadly force was necessary."[50]

Despite these harsh circumstances, black Tampans still found ways to sustain themselves. They maintained a strong family unit with over 70 percent of African American children living in two-parent households. They created a number of organizations and institutions to promote self-help and advancement like the Clara Frye Hospital in 1910, the Afro-American Civic League in 1912, and the *Afro-American Monthly* in 1912. Black women created a number of women's organizations like the Mary Talbert Club, the Harriet Tubman Mother's Club, and the Florence Nightingale Nurses Club. Blanche Armwood acted as the Superintendent of "Negro Schools" and black Tampans commonly referred to her as "their female Booker T. Washington." Armwood graduated from Saint Peter Claver Catholic High School in Tampa, earned a law degree from Howard University, and then worked as executive secretary of the Tampa Urban League. As with Wells-Barnett, Armwood spoke out against mob violence and lynching, but "like Booker T. Washington and other proponents of racial uplift and industrial training," she tried to "maintain a delicate balance between serving the Black community and working with the white," Nancy Hewitt surmised. Christina J. Meacham, another female African American educator and leader in Tampa, became the first female principal of Harlem Academy and helped to organize the Florida Negro Teacher's Association. So by the time of the Tuskegean's arrival, the city was primed to receive his message of self-help and racial uplift.[51]

Many black and white people showed up to hear Washington because of the Tuskegee leader's popularity and their belief in his philosophy. Around March 2, an announcement went out that an admission fee of 50 to 75 cents would be charged until all expenses were met at the Tampa Bay Casino; after which, those unable to pay would be let in for free. But the coordinators of the affair did not follow their own rules. To Washington's chagrin, they continued to charge people even after they had raised enough money to cover expenses. "The greater grew the pile [of money], the better it looked to the ebony eyes, and it kept on growing," a white Tampa reporter mused. When Scott learned of this, he insisted that they stop collecting extra money.[52]

After Washington found out, he considered not speaking at all because, according to the *Tampa Morning Tribune*, "he was not out in Florida trying to make money for himself, and he wasn't going to trade on the name he has made to benefit the Tampa negroes." All of this delayed Washington's speech. One reporter claimed that as they waited for Washington to speak, "some of the dressed up darkies sweat[ed] axle grease." Ultimately, Scott, Horace D. Slatter, and others in the party prevailed upon Washington to give the lecture to the thousand or more people who had paid and were getting anxious. Seating in the casino remained divided by race, and a number of Northern tourists visiting Tampa also heard his address. After the program, the Tampa Business League provided the party a "good Spanish supper" at Ybor City and then they attended a smoker where cigars were furnished by J. Andrew Williams of the Williams Cigar Company.[53]

Unfortunately, Washington became very ill by the time he retired for the evening. According to Moton who slept in an adjoining room, Washington's condition led him to believe the Tuskegean would "not live through the night." Fortunately, John A. Kenney and

George C. Hall, two leading black medical doctors, were with him on the trip and attended to him all night. Despite Moton's premonition to the contrary, Washington bounced back the very next day. "To all appearances, he was in better condition than those of us who had not been ill," Moton observed. "I recall the frequent surprise of Mr. Emmett J. Scott and the two physicians as well as the rest of us at the apparently excellent condition in which we found Doctor Washington on the days following…" Indeed, the next morning, while waiting for the Lakeland meeting to begin, Washington went fishing at a nearby lake and those with him said he was "the most enthusiastic angler" of the group.[54]

Next, Washington and his party arrived at Lakeland. Six African Americans had recently been lynched in Lakeland and some considered "it notorious as a place for treating colored people harshly." There, a procession began at the corner of Florida Avenue and Main Street and proceeded to the baseball field. About two thousand black and white people paid 50 cents to attend. "All the colored school children occupied one side of the bleachers, and sang 'America' and waved the national flag as he ascended the rostrum," a newspaper reported. Several hundred whites occupied another portion of the bleachers although they "looked sullen and somewhat vicious," according to the *Baltimore Afro-American Ledger*. Washington spoke at twelve thirty in the afternoon and was supposed to be introduced by Lakeland Mayor, S. L. A. Clonts; instead, former confederate general, J. A. Cox, who represented the county school board, introduced Washington.[55]

In his introduction Cox, "in a feeling manner," reflected on the experiences he had with slaves as a child on his father's plantation and to the fidelity of his own slaves when he went to war.

> The General declared that when he set forth to the war there was a fight between six of his men slaves as to which should accompany him, and that to the herculean efforts of his aide, he now owed his life. This boy…bore him off the field wounded when the Federal soldiers were within fifty yards of his body, and that while no white person save his wife, aged father and child were left on the plantation, they were tenderly cared for and protected by the thirty odd slaves remaining. "God forbid that I should now say one word or do one thing against the negro."[56]

"I have but one object in view in coming into this state at this time," Washington told the Lakeland audience as he began his speech, "and that is to see for myself something of the progress made among the colored people and the existing relations between [the] white man and black man." He also wanted to say something that would make black people more useful and enhance friendly relations between the two races. Since many blacks worked on farms in Florida, Washington began by encouraging them to become better farmers. Echoing his previous sentiments about outsiders not appreciating the relationship between blacks and whites in Southern communities, he stated: "Wherever one goes into a community he will find that every negro has a white friend and every white man has one negro that he absolutely trusts and depends on. Whenever a negro gets into trouble in any community, he goes to a white man who helps him out of trouble, in fact, the average negro in Lakeland...keeps his white man picked out to use in troublesome times."[57]

Next, Washington spoke on the importance of blacks securing an education. "The negro in the South is going to secure education of some kind or other," the Tuskegean advised, thus "it seems to me that it is the wisest and best policy for the people of both races to unite and see that he gets the right kind of education, the education that will make him a better man, a better citizen and a more useful and more valuable laborer." Moreover, "the negro wants education for his children. He has ambition to improve the life of his family," Washington asserted, and told the whites that African Americans would be inclined to move to areas where schools operated on eight- or nine-month terms as opposed to three or four. "Our white friends can help us and help themselves...by seeing to it that the negro family is provided with just as good school accommodations in the country as in the city," said Washington. African Americans took these words by the Tuskegee Wizard as advocacy on their behalf. Surely, they desired longer school terms and a better quality of life and they finally had someone of stature explaining this to whites in a palatable manner. After his talk, the black leader and members of his party were taken on a tour of the city and then to the homes of various leading African Americans where they were entertained throughout the day. "Though many of the whites angrily stared at the Tuskegee party, everything passed off calmly," a newspaper reported. Washington stayed at the home of Reverend A. L. Brunson in Lakeland.[58]

One "intensely Southern" white newspaper editor, criticized for giving so much coverage to Washington's visit, made no apologies for doing so and stated that his newspaper admired character and ability wherever they were found. The editor said he also respected accomplished men regardless of nationality, race, or calling. Then he praised Washington for his achievements, courtesy, and kindness and described the Tuskegean as being "as brave and true a Southerner as ever wore the gray." Equally important, the writer felt that if blacks followed Washington's advice, there would be no race problem in the country.[59]

This editor closed his remarks hoping that Washington's "words of wisdom will *linger long in the minds of the colored people* of this section, and *be to them* an inspiration to the things their leader stands for—honesty, industry, frugality and the general uplift of their race" (emphasis mine). This not only illustrates how some, if not most, whites left the Tuskegee leader's speeches with a unilateral perspective, it also shows how successfully he mastered the art of double-talk. The paternalistic editor seems to have seized upon Washington's advice for blacks but made no mention of the advice he had for whites. While the journalist openly publicized Washington's visit and advice he had for African Americans, he consciously or unconsciously did not recount the advice he had for whites. Ultimately, blacks walked away from Washington's speeches with a different message as they appreciated the advice he had for whites too. Blacks also remembered his calls for better schools and longer school terms, better economic opportunity from whites, better treatment by whites, and an end to lynching and other forms of violence by whites.[60] Many contemporary historians have erred by mostly focusing on Washington's message to blacks and neglecting his message to whites.

The next stop on the tour was all-black Eatonville, home of the Robert Hungerford Normal and Industrial School. Started in 1899 by Tuskegee graduate Russell C. Calhoun, the Hungerford School became extremely successful. When Calhoun died in 1910, his wife, Mary, who also attended Tuskegee from 1885 to 1890 but did not graduate, took over and continued to run the school effectively. The Calhouns patterned Hungerford's curriculum after Tuskegee Institute's and Washington helped the school procure its first large building. Because of his assistance, leaders of the school named this most prominent structure Washington Hall. The multipurpose building provided a dining room, kitchen, and an assembly hall for guests on the first floor and a girls' dormitory on the second.[61]

In Eatonville, Washington's itinerary got mixed up, so several thousand blacks as well as a number of tourists with winter homes in the area gathered to hear him around ten o'clock in the morning. Washington did not arrive until five o'clock in the evening the afternoon of March 6, but the anxious crowd had not abated. Upon his arrival, Washington and his entourage met with "enthusiastic applause and the school's yell of 'W-A-S-H-I-N-G-T-O-N.'" The program began with students singing plantation spirituals, followed by an introduction by Napier. Napier introduced the Tuskegean as being "the very greatest Negro who ever lived on earth." Washington's words to the students "were full of pathos and humor as he reminded them of the homes they had left to come to school, and how they would find them on their return, and how they could help to better their condition." One member of his party marveled at how the Tuskegee principal still "spoke with as much vigour and as effectively as I had ever known him to speak" in both Lakeland and Eatonville. Remarks by several other members of Washington's party followed his speech.[62]

The next day, on March 7, Washington went to Daytona Beach and Palatka. He and his entourage were the guests of the Daytona Normal and Industrial Institute for Training Negro Girls headed by Mary McLeod Bethune who founded it in 1904. Bethune promoted her school as a place where people could actually see "The Booker T. Washington Idea of Education Demonstrated." Like Washington, Bethune later became a national figure serving as president of the National Association of Colored Women, vice president of the National Urban League, founder and president of the National Council of Negro Women, and president of the Association for the Study of Negro Life and History, just to name a few. At Daytona, Washington gave one speech at the First Presbyterian Church to a large black audience and another at the new Daytona Theater to an audience composed of mostly white people, winter tourists, and "natives of the community." Both groups were responsive to his remarks and showered him with applause. Several of the men with Washington also spoke to the groups. After the lectures, the party had dinner at Bethune's school before leaving Daytona Beach for Palatka.[63]

At Palatka, the party visited some of the African American schools, and Washington spoke at the Howell Theater. As with Ocala, Palatka had a reputation for easy race relations. At the time of Washington's visit, two blacks, Joseph A. Adams and Lee N. Robinson, sat on the city council. One month after the Tuskegean's visit, both men were reelected to another term. As late as 1924, Palatka still had two black men on its governing authority.[64]

The last and, perhaps, the most colorful stop on Washington's tour was in Jacksonville, which some considered "the biggest event of the kind that has been witnessed in the city for many years." In describing the black community in this city, one writer asserted that "Jacksonville not only surpasses Ocala in business, thrift, and general progress among the colored people but equals any other city of its size in these respects and indeed outstrips most cities." The writer went further to state that Jacksonville also provides an example of what African Americans could accomplish "under good conditions and with fair educational facilities."[65]

In order to meet this last engagement, the party had to go to Jacksonville by special train from Daytona. A Jacksonville newspaper reported this as "probably the first time a special train has been made up in this State to accommodate a negro." Washington arrived in Jacksonville on the evening of March 7. The Jacksonville Negro Business League, perhaps the strongest local league in the state, expended a considerable amount of time preparing for Washington's visit. A number of Jacksonville's leading black citizens were members of the League. They included Abraham Lincoln Lewis, Joseph Haygood Blodgett, Charles Harry Anderson, Lawton Leroy Pratt, William Seymour Sumter, and others.[66]

A brief examination of some of these members provides a good snapshot of the functionaries serving the Tuskegee Machine in Florida. These men were notably successful in their endeavors. Abraham L. Lewis, a founder of the Afro-American Life Insurance Company and a real estate mogul, helped Washington found the NNBL. By 1926, Lewis was earning $1,000 per month while comparatively speaking auto mechanics were earning $48 per month and brick masons were earning $1.25 an hour. By 1947, Lewis paid more property tax and owned more property than any other African American in Florida.[67] Joseph H. Blodgett did not receive any formal education because he had to work on a farm as a youth. Nevertheless, he overcame tremendous odds and became a successful businessman. He went into the drayage business, had a wood yard, operated a farm and a restaurant, and became a real estate developer and builder in 1898. His two-story home called "Blodgett Villa" was "one of the finest owned by colored people anywhere." He entertained Washington as well as many other prominent blacks in his home. Blodgett owned over one hundred rental properties in Duval County and built 258 homes in Jacksonville after "the great fire" of 1901. He even built Lewis's "grand home." According to one source, "Blodgett and Lewis were acknowledged as the first black millionaires in Florida."[68]

Charles Anderson successfully operated the Anderson Fish and Oyster Company. The motto of his company was to "sell goods that won't come back, to customers that will." He later founded a bank in Jacksonville called Anderson and Company, housed on the ground floor of the Masonic Temple Building on Broad Street. Lawton Pratt founded the L. L. Pratt Undertaking Company. After graduating from Cookman Institute, he completed a program at the Parks School of Embalming at Cincinnati, Ohio. Pratt later returned to Jacksonville and started a successful undertaking business with only $60. By 1919, his holdings had grown so much that he ranked among the foremost of Jacksonville's businessmen, noted one source. Likewise, William Sumter founded the Union Mutual Insurance Company in 1904. This company grew from 10 employees in 1900 to about 125 with 40 agencies throughout the state by 1919.[69]

Washington addressed one of his largest crowds of the entire Florida tour in Jacksonville. Some two thousand five hundred black and white persons attended his lecture at the Duval Theater. But the black community was on edge during his visit because a few days earlier, Eugene Baxter, described in one paper as "a tall light-skinned darky," had been charged with murdering Simon Silverstein, a white grocer, robbing his store and severely beating his wife, son, and daughter. Tom White and Sam Richardson, Baxter's roommates, and two other blacks were also arrested and implicated in the crime.[70]

This murder stirred such intense racial feeling that some of Washington's friends foresaw the likelihood of a lynching and, fearing for his safety, encouraged him to cancel his engagement in Jacksonville. Washington refused to do this, however, and "insisted that because there was special racial friction it was especially necessary that he should keep his engagements in the city." As the Tuskegee leader rode to the Duval Theater, one of the automobiles in his entourage was stopped "by a crowd of excited white men who angrily demanded that Booker Washington be handed over to them." When they did not see Washington, the men allowed the car to pass "without molesting the Negro occupant, who enjoyed to an unusual degree the confidence and respect of both races in the city."[71]

When Washington arrived at the theater, the program began with a few musical selections and the invocation. Blodgett introduced George C. Bedell, a white lawyer in Jacksonville who also served as president of the Board of Public Instruction. Bedell in turn introduced Washington who spoke on many of the same points he covered at previous stops. The Tuskegee Wizard discussed the abundance of work available for blacks in Florida, the value of performing manual labor, and that blacks "must get rid of the immoral leaders everywhere, whether they are ministers or teachers, and let them understand that our pulpits and our school teachers' desks must be clean." Washington also urged blacks to buy as much land as possible in Florida "while it is reasonably cheap, but I warn you that land in a State like Florida will not always be cheap," he correctly advised.[72]

In the midst of his speech Washington heard the howls of a mob in the distance on its way to lynch the accused murderers of Silverstein at the jail. Without addressing that occurrence, Washington, "to the alarm of his friends, launched into a fervid denunciation of lynching and ended with an earnest and eloquent appeal for better feeling between the races." This served as a bold move for Washington as his adversaries had often criticized him for not speaking out more boldly against lynching. The mixed audience applauded his sentiments and one observer believed "undoubtedly they were applauding not so much the views expressed as the courage shown in expressing them at that place and under those circumstances."[73]

The Tuskegee leader iterated that those who lived outside of the South always heard the worst things that happened between the races, but seldom heard the "best things that occur. One living outside the South hears of the lynchings, the burnings, and the work of the mob, but he rarely hears of what white people are doing in nearly every community of a State like Florida to help and encourage the colored people." Moreover, "the worst that occurs between the races is flashed by telegraph all through the world, while the best that occurs is seldom heard of outside of our immediate local communities. In no other part of the world can there be found white and black people in so large numbers who are living side by side in such peaceful relations as is true in our Southern States," Washington claimed. "This I say despite much that is wrong and unjust, despite the work of the mob which so often disgraces both races."[74]

These were obviously the wisest words for Washington to use in that climate. Had he urged armed resistance during his oration there probably would have been a race riot inside and outside of the theater and hundreds, if not thousands, would have been injured and killed. Moreover, had Washington chosen to leave Jacksonville because of the threat of violence, his enemies would have seized upon his rapid departure and used it to make the Tuskegean look weak and timid. They also would have argued that Washington did not follow the advice he gave others when they were dealing with similar circumstances. Washington understood how allegations of cowardice could negatively impact him as he used this tactic to discredit one of his adversaries, Jesse Max Barber, editor of the *Voice of the Negro*, after the Atlanta race riot in September 1906. So ultimately, Washington had few choices and could not bypass Jacksonville without speaking.[75]

"It was feared trouble would start when the Booker T. Washington meeting came to a close and a careful watch was kept on the mobs at this time," a newspaper reported. "There was no movement about the theater, however, and the negroes went to their homes without being molested." Nevertheless, the lynch mob repeatedly tried to storm the jail and take the prisoners leading Judge R. M. Call to take steps to "save Duval County from the disgrace of a lynching." So Baxter, White, and Richardson were moved from the jail on March 7 and sent far away from Jacksonville, but the citizens were promised "an immediate trial and punishment, if the prisoners are found guilty."[76]

A reception took place after Washington's speech at Odd Fellows Hall where some leading citizens of Jacksonville conducted another short program. No women were allowed to attend this event, which represents another manifestation of how men during that era displayed "manhood." Dr. A. H. Attaway, president of Edward Waters College spoke on "Our State"; Professor N. W. Collier, president of Florida Baptist College spoke on "Our Schools and Colleges"; Lewey spoke on the "State Business League and Commercial Enterprise"; C. C. Manigault spoke on "Fraternal Societies"; and Dr. A. W. Smith talked about "Our Professional Men." A discussion followed on "The Press" by Lewis, and then Anderson recognized all the distinguished visitors. Washington and Scott were guests in the home of Mr. and Mrs. Lewis. Robert L. Smith stayed with Attorney I. L. Purcell, his old college classmate, and the rest of the party stayed at the black-owned Richmond Hotel. The next morning, Washington toured the city and visited some of the schools, businesses, and homes owned by African Americans, and then left Jacksonville for Chicago to handle business related to Tuskegee Institute.[77]

All of these contributions by black entrepreneurs, educators, and others worked to provide a better quality of life for African Americans in Duval and surrounding counties. Moreover, the accomplishments of the aforementioned people did not just represent personal achievements on their behalf, they signified something much greater. At a time when black manhood and womanhood, as well as the basic humanity of African Americans, was being called into question, these amazing successes smacked in the face of the racial demagoguery of that day. Every time African Americans in Jacksonville and throughout the nation scored a success in business, it literally sent shock waves throughout the white community because it contradicted prevailing notions about black inferiority and shiftlessness. In a word, by being successful in so many business endeavors blacks were demonstrating they were civilized and that they were "men" and "women" in the Victorian sense of the terms.[78]

If Jacksonville was the most refreshing venue on Washington's tour, Lake City was the most hostile. Although he did not speak to as many people in Florida as he had in other states, on the whole, the Tuskegean's Florida educational campaign proved to be just as successful as his previous tours throughout the South, even considering that the NAACP continued to win over new supporters. In a letter to Henry Lee Higginson, a Boston investment banker in the firm of Lee, Higginson and Company, Washington said that he had been "reaching large numbers of both white and colored people and arousing them on the subject of education and speaking out against lynching and other crimes and trying to bring about better relations between black people and white people." He correctly concluded: "I am glad to say that the trip is a great success."[79]

While it is difficult to measure the direct impact of Washington's trip on black Floridians, undoubtedly the Tuskegee Wizard achieved his objectives. He successfully sold his agenda for racial uplift and attracted new followers. In addition, the way he handled the Jacksonville incident surely won him even more admirers. The trip continued to help him bolster his position among blacks and whites as the legitimate leader of African Americans. This "legitimacy" remained important to Washington because of growing competition from the NAACP. Moreover, by demonstrating the progress blacks were making, he dealt another major blow to white claims of black inferiority and degeneration.

Washington, along with his entourage, gained a great deal of publicity and exposure throughout Florida and the nation during the trip from the black press, North and South. The *New York Age*, *Baltimore Afro-American-Ledger*, *Washington Bee*, *Indianapolis Freeman*, *Southern Workman*, and presumably the *Florida Sentinel*, among others, all reported stories. It seems that although Du Bois, secretary of the NAACP, editor of the *Crisis*, and one of Washington's most vociferous critics, did not think much of Washington's tour, he continued to blandly acknowledge the Tuskegean's trip as he had in the past with one sentence in the *Crisis*. "Mr. Booker T. Washington and friends have been in the State of Florida making speeches," the magazine reported.[80] As stated earlier, Du Bois probably remained purposefully guarded in not criticizing Washington's trip because he recognized the greater good that could result. Instead of lambasting the Tuskegee leader for grandstanding or self-promotion, he practiced restraint and said very little, which, perhaps, shows he realized how these tours worked to vindicate the race and undermine white supremacy, the same force he continued to struggle against. Major white newspapers also covered Washington's trip. Likewise, the endorsement of Florida's leading black citizens showed the Tuskegee leader's adversaries, like Du Bois, Trotter, and other blacks and whites, that he had support not only from the black underclass, but also from black leaders and black aristocrats in the Sunshine State.

CHAPTER 9

Conclusion

Washington became the most powerful African American leader of his day. His influence was very broad and extended to the black press, the Talented Tenth, white philanthropists, white politicians (including Presidents Roosevelt and Taft), the NNBL, the Tuskegee Institute, the Tuskegee Farmer's Conference, and others. Also, the Tuskegean had close connections with leading black doctors, lawyers, businessmen, educators, bishops, ministers, and Masonic leaders throughout the country, all of which gave him inordinate power. The Tuskegee leader shrewdly exploited these relationships making him the virtual boss of black America.

The Southern educational pilgrimages of Washington took place at an awful time for blacks in American history, an era that necessitated the tours. African Americans were placed in a position where they had to struggle just to establish their humanity. In effect, after Reconstruction ended, blacks were engaged in a full-scale psychological war where an effort was being made to force them to have an inferiority complex and to hate themselves in deference to whites. White psychologists, criminologists, doctors, historians, clergymen, educators, politicians, and other interlocutors argued in one way or another that African Americans were subhuman and/or were regressing into barbarism in the absence of slavery. Blacks were described as "uncivilized" beasts that had uncontrollable urges requiring oppressive treatment just to keep them in "place." It was that type of general thinking that allowed Ota Benga to become "the pygmy in the zoo."

African Americans continued to suffer during the Age of Booker T. Washington; however, by placing black progress on display, the Tuskegee Wizard engaged in a systematic effort to vindicate the race and helped undermine at least a part of the American system of racial oppression. It is against this environment that the merits of Washington's tours should be evaluated. It is clear that a number of lessons can be learned from Washington's pilgrimages through the South. By touring Southern states, Washington garnered tremendous publicity. Newspapers throughout the country, both black and white, covered his travels with precise detail, and the Tuskegean utilized these tours to garner support for Tuskegee Institute and to promulgate his racial philosophy for advancing the race. Doubtless, he also used these tours to consolidate power as the HNIC against a rising tide of opposition in the African American community. Moreover, Washington wanted to show African Americans that they were progressing and that they should continue to excel. Perhaps most significant, his trips over time became important in the orbit of the Tuskegee Machine, especially as Washington and other African Americans struggled to undermine white supremacy.

A major benefit of the Southern educational tours was that they effectively placed black progress and manhood on display, which undermined mounting arguments by racial demagogues and other interlocutors that the race was "uncivilized" and degenerating in the absence of slavery. Each time Washington publicized the elegant homes of the black middle class, the colleges, normal schools, and industrial schools constructed by blacks, the Masonic temples, and the businesses they owned, he provided concrete proof of racial advancement. By exposing the country to professional black individuals who were lawyers, doctors, journalists, professors, college presidents, teachers, bishops, and businessmen, among others, he showed that even under very difficult circumstances and with the deck stacked against them, African American men were demonstrating manly character and respectability. Thus, every trip, every little stop, every sign of black progress provided through these venues began chipping away at the notion of black inferiority and regression. The tangible examples displayed by Washington and his entourage on these trips made it difficult for critics of the race to argue the contrary.

A person who does not understand the era may wonder why no women traveled with Washington's entourages. To the contemporary reader, at first glance it might appear as male chauvinism. However, as Gail Bederman and Martin Summers have aptly explained, these men were engaged in gender identity formation that signified what "manliness," during the Victorian Age, was supposed to represent. These trips helped black men to affirm their gender identity publicly. Undoubtedly, black women supported their men in this endeavor and did not view it as chauvinistic. They, too, understood that black men needed to illustrate their "manliness."[1]

Nonetheless, African American women did more than just provide moral support to the black men. Typically, the wives of the men in local communities played a crucial role in ensuring the success of these tours on a variety of levels. Although much of what they did occurred behind the scenes, on occasion, their contributions were highlighted in the newspapers as well. For example, when Washington stopped at the home of Bishop Cottrell in Holly Springs, Mississippi, Mrs. Cottrell and other women took care of the food and entertainment for the reception. After the group had dinner, they were given a dessert with Washington's initials carved on it. The hostesses served the men punch and then Cottrell's daughter and another young lady serenaded the group with songs accompanied by piano. Publicizing these things showed womanliness, genteel behavior, and demonstrated that black women and children could conform to the prevailing rules of social etiquette required of Victorians.

Likewise, by touring the South with such an accomplished entourage and by demonstrating clear signs of respectability, Washington helped demonstrate black "manliness." "Gender identity formation," according to Summers, "involved a relational process that was organized around gender, class, status, and age," all characteristics clearly delineated among the Tuskegean's group. The men with Washington also realized that by traveling together they were not only placing black progress on display, but also projecting black "manliness." Indeed, they were demonstrating that African Americans were, in fact, men! This was important because whites argued the contrary and used that argument to legitimize the abuse blacks suffered and their political and social disfranchisement. Black men clearly understood that these demonstrations were one way of gaining respect and civic power. Simultaneously, by taking these tours they desired to transmit their bourgeois values to working-class blacks, thereby elevating the entire race. This show of black progress caused many whites to experience cognitive dissonance. White men had established a system guaranteed to ensure black failure, but despite the obstacles placed before them, African Americans were still making progress. These facts generated considerable anxiety and self-doubt among some white men and effectively made them question their own manhood, a point not lost on other black leaders.[2]

Du Bois remained guarded in his criticism of Washington for taking these trips. Although he may have given only a brief mention of the tours in the *Crisis*, he did not unleash any serious attack on Washington or his entourage for taking them. Perhaps he understood that no matter what their differences, Washington's tours were countering white racist arguments of black degeneration and therefore served a greater purpose than just self-promotion for the Tuskegean. In addition, Du Bois surely understood that the men traveling with Washington and participating with him were the same Talented Tenth he thought so highly of. These men were showing America the remarkable progress of the black race and that black men, despite arguments to the contrary, were manly. They were successful, educated, well-dressed, well-spoken, economically secure, and respectable. While Washington and Du Bois were in a race for leadership, both men realized that they had common enemies—white supremacy and white racism. In the absence of those factors, there would have been no need for "race men" in the first place.

It was imperative for blacks who attended these affairs to conduct themselves respectfully and abstain from conduct that was seen as "uncivilized." If their behavior was anything to the contrary, it would have added fuel to arguments of black underdevelopment and degeneration. In Tampa, while African Americans waited patiently for the program to start because of delays associated with money being collected to enter the venue, it remained essential for them to conduct themselves in a fashion that would not add to stereotypical notions about black irascibility.

Thus, the African Americans who attended these programs in large numbers also played a crucial role in Washington's tours. They showed they were not beasts, but were "civilized" people who had self-control and who could share an auditorium with whites without manifesting any of the horrible traits so often ascribed to them. The patience the masses of blacks demonstrated at many venues, especially when Washington's arrival was delayed, manifested discipline. This is significant because self-control was a perceived genetic trait not possessed by blacks. They dressed in their finest clothes and arrived at his presentations with their families intact, projecting the image of stability and order. Black children also attended and participated in the programs and demonstrated that they, too, were disciplined and well-mannered. These images contradicted those picturing blacks as "uncivilized" and served as a powerful tool in the effort to uplift the race. Indeed, the black presence at these events reflected a collective sort of "civilization" among African Americans.

The powerful symbolism of Washington and other black men sharing an integrated platform, even when many of the places at which Washington spoke were segregated, provided some people with a glimmer of optimism. It also showed that blacks were "civilized" enough to share the stage with white men, thus placing them on equal ground. Washington was very calculated in insisting on the "best whites" joining him on the platform. He wanted them to participate in the program and a representative number to be in attendance. If Washington spoke to black-only audiences and had no white participation at these venues, the trips would not have had the same effect or generated as much publicity. Indeed, the endorsement of prominent whites helped to legitimize Washington to blacks and whites alike.

At Salisbury, North Carolina, when Washington's railcar backed up to Vice President James Schoolcraft Sherman's and the two met, shook hands, and exchanged greetings, it projected an image of cooperation and hope that many were not accustomed to seeing. It also demonstrated "civilized" behavior and showed "manliness." It appeared that the leader for African Americans was being projected as being on the same manly level with the vice president of the United States. When the crowd witnessed this they began to cheer vigorously. Undoubtedly, the symbolism of this encounter went a long way in undermining arguments of black backwardness and degeneration.

Another thing that can be gleaned from this study of Washington's pilgrimages is how his perspective on Europeans changed after he traveled to Europe. Growing up in America, the Tuskegean had been brainwashed into thinking that Europeans were so much more "civilized" than the African and his descendants. However, when he went to Europe and visited over ten countries he was struck by the fact that he saw filth in many places, mud houses, and homes with dirty floors. In one home, six men were eating from the same bowl, which literally disgusted the Tuskegee leader. He also saw a plentiful supply of beggars and some families, he said, were even working for as little as $.17 per day.

Washington incorporated a number of the lessons he learned from his European travels into the speeches he made when he returned to the United States. Basically, the Tuskegean believed that "the man farthest down" in Europe had nothing on "the man farthest down" in the United States, that is, African Americans. Washington became even more optimistic for the future of blacks and many times he explained that "compared with the condition and the outlook of the working classes in Southern Europe especially, the Negro has a chance in the South that is from 50 to 100 per cent more hopeful than is true of the working classes in Southern Europe." These circumstances often led Washington to assert that black Americans have a great advantage over Europeans. "The Negro in the South for the main part does not have to seek labor. Work seeks him," Washington often claimed.[3]

In addition to his growth in that area, Washington continued to publicly confront racial violence against blacks during his tours. Almost forty years ago, historian Emma Lou Thornbrough noted that throughout his life "Washington consistently condemned lynching and mob violence...in his speeches and writings." "A careful reading of his utterances," she continued, "also shows that they nearly always contained criticism of other forms of racial injustice and appeals to the 'best class' of whites for more equitable treatment of Negroes." Indeed, after he was beaten severely in New York in 1911 by Ulrich necessitating sixteen stitches, Washington continued to speak out on assaults against African Americans.[4] This incident exposed the vulnerability of even the "best blacks." Although he had always called for friendly relations between the two races and urged them to maintain peace and tranquility, Washington admitted publicly during his Florida tour that the way blacks were treated in America was "wrong and unjust" and he criticized whites for joining mobs and not allowing the justice system to run its course. He asserted that the work of the mob disgraced not only the black race, but the white race as well.

One of the things that can be attributed to Washington's success on these trips was that he knew *how* to talk to black and white Southerners—he mastered the art of double-talk. The Tuskegee leader learned how to effectively deliver one speech to blacks and another one to whites during the same presentation. This fact is very important because many historians have taken a literalist approach in interpreting Washington's speeches and writings. They simply argue that if he said or wrote certain things, he meant them—literally.[5] In light of the abundance of evidence to the contrary, this interpretation seems fallacious. As a matter of fact, blacks "wore the mask" and did not reveal their true intentions to whites. This was common knowledge among black people, although not suspected or believed by many whites. Underlying this sort of thinking is a racist assumption that Washington, a black man, did not have the capacity to be so calculating, shrewd, perspicacious, and devious.

Many scholars have chosen the term "accommodationist" as the best adjective to describe Washington. For example, in his study *Middle Passages* (2006), James T. Campbell calls Washington "the great apostle of racial accommodation."[6] By using this label to describe Washington's entire platform for racial uplift, historians have effectively placed him in a box, which does not provide for any deviation from their perceived archetype. Instead of labeling Washington as an "accommodator," it seems that a more appropriate term would be "master manipulator." Indeed, he masterfully manipulated blacks and whites alike, a fact that requires scholars to conduct more than super ficial (or simply literal) analysis when studying the Wizard of Tuskegee. The fact of the matter is that everything Washington said or wrote cannot be interpreted literally.

Over his lifetime, surely "accommodation" may describe some of Washington's actions, but certainly not all of them, as his approach to racial uplift varied depending on the situation. The same can be said of Du Bois at different points in his life. For example, historian Mark Ellis asserts that Du Bois's essay "Close Ranks"—published in the July 1918 issue of the *Crisis* during World War I—for example, "seemed to contradict the mounting radicalism of black politics and all that Du Bois, in particular, stood for." In "Close Ranks," Du Bois encouraged blacks to "forget our special grievances and close ranks shoulder to shoulder with our own white fellow citizens and the allied nations that are fighting for democracy. We make no ordinary sacrifice, but we make it gladly and willingly with our eyes lifted to the hills." It did not help that at the time he wrote the essay Du Bois was discreetly seeking a commission as a captain in the Military Intelligence Branch, described as "an antiradical agency of the United States Army General Staff." At best, this act can be classified as "accommodation." At worst, it was a self-serving act of the worst kind.[7]

Du Bois's contemporaries lambasted him through the black press calling him a "traitor" and a "Benedict Arnold." Even his former associate Trotter, editor of the *Boston Guardian*, expressed serious disappointment. He wrote that Du Bois "was 'no longer a radical,' but 'a rank quitter in the fight for equal rights,' betraying his race just when demands for equality and liberty should be most vigorously advanced." After thoroughly examining this issue, Ellis concluded that Du Bois's editorial "was a conscious deviation in the trajectory of his wartime writings and was specifically included in the July 1918 issue of the *Crisis* to help him into military intelligence." Furthermore, "the meekness of the July editorial was an astonishing departure from the magazine's declared commitment to expose and attack all racial injustice. Above all, it did not square with the editor's [Du Bois's] known rejection of accommodationism," Ellis asserted.[8]

In the end, according to Ellis, Du Bois "distorted his real beliefs and paid a heavy price." But even with the transparency of these facts, contemporary historians do not label Du Bois as an accommodationist, a traitor, an Uncle Tom, or a sellout. He does not fit the accommodationist model because he has been placed in a box labeled "radical" that does not allow for such a classification. At the same time, if Du Bois, Turner, or Trotter had risked their lives or even their institutions to save the life of a fellow "militant," as Washington did with Thomas A. Harris when he saved him from a Tuskegee mob, it would be viewed as a defining moment in their militancy. Historians would utilize that example over and over again to demonstrate their "radicalism." However, when Washington does the same thing, he does not qualify as a radical because he has been relegated to an "accommodationist" box. Ultimately, historians should not judge a person's career based on one blunder or the selective use of evidence that may point in only one direction. In reality, no leaders should be placed in boxes, Washington included, and when history judges them it should be based on a comprehensive examination of their overall work and effectiveness in historical context.[9]

Thus, historians should analyze the context and possible reasons for why Washington and other Bookerites said some of the things they did on these Southern educational tours. Many times, they "had to lie" and say things they did not mean to ensure their survival. This tactic may have been Machiavellian, but as long as the end justified the means, they considered it proper and necessary. These men were pragmatists who sometimes used deception to manipulate whites in order to achieve their particular aims. The numerous examples offered by the life of Washington and countless other Bookerites, such as Merrick and Banks, more than make the point.[10] On one occasion, Banks frankly told Washington that he adopted the policy of telling whites they deserved credit for black progress in Mississippi simply to remove any fear they had in terms of how black achievement would impact them. When he told them they deserved credit, however, it was strictly for white consumption and not because he really believed it. Banks took this position because he knew that white envy and jealousy over black progress could result in all sorts of egregious crimes against black lives and property.

On numerous occasions during his tours, Washington spoke of behaviors in the past that he wanted to see in the present and the future. Often, he mentioned how Southern whites were black people's "best friends" and that whites were doing "all they could" to help African Americans. However, these comments were made strictly for white consumption. By using this kind of metalanguage, Washington effectively described the behavior he wanted whites to live up to, making it a self-fulfilled prophecy. Indeed, Washington gave suggestive messages filled with "prophecy" throughout his tours. The way he and other Bookerites used their words remained a coded but tactful way of placing demands on whites in a manner that did not breach the code of racial etiquette by bluntly telling them what to do. This approach simply became another method of black survivalism used by African Americans to navigate the perils of Jim Crow.

In terms of an overall assessment of Washington's tours, they helped blacks in their efforts to project the image of "civilized" behavior, to place black progress on display, and to show, in the main, that black men were manly. There were some negative factors associated with these tours, one clearly being the toll they took on Washington's health. Washington was constantly traveling from place to place and had to speak before large crowds under all sorts of weather and other conditions. While they were in Tampa, Moton thought Washington was on the brink of death. Fortunately, after receiving assistance from the physicians accompanying him, the Tuskegean bounced back and finished the tour of the state in robust fashion.

Nonetheless, over time, these factors affected his health, but Washington continued to persevere. Next, one can only imagine the toll these tours took on the psyche of whites who viewed blacks as subhuman and inferior. These bombastic examples of black success provided by Washington could have stimulated fear and consternation on the part of whites and led them to take a more defensive posture when they felt threatened. Ultimately, if blacks followed Washington's advice, as Thomas Dixon warned, they would become less dependent on whites. The notion of black independence surely alarmed some whites, and it is difficult to ascertain how they processed and dealt with that notion.

The total destruction of all-black towns like Rosewood, Florida, provides an example of how white fury could gestate and explode over the appearance of black independence. In this case, a white mob overran and destroyed Rosewood for a crime allegedly committed by only one African American. It seems that local whites were just looking for an excuse to eliminate the town because it provided a source of economic competition. Similar motivations manifested themselves in Memphis, Tennessee. After Thomas Moss, Calvin McDowell, and William Stewart opened the People's Grocery store in a black Memphis neighborhood across the street from a white grocer and began taking business away from him, all three were brutally tortured and lynched. One scholar concluded that "the lynchers' motivations seemed crassly economic. The three victims," she wrote, "had committed the 'crime' of opening a successful store...which competed with a nearby white-owned grocery."[11]

Ida B. Wells-Barnett became infuriated over this event because she knew these men personally and they all were upstanding members of the community. She surmised that these men were acquiring property and wealth and whites just wanted to "keep the race terrorized and keep the nigger down."[12] Thus, even progressive African Americans found themselves having to walk a tightrope as they navigated the perils of Jim Crow while working to uplift the race.

Washington's tours brought some benefits to black people— tangible and intangible. These tours represented a form of empowerment and gave African Americans hope. Black people were receptive to the possibilities provided through Washington's speeches on the tours. Some were inspired and encouraged to improve their communities, build new businesses, improve their schools, and attend church. In some cases, Washington's efforts succeeded. For instance, in Ocala, Florida, just over a year after his visit, black businessmen in the town opened the Metropolitan Savings Bank. The founders of the bank had been Washington's hosts during his Florida tour and were members of the NNBL and the FSNBL. Thus, it is not difficult to associate the creation of the bank in some way with Washington's visit.

On an individual level, it is difficult to measure the direct benefits of the trip for those who attended. However, it seems reasonable to assume that some people would have been inspired and encouraged by Washington's message and by the pomp and circumstance of the programs. Washington also provided the people with concrete advice that could improve their everyday lives, if put into practice. On the group level, Washington and his entourage provided living examples of "civilized" African Americans who were progressing as a race. Black people also benefited collectively because those attending these events were in essence placed on display. When stories circulated throughout the country about these events, it brought pride to the race and helped improve their overall standing in terms of how African Americans were perceived.

In the end, Washington probably reached close to a million individuals directly or indirectly through these tours. In his dedicated effort to uplift the race, he used these Southern educational tours to advance the image of African Americans and to undermine white supremacy. To be sure, the continued display of African American progress chipped away at arguments of black degeneration. How successful was he in this effort is hard to tell, but what would have conditions been like if he never toured the South and placed black progress on display? What if racist claims of black bestiality went unchallenged? Those factors should be considered when we examine Washington's tours and how his savvy guided him to use the trips to place black progress on display as a means of elevating the race while undermining a very oppressive and racist system.

Appendix: Roster of Selected National Negro Business League Members in Mississippi, Tennessee, North Carolina, Texas, and Florida from 1900 to 1915

Mississippi		
Name	*City*	*Occupation*
S. J. Alford	Mound Bayou	Druggist/Surgeon/Physician
W. A. Attaway	Greenville	Physician
Charles Banks	Mound Bayou	Banker
J. B. Banks	Natchez	Physician
Mrs. Charles [Trenna] Banks	Mound Bayou	—
Richard Barnett	O'Reilly	Planter
Wallace N. Battle	Okolona	—
Augustus G. Bell	Brookhaven	—
Eugene P. Booze	Mound Bayou	Merchant
Theodore H. Black	Mound Bayou	General Merchandise
Mary C. Booze	Mound Bayou	Postmistress
J. F. Brook	Mound Bayou	General Merchandise
E. P. Brown	Greenville	Physician
G. H. Brown	Vicksburg	School Principal
W. Burns	Leland	Merchant
G. W. Burt	Mound Bayou	Photographer Book Agent

Continued

Continued

Name	City	Occupation
J. P. Cain	—	Merchant
John C. Chapple	Greenville	Publisher Editor
Orange Christmas, Jr.	Mound Bayou	Farmer
J. B. Combs	Corinth	Teacher
Auger A. Cosey	Mound Bayou	Minister
Elias Cottrell	Holly Springs	Bishop
Wayne W. Cox	Indianaola	Postmistress
Reverend M. [N] E. Davis	Natchez	State Business League
A. Dixon	Mound Bayou	General Merchandise
Mrs. E. P. G. Frances	Mound Bayou	General Merchandise
John W. Frances	Mound Bayou	Banker/Merchant
D. J. Foreman	Vicksburg	Real Estate
James B. Garrett	Mound Bayou	Secretary
D. W. Gary	Mayersmith	Farmer
C. W. Gilliam	Okolona	Merchant
H. A. Godbold	Mound Bayou	General Merchandise
G. S. Goodman	Holly Springs	Teacher
F. A. Gray	Greenwood	—
E. W. Green	Fayette	Farmer
L. O. Hargrove	Mound Bayou	Hardware Blacksmith
Joseph T. Harris	Michigan	Farmer
S. H. Highland	New Gerry	Farmer
William H. Holtzclaw	Utica	Principal/Utica Institute
Perry W. Howard	Jackson	Lawyer
R. W. Hood	Mound Bayou	Blacksmith
O. V. Jarmen	Grannitt	—
W. H. Jefferson	Vicksburg	Funeral Director
Mrs. L. C. Jefferson	Vicksburg	Funeral Director
E. P. Jones	Vicksburg	—
G. B. Jones	Mound Bayou	General Merchandise
Laurence C. Jones	Braxton	School Work

Name	City	Occupation
Dan Jordan, Jr.	Mound Bayou	General Merchandise
Thomas I. Keys	Ocean Springs	Stationary Merchant/ Real Estate
W. J. Latham	Jackson	State Business League/ Lawyer
M. A. Lee	Mound Bayou	Drugs/Physician
Rev. W. W. Lucas	Meridian	Minister
Mrs. W. W. Lucas	Meridian	—
P. R. McCarty	Mound Bayou	General Merchandise
Richard M. McCarty	Mound Bayou	Farmer
P. McIntosh, Sr.	Okolona	Merchant
E. H. McKissack	Holly Springs	—
L. W. W. Mannaway	Jackson	Minister
J. M. Marr	Mound Bayou	Tonsorial Artist
Rev. Eugene G. Mason	Shaw	Minister/Banking
George H. Mays, Jr.	Mound Bayou	Cotton Oil Mill
Miss J. B. Mazique	Natchez	—
Mrs. Emma Miller	Yazoo City	—
Willis E. Mollison	Vicksburg	Lawyer/Banker
Isaiah T. Montgomery	Mound Bayou	Real Estate
Mrs. Martha R. Montgomery	Mound Bayou	General Merchandise
W. A. J. Morgan	Shelby	—
Alexander Myers	Mound Bayou	Blacksmith
George H. Oliver	Clarksdale	Principal
L. K. Otund [sic]	Jackson	Lawyer
Mrs. S. J. Owen	Natchez	—
S. H. C. Owen	Natchez	—
C. P. Parnell	Mound Bayou	Farmer
W. W. Phillips	Kosciusko	Educator
J. H. Powell	Alcorn	—

Continued

Name	City	Occupation
Elizabeth Richards	Mound Bayou	Restaurant/Butcher
W. A. Scott	Jackson	—
J. Beverley F. Shaw	Meridian	Educator/Meridian Academy
D. W. Sherrod	Meridian	Physician
C. C. Sims	Jackson	Contractor
J. W. Smith	Meridian	Grocer
Jerry M. Smith	Boyle	Planter
John W. Strauther	Greenville	Funeral Director/Banker
W. L. Smith	Mound Bayou	Order of Twelve
Columbus R. Stringer	Mound Bayou	General Merchandise
A. L. Swanger	Mound Bayou	Farmer
Rev. E. B. Tapp	Jackson	Editor/Minister
N. S. Taylor	Greenville	Lawyer
A. L. Thompson	Mound Bayou	—
J. E. Walker	Garrison	—
J. C. Wall	Okolona	—
C. B. Wallis	Rosedale	Cotton Buyer
John L. Webb	Yazoo City	—
C. L. Webster	Mound Bayou	General Merchandise
L. J. Wieston	Greenville	Lawyer
Mrs. L. M. Young	Edwards	Masonic Benefit Association

Tennessee		
Name	City	Occupation
P. Adams	Nashville	Lawyer
C. W. Anderson	Jackson	Farmer
I. H. Anderson	Jackson	Merchant
Joseph Anderson	Jackson	Farmer
W. M. Anthony	Jackson	Farmer

Continued

Name	City	Occupation
J. M. Barnett	Jackson	Farmer
Sam Bivens	Jackson	Farmer
John B. Bosley	Nashville	Real Estate
Lewis Bond	Jackson	Farmer
Henry A. Boyd	Nashville	Newspaper Editor
Robert F. Boyd	Nashville	Banker/Physician/Businessman
Miss Mamie E. Braden	Nashville	Dean of Music Department Walden University
S. S. Brown	Memphis	Banker
Ira T. Bryant	Nashville	Publisher
James Bumpas	Nashville	Real Estate
A. C. Cain	Jackson	Merchant
Allen A. Carter	Nashville	R. R. Mail Service
John W. Christmas	Trenton	Agent
R. E. Clay	Bristol	Coal Dealer/Barber
George Crawford	Memphis	—
I. S. Cunningham	Springfield	Physician
Thomas Davis	Jackson	Merchant
S. M. Diggs	Jackson	Farmer
J. N. Ervin	Johnson City	Teacher
Jackson Estes	Jackson	Farmer
George W. Franklin, Jr.	Chattanooga	Undertaker
D. W. Featherston	Jackson	Minister
Leland Forest	Jackson	Farmer
George A. Gates	Nashville	Doctor
Harrison Golden	Jackson	Farmer
J. B. Goodrich	Jackson	Porter
J. C. Grant	Jackson	Farmer
Green P. Hamilton	Memphis	Principal
George Harper	Jackson	Farmer
Thomas H. Hayes	Memphis	—

Continued

Continued

Name	City	Occupation
R. G. Hayes	Jackson	Farmer
George Henning	Jackson	Farmer
E. M. Higgins	Bristol	—
Dick Hirsch	Jackson	Farmer
W. H. Hodgkins	Nashville	Lawyer
Robert Horton	Jackson	Farmer
W. H. Hurt	Jackson	Farmer
A. S. Ingram	Jackson	Farmer
E. B. Jefferson	Nashville	—
Andrew N. Johnson	Nashville	Undertaker
Thomas A. Johnson	Nashville	Real Estate
Jesse Jones	Memphis	—
Hightower T. Kealing	Nashville	Editor
Edward R. Kirk	Memphis	Real Estate
H. R. Ladder	Memphis	Lawyer
C. N. Langston	Nashville	Cashier
J. A. Lester	Nashville	Physician
Williams M. McGavock	Nashville	Undertaker
Moses McKissack	Nashville	Architect
E. N. Martin	Nashville	Tailor
Hubbard May	Jackson	Farmer
M. D. Meachem	Jackson	Farmer
E. M. Merriwether	Jackson	Farmer
George W. Moore	Nashville	Minister
T. Clay Moore	Nashville	Real Estate
James C. Napier	Nashville	One Cent Savings Bank
J. J. Pace	Bristol	Grocer
William M. Payne	Jackson	Farmer
J. P. Rhines	Nashville	Lawyer
Jeff Robinson	Jackson	Stock Dealer
V. M. Roddy	Memphis	Banker

Continued

Name	City	Occupation
Alfred Rogers	Jackson	Farmer
Allen Rogers	Jackson	Farmer
Mrs. J. J. Scott	Memphis	Undertaker
Josiah T. Settle	Memphis	Banker/Lawyer
H. C. Sheyshood	Memphis	Banker
H. Springfield	Jackson	Farmer
G. B. Taylor	Nashville	School
Preston Taylor	Nashville	Undertaker
J. Hamilton Trimble	Jackson	Druggist
J. Thomas Turner	Nashville	—
Charles Varner	Memphis	Vegetable Producer
A. B. Warton	Jackson	Farmer
Washington Weddle	Jackson	Farmer
I. H. Welch	Chattanooga	Minister
Sam Whorton	Jackson	Farmer
W. J. Whorton	Jackson	Farmer
P. T. Williamson	Jackson	Farmer
L. V. Willis	Jackson	Farmer
M. D. Willis	Jackson	Farmer
S. M. Willis	Jackson	Farmer
Mrs. C. Woods	Jackson	Farmer
Dawn Woods	Jackson	Farmer

North Carolina		
Name	City	Occupation
B. A. Adkins	Greensboro	Real Estate
S. G. Atkins	Winston-Salem	Real Estate
J. M. Avery	Durham	Insurance
J. H. Benford	Greensboro	—
George W. Clinton	Charlotte	Bishop

Continued

Continued

Name	City	Occupation
Warren Coleman	Concord	Coleman Manufacturing Company
James B. Dudley	Greensboro	A&M College
John S. Fitts	Winston	—
J. R. Hawkins	Kittrell	Fire Insurance
J. R. Hemphill	Charlotte	Tailor
E. A. Johnson	Raleigh	—
John Merrick	Durham	Insurance/Barber
G. H. Mitchell	Greensboro	Lawyer
Aaron M. Moore	Durham	Insurance/Physician
Charles H. Moore	Greensboro	Organizer Local Business League
G. W. Powell	Durham	Insurance
J. K. Scott	Goldsboro	House Mover
Isaac H. Smith	New Bern	Real Estate
C. C. Spaulding	Durham	Banking/Insurance
Thaddeus L. Tate	Charlotte	Real Estate
S. H. Vick	Wilson	—
A. L. E. Weeks	New Bern	Principal/Minister

Texas		
Name	City	Occupation
E. W. D. Abner	Austin	—
S. P. Allen	Fort Worth	Banker
L. C. Anderson	Austin	Austin Negro Business League
R. T. Andrews	Houston	Grocer
George Ash	Galveston	Painter
Mrs. J. W. Ballew	Galveston	Restaurant
J. T. Barnes	Willis	Grocer
John B. Bell	Houston	Real Estate

Continued

Name	City	Occupation
E. L. Blackshear	Prairie View	Principal/Prairie View State Normal and Industrial College
S. W. Broome	Tyler	Education
James T. Bush	Houston	Education
William M. Calvin	Fordyce	Merchandise
L. L. Campbell	Austin	Austin Negro Business League
R. Carter	Galveston	Wood Dealer
H. Clay	Galveston	Saloon/Show House Keeper
William Conoway	Galveston	Barber
John Covington	Houston	General Merchandising
Mr. [sic] Cox	Galveston	Barber
J. H. Crawford	Prairie View	Teacher
O. C. Crook	Fort Worth	Messenger
J. Cuney	Galveston	Barber
J. P. Diggs	Waxahachie	Grocer
F. L. Etter	Paris	Physician
S. Fieffer	Galveston	Wood Dealer
L. H. Flenegan	Paris	Teacher
J. M. Frierson	Houston	Undertaker
O. A. Fuller	Marshall	Teacher
J. V. Gibson	Galveston	Teacher
Warren E. Glenn	—	—
E. M. Griggs	Palestine	Banker
George M. Guest	Paris	Undertaker
Mrs. R. T. Hamilton	Dallas	Teacher
Amos Harper	Galveston	Barber
L. Harper	Galveston	Artist
Wheeler Haywood	Texarkana	—

Continued

Continued

Name	City	Occupation
W. R. Hill	Galveston	Barber
J. H. Hines	Waco	Banker
J. W. Hoffman	Prairie View	Professor
Mrs. D. V. Hooper	Dallas	Druggist
R. C. Houston, Jr.	Fort Worth	Undertaker
R. C. Houston	Houston or Fort Worth	Undertaker
G. I. Jackson	Dallas	Penny Savings Bank
G. W. Jamerson	Texarkana	Physician
H. C. Johnson	Waco	—
James P. Jones	Houston	Grocer
Josh Jones	Galveston	Wood Dealer
R. Jones	Galveston	Contractor
W. T. King	Dallas	Publisher
E. Laurance	Galveston	Barber
William Lane	Galveston	Saloon Show House Keeper
D. N. Leathers	Corpus Christi	Grocery Merchant
C. A. Lewis	Galveston	Contractor
J. Vance Lewis	Houston	Lawyer
O. A. Lewis	Dallas	Dry Goods
W. H. Love	Galveston	Barber
M. McKinney	Galveston	Barber
J. McNeil	Galveston	Barber
R. McPherson	Galveston	Barber
B. Martin	Galveston	Huckster
P. Matthews	Galveston	Contractor
N. Moore	Galveston	Contractor
M. V. Morris	Houston	—
H. S. Newlin	Texarkana	Hotel
W. H. Nobles, Jr.	Galveston	Newspaper
Mrs. L. Parker	Galveston	Barber

Name	City	Occupation
A. Perkins	Galveston	Contractor
W. A. Pete	Tyler	Education/ Newspaper
Albert Piner	Galveston	Barber
Rev. N. P. Pullum	Houston	Brick Manufacturer/ Minister
D. R. Rawls	St. Augustine	Teacher
J. B. Rayner	Calvert	Laborer
W. J. Redwine	Tyler	Banker
Ben Reed	Galveston	Barber
S. S. Reid	Marshall	Teacher
L. G. Robinson	Galveston	Grocer
Wade C. Rollins	Prairie View	—
H. W. J. Scott	Dallas	Grocer
Calet Smith	Marshall	Undertaker
George Smith	Galveston	Blacksmith
R. L. Smith	Paris	—
S. J. Spencer	Texarkana	Mercantile
William Tears	Austin	Undertaker
George Terry	Galveston	Painter
Andrew Thomas	Galveston	Saloon/ Show House Keeper
T. H. Thomas	Galveston	Barber
L. M. Thornton	Galveston	Barber
T. W. Troupe	Paris	Farmer
A. B. Trowell	Galveston	Barber
B. F. Walker	Galveston	Barber
N. T. Wallis	Fort Worth	Dentist
William Wallis	Galveston	Contractor
James S. Walton	San Antonio	Physician
James T. Walton	San Antonio	Real Estate Coordinator

Continued

Continued

Name	City	Occupation
Jesse W. Washington	Marlin	—
R. E. Wells	Temple	—
F. W. Wheeler	Avinger	Industrial Education
Q. M. White	Texarkana	—
J. H. Wilkins	Galveston	Barber
F. E. Williams	Marshall	Grocer
L. H. Williams	Marshall	Merchant
T. H. Williams	Galveston	Wood Dealer
L. W. Woods	Houston	Merchant
W. B. Woods	Houston	Grocer
A. York	Galveston	Contractor
E. G. Young	Texarkana	Minister/Merchant

Florida		
Name	City	Occupation
M. S. G. Abbott	Pensacola	Physician
Charles H. Alston	Pensacola	Lawyer
Charles H. Anderson	Jacksonville	Merchant/Banker/ Fish and Oyster
R. B. Ayer	Gainesville	—
Joseph H. Blodgett	Jacksonville	Real Estate
Henry S. Bryant	Jacksonville	Manufacturer
Samuel Charles	Pensacola	Shoe Dealer
N. W. Collier	Jacksonville	Principal/Florida Baptist Academy
J. D. Cunningham	Pensacola	Grocer
Evigan Edwards	Pensacola	Drayman/Real Estate
Mrs. Evigan Edwards	Pensacola	School Teacher
George B. Green	Pensacola	Furniture Dealer Real Estate
Lewis C. Griffin	Belleview	Minister
J. M. Harvey	Pensacola	Contractor/Real Estate

Name	City	Occupation
Joe H. James	Pensacola	Grocer
A. M. Johnson	Pensacola	Grocer
Nathan Jones	Pensacola	Tailor
B. A. Joseph	Pensacola	Tailor
Henry King	Pensacola	Contractor/Sawmill Owner
Matthew M. Lewey	Pensacola	Publisher
Abraham L. Lewis	Jacksonville	Insurance
H. H. Lewis	Pensacola	Contractor/Builder
J. D. McDuffy	Ocala	Farming and Livery
John M. Murphy	Pensacola	Painter/Secretary of Painter's Union
Mr. Oliver	Pensacola	Grocer
H. S. Pons	Pensacola	Contractor
A. C. Porter	St. Petersburg	—
Isaac L. Purcell	Pensacola	Lawyer
Rufus Roberts	Pensacola	Secretary of Bricklayer's Union
C. V. Smith	Pensacola	Physician
A. W. Spears	Pensacola	Lawyer
D. T. Straghn	Pensacola	Druggist/People's Drug Store
Edward Sunday	Pensacola	Contractor
John Sunday	Pensacola	Real Estate
George E. Taylor	St. Augustine	—
F. E. Washington	Pensacola	—
W. A. Watts	Pensacola	Dry Goods
A. H. Whorley	Pensacola	Real Estate
Joseph L. Wiley	Fessenden	Principal/Fessenden Academy
H. G. Williams	Pensacola	Physician/Surgeon Pensacola Drug Co.

Continued

Continued

Name	City	Occupation
J. Andrew Williams	Tampa	Cigar Manufacturer
E. I. Alexander	Jacksonville	Dry Goods
Mrs. Emily Bagley	Jacksonville	Grocer/Boarding House
H. G. Reed	Jacksonville	Editor
R. B. Robinson	Jacksonville	Grocery Merchant
H. F. Russell	Jacksonville	Grocer
A. D. Saunders	Jacksonville	Restaurant
G. Simon	Jacksonville	Grocery Merchant
C. J. Sinkler	Jacksonville	Merchant Tailor
F. R. Smith	Jacksonville	Butcher
Mrs. Stragn	Jacksonville	Restaurant
Mrs. A. E. Stringer	Jacksonville	Grocery and Confection
Charles Thomas	Jacksonville	Restaurant
Edward Thompson	Jacksonville	Grocery Merchant
S. Toby	Jacksonville	Proprietor/Barber Shop
Rev. J. M. Trammell	Jacksonville	Publisher
David Trent	Jacksonville	Horseshoe Business
J. L. Usher	Jacksonville	—
C. N. Vought	Jacksonville	Grocery Merchant
George W. Whetmore	Jacksonville	Real Estate Agent
H. A. Williams	Jacksonville	Contractor and Builder
H. H. Yates	Jacksonville	Contractor and Builder
H. Adams	Tampa	Butcher
H. Anderson	Tampa	Plumber
J. Beasley	Tampa	Restaurant/Grocer
J. Belton	Tampa	Liveryman
D. Bradley	Tampa	Liveryman

Continued

Name	City	Occupation
Mrs. D. Bradley	Tampa	Restaurant
M. B. Brunson	Tampa	Barber
A. Curry	Tampa	Barber
F. Daniels	Tampa	Barber
R. Donaldson	Tampa	Saloon Keeper
R. W. Dupree	Tampa	Peddler
W. E. Durham	Tampa	Shoemaker
R. Fleming	Tampa	Tailor
S. Gilbanks	Tampa	Tailor
F. W. Glover	Tampa	Liveryman
Thomas Glover	Tampa	Restaurant
W. H. Green	Tampa	Manager/ Undertaking Business
J. H. Hill	Tampa	Tailor
Mrs. W. Houston	Tampa	Restaurant
J. C. Hunter	Tampa	Peddler
J. Jefferson	Tampa	Bicycles
J. M. Johnson	Tampa	Shoemaker
William Larkins	Tampa	Grocer
W. W. Leak	Tampa	Grocer
S. Lee	Tampa	Barber
William Lee	Tampa	Liveryman
J. Lighbourn	Tampa	Tailor
B. J. McCullough	Tampa	Tailor
J. W. McConnall	Tampa	Tailor
Y. K. Meeks	Tampa	Jeweler
J. H. Miller	Tampa	Liveryman
Mrs. A. P. Mills	Tampa	Restaurant
A. E. Minns	Tampa	Cigar Factory
William Morris	Tampa	Barber
M. Nilback	Tampa	Tailor

Continued

Continued

Name	City	Occupation
C. W. Patterson	Tampa	Cigar Factory
W. O. Perry	Tampa	Cigar Factory
W. B. Reed	Tampa	Shoemaker
W. C. Richardson	Tampa	Grocer
B. B. Roberts	Tampa	Shoemaker
John L. Saulter	Tampa	Saloon Keeper
Isaac H. N. Smith	Tampa	Tailor
Mrs. J. Taylor	Tampa	Restaurant
T. E. Taylor	Tampa	Cigar Factory
H. Vaughn	Tampa	Barber
W. C. Vester	Tampa	Peddler
J. A. Walker	Tampa	Grocer
E. E. West	Tampa	Grocer
H. W. Wiggins	Tampa	Shoemaker
H. Williams	Tampa	Chop House
J. W. Williams	Tampa	Barber
T. C. Williams	Tampa	Plumber

NOTES

I INTRODUCTION

1. Harlan, "Booker T. Washington," 3, 4; Harlan, *Wizard of Tuskegee*, 145; Du Bois, *Dusk of Dawn*, 49.
2. Harlan, *Making of a Black Leader*, 206; Similarly, James Napier believed that black participation in the Tennessee Centennial Exposition would give them a chance to " 'correctly' demonstrate their progress since slavery. Napier believed that what elite blacks 'had done and were doing' best demonstrated progress since slavery," Lovett explained. See Lovett, "James Carroll Napier (1845–1940)," 85–86.
3. See, for example, Anderson, *Education of Blacks in the South*, 65, 77, 104; and Moore, *Booker T. Washington, W. E. B. Du Bois and the Struggle for Racial Uplift*.
4. Fredrickson, *White Supremacy*, xi–xii; Neely Fuller is cited in Welsing, *The Isis Papers*, 3.
5. Booker T. Washington to Charles Banks, October 23, 1907; Booker T. Washington to I. T. Harahan, September 16, 1908, Booker T. Washington Papers, Microfilm. Hereafter cited as BTWPF. Washington, *My Larger Education*, 183–184; See all of Chapter 3 entitled "My Educational Campaigns through the South and What They Taught Me"; Hemmingway, "Booker T. Washington in Mississippi," 29–42; Denton, *Booker T. Washington*, 102–105.
6. "The Washington Tour in Florida," 198; Denton, *Booker T. Washington*, 102–105.
7. Rules and Regulations in the program of Third Annual Session of the NNBL, August 25–27, 1902, National Negro Business League Papers; Circular letter from Washington to Local Negro Business Leagues, September 24, 1915, BTWPF.
8. For further reading on the NNBL, see Nichols and Crogman, *Progress of a Race*, 211–229; Burrows, "The Necessity of Myth;" Borchert, "The National Negro Business League."
9. Jackson, *Chief Lieutenant*, 90.
10. Jackson, "Growth of African American Cultural and Social Institutions," 316–317.
11. Harlan, *Making of a Black Leader*, 254–255, 271.
12. Simkins, *Pitchfork Ben Tillman*, 399–400.

13. Ibid.
14. Walker, *Metamorphosis of Sutton Griggs*, 13; Blight, *Race and Reunion*, 332; See also Bay, *The White Image in the Black Mind*, 8.
15. Blight, *Race and Reunion*, 332.
16. Ibid., 333.
17. Lovett, *African-American History of Nashville*, 110–112.
18. Harlan, *Wizard of Tuskegee*, 263.
19. Ibid., 262–263.
20. See, for example, Lovett, *African-American History of Nashville*, 112. Lovett quotes Frederick Douglass as saying, "I found myself better appreciated by the whites than by my own people in Nashville, and much of the attention paid by the colored people was due to the respect paid me by the whites."
21. Booker T. Washington to Whom It May Concern, November 20, 1909, BTWP, 10: 237–238.

2 THE THREE R's: RECONSTRUCTION, REDEMPTION, AND RACISM

1. See, for example, Equiano, *Interesting Narrative*, 93–100; Blassingame, *Slave Community*; Davis, *Inhuman Bondage*, 31, 37, 93, 95–96, 179–180, 201, 255; Kolchin, *American Slavery*, 7, 10, 13, 20, 57–59, 121–122; Stampp, *Peculiar Institution*; Clarke, *Critical Lessons In Slavery*; Thomas, *The Slave Trade*.
2. Hine, Hine, and Harrold, *African American Odyssey*, 285–288; Fredrickson, *Black Image*, 186.
3. Ibid., 187; Jackson, *Chief Lieutenant*, 2–3.
4. Honey, "Class, Race, and Power in the New South," 178; Anderson, *Race and Politics in North Carolina*, 5; Lovett, *African-American History of Nashville*, 217; Du Bois, *Black Reconstruction*, 575; Lamon, *Blacks in Tennessee*, 49; Pitre, *Through Many Dangers, Toils and Snares*, 223–226; Williams, *Bricks without Straw*, 57–59, 45–72.
5. Brown, *Florida's Black Public Officials*, 92–93, 135–136.
6. Foner, *Freedom's Lawmakers*, 28, 47, 113, 257, 245–259.
7. Hine, Hine, and Harrold, *African American Odyssey*, 286; Foner, *Freedom's Lawmakers*, xiv–xi, 296.
8. Hine, Hine, and Harrold, *African American Odyssey*, 277; Fredrickson, *Black Image*, 187.
9. Ibid., 195; See also Logan, *Betrayal of the Negro*.
10. Quoted in Fredrickson, *Black Image*, 195–196.
11. Ibid., 196.
12. Hine, Hine, and Harrold, *African American Odyssey*, 277, 291, 297–299.
13. Clark, "The Public Career of James Carroll Napier," iv.

14. Hine, Hine, and Harrold, *African American Odyssey*, 395; Franklin and Moss, *Slavery to Freedom*, 325; Dray, *At the Hands of Persons Unknown*, 190–193, 196–207; Turner, *Ceramic Uncles and Celluloid Mammies*, 51–52, 82–83.

15. Fredrickson, *Black Image*, 282.

16. Oshinsky, *Worse than Slavery*, 33; Hine, Hine, and Harrold, *African American Odyssey*, 313.

17. Thompson, *Lynchings in Mississippi*, 11–12; McMillen, *Dark Journey*, 40, 41, 43; Franklin and Moss, *Slavery to Freedom*, 259–260.

18. Thompson, *Lynchings in Mississippi*, 11–12.

19. Hine, Hine, and Harrold, *African American Odyssey*, 318; for more extensive studies on white violence against blacks see Dray, *At the Hands of Persons Unknown*; and Litwack, *Trouble in Mind*.

20. Hale, *Making Whiteness*, 201; Bennett, *Before the Mayflower*, 277; Patterson, *Rituals of Blood*, 169–232.

21. Fredrickson, *Black Image*, 282.

22. Hine, Hine, and Harrold, *African American Odyssey*, 272; Franklin and Moss, *Slavery to Freedom*, 225.

23. Oshinsky, *Worse than Slavery*, 32, 35; Hine, Hine, and Harrold, *African American Odyssey*, 329.

24. Turner, *Ceramic Uncles and Celluloid Mammies*, 11.

25. Ibid., 51–52.

26. Clinton, *The Plantation Mistress*, 201–202; Turner, *Ceramic Uncles and Celluloid Mammies*, 43–44.

27. Goings, *Mammy and Uncle Mose*, xiii, 8; Litwack, "Trouble in Mind: The Bicentennial and the Afro-American Experience," 326.

28. Goings, *Mammy and Uncle Mose*, 13.

29. Ibid., 14.

30. Ibid., 40.

31. Hale, *Making Whiteness*, 200.

32. Ibid., 21.

33. Ibid., 128–129.

34. Brinkley, *American History*, 653–655.

35. Johnson, *Myth of Ham*, 95–96.

36. Hine, Hine, and Harrold, *African American Odyssey*, 334; Fredrickson, *Black Image*, 295.

37. Bederman, *Manliness & Civilization*, 23, 25.

38. Ibid., 25, 72–73.

39. Ibid., 27, 29.

40. Shufeldt, *The Negro: A Menace to Civilization*, 124, 128, 134; Also, see Oshinsky, *Worse than Slavery*, 94–95.

41. Carroll, *The Negro a Beast*, 114, 124–136. Also, see inside title page for claim of "fifteen years" of research.

42. Ibid., 125.

43. Johnson, *Myth of Ham*, 33, 35; Fredrickson, *Black Image*, 188.

44. Johnson, *Myth of Ham*, 10, 12, 20, 28, 33, 39.

45. Ibid., 12.
46. Ibid., 12–13.
47. Ibid., 37–38, 40–41.
48. Both quotes cited in Moore, *Leading the Race*, 81–82.
49. Hoberman, *Darwin's Athletes*, 152.
50. Ibid., 160.
51. Gayarre', "The Southern Question," 485, 493, 495; Fredrickson, *Black Image*, 220, 229, 236–239, 246–247, 249–252; Barringer, *The American Negro: His Past and Future*, 3, 5, 14–15.
52. Hoberman, *Darwin's Athletes*, 153.
53. *New York Times*, September 10, 11, 1906; Bradford and Blume, *Ota Benga*, 181. For the entire story, see Bradford and Blume's *Ota Benga*. These authors give the complete story of the tragic life of Ota Benga who eventually committed suicide before being transported back to Africa. Harriet Washington also discusses Benga's dreadful story in *Medical Apartheid*, 75–79, sharing that before being taken from the Congo, Ota had been married with children. However, once when he returned from a hunting trip around 1903, Benga's village had been burned to the ground and his entire tribe, including his wife and children, had been exterminated by Force Publique "thugs," a group supported by Belgium's government.
54. *New York Times*, September 18, 1906; Bradford and Blume, *Ota Benga*, 185, 187; Washington, *Medical Apartheid*, 75–79.
55. *New York Times*, September 10, 11, 18, 19, 1906; Bradford and Blume, *Ota Benga*, 182, 183, 189.
56. Du Bois, *Black Reconstruction*, 711–729; Walker, *Metamorphosis of Sutton Griggs*, 15.

3 BOOKER T. WASHINGTON AND THE PSYCHOLOGY OF "BLACK SURVIVALISM"

1. Wiggins, *The Life & Works of Paul Lawrence Dunbar*, 184.
2. Garvey, *Message to the People: The Course of African Philosophy*, 75.
3. Harlan, "The Secret Life of Booker T. Washington," 393; Flynn, "Booker T. Washington: Uncle Tom or Wooden Horse," 262; Dagbovie, "Exploring a Century of Historical Scholarship on Booker T. Washington," 239–264.
4. *Jacksonville Florida Times-Union*, February 13, 1900.
5. Washington, *Up from Slavery*; Franklin and Moss, *From Slavery to Freedom*, 244–246; Harlan, *The Making of a Black Leader*; Washington, "Industrial Education Is the Solution," 277–279; Summers, *Manliness & Its Discontents*, 27.
6. Franklin and Moss, *From Slavery to Freedom*, 244–248; Thornbrough, "Booker T. Washington as Seen by His White Contemporaries," 161–182. See also Spivey, *Schooling for the New Slavery*.

7. Harlan, "The Secret Life of Booker T. Washington," 393–416; Lovett, *African-American History of Nashville*, 239; Calista, "Booker T. Washington: Another Look," 240.

8. Watkins, *On the Real Side*, 235–236.

9. Ibid., 236.

10. Harlan, "Secret Life of Booker T. Washington," 393–416; Lovett, *African-American History of Nashville*, 239; Daniel, "Up from Slavery Down to Peonage," 654–670; Daniel, *Shadow of Slavery*, 65–81.

11. Lewis, *W. E. B. Du Bois, 1868–1919*, 258.

12. Harlan, *Making of a Black Leader*, 171, 175. For the entire story on Harris, see pages 171–175. For more examples of this type of deception by Washington, see Harlan, "The Secret Life of Booker T. Washington."

13. Thompson, *Lynchings in Mississippi*, 7.

14. Blassingame, *The Slave Community*, 312–315.

15. Ibid.; Watkins, *On the Real Side*, 75.

16. Cone, *The Spirituals & the Blues*, 27.

17. Watkins, *On the Real Side*, 75.

18. Ibid., 448.

19. Levine, *Black Culture and Black Consciousness*, 122–123; Cone, *The Spirituals & the Blues*, 28.

20. Levine, *Black Culture and Black Consciousness*, 122–123.

21. Ibid., 127; Watkins, *On the Real Side*, 448–449.

22. Calista, "Booker T. Washington: Another Look," 250–251; Harlan, "Secret Life of Booker T. Washington," 395.

23. The following scholars have been more critical in their analysis of the speeches and writings on Washington. They both have examined their deeper meanings. See Willard, "Timing Impossible Subjects: The Marketing Style of Booker T. Washington," 624–668; Dagbovie, "Exploring a Century of Historical Scholarship on Booker T. Washington," 239–264.

24. Higginbotham, "African-American Women's History and the Metalanguage of Race," 261.

25. Ibid., 254, 267.

26. *El Paso Morning Times*, September 25, 1911; "An Account of Washington's Tour of Texas," in BTWP, 5: 11, 323, 329–330; Biehler and Snowman, *Psychology Applied to Teaching*, 161.

27. Weare, *Black Business in the New South*, 52.

28. Banks, "Negro Town and Colony, Mound Bayou, Bolivar Co., Miss., Opportunities Open to Farmers and Settlers," 11.

29. Charles Banks to Robert W. Taylor, June 22, 1908, BTWPF; Charles Banks to Robert Park, April 25, 1907, BTWPF.

30. Wiggins, *Life & Works of Paul Lawrence Dunbar*, 184.

31. Charles Banks to Mr. W. L. Park, February 6, 1911, BTWPF.

32. Charles Banks to Booker T. Washington, October 20, 1907, BTWPF.

33. Crockett, *The Black Towns*, 103.

34. Ellsworth, *Death in a Promised Land*; D'Orso, *Like Judgment Day*.

35. "Whites, Blacks Join to Stop Lynching," *Memphis Commercial Appeal*, ca. December 13, 1913.

36. Ibid.

37. Harlan, "Secret Life of Booker T. Washington."

38. Thomas Owen to Charles Banks, March 24, 1912, BTWPF.

39. L. K. Salsbury to Charles Banks, April 1, 1912; see also Leroy Percy, U.S. Senator to Andrew Carnegie, April 8, 1912, BTWPF.

40. Thompson, *Lynchings in Mississippi*, 11, 24.

41. Jackson, *Chief Lieutenant*, 41–43; Harlan, "Booker T. Washington and the Voice of the Negro," 145; Calista, "Booker T. Washington: Another Look," 253; Fredrickson, *Black Image*, 295.

42. Potter, "Booker T. Washington: A Visit to Florida," 744; See also Allen, Ware, and Garrison, *Slave Songs of the United States*.

43. Haskin, *Black Music in America*, 27.

44. Ibid., 27, 29.

45. Ibid.

46. Cone, *The Spirituals & the Blues*, 4, 5; Haskin, *Black Music in America*, 6.

47. Cone, *The Spirituals & the Blues*, 13.

48. Ibid., 14–15.

49. Pinn, *Why, Lord? Suffering and Evil in Black Theology*, 21–38.

50. Cone, *The Spirituals & the Blues*, 15, 16, 32, 35. See also Pinn, *Why, Lord? Suffering and Evil in Black Theology*, 57–89.

51. Cone, *The Spirituals & the Blues*, 32; Haskin, *Black Music in America*, 9.

52. Cone, *The Spirituals & the Blues*, 32; Haskin, *Black Music in America*, 9.

53. Ponton, *Life and Times of Henry M. Turner*, 60, 64; Washington, *My Larger Education*, 199.

54. Ponton, *Life and Times of Henry M. Turner*, 146.

55. Angell, *Bishop Henry McNeal Turner and African-American Religion in the South*, 89.

56. Washington, *My Larger Education*, 66, 216–217; for information on Washington's pragmatism, see West, *The Education of Booker T. Washington*, 13–14, 24–29.

57. Lewis, *W. E. B. Du Bois, 1868–1919*, 258.

58. Harlan, *The Wizard of Tuskegee*, 307; *Jackson Clarion-Ledger*, October 24, 1901; *Springfield Republican*, January 22, 1903; Thornbrough, "Booker T. Washington as Seen by His White Contemporaries," 179.

59. To the Editor of *The Montgomery Advertiser*, August 20, 1905, in BTWP, 5: 8, 343–344.

60. Thomas Dixon, Jr., "Booker T. Washington and the Negro: Some Dangerous Aspects of the Work of Tuskegee," *Saturday Evening Post [Philadelphia]* August 19, 1905.

61. Ibid.
62. Ibid.
63. Congress had done the same thing in the 1860s and 1870s, but allowed those rights to be taken away.
64. See Washington, "My View of Segregation Laws," quoted in Calista, "Booker T. Washington: Another Look," 254–255.
65. Norrell, "Understanding the Wizard," 74.
66. Ibid.; Lewis, *W. E. B. Du Bois, 1868–1919*, 258–259.
67. Norrell, "Understanding the Wizard," 76.

4 TOUR OF THE MAGNOLIA STATE, OCTOBER 1908

1. McMillen, *Dark Journey*, 9, 10, 11, 1–32.
2. Ibid., 5.
3. Ibid., 10; Wharton, *Negro in Mississippi*, 230–233; See also Rabinowitz, *Race Relations in the Urban South*.
4. McMillen, *Dark Journey*, 31.
5. Ibid., 120–121, 233–234; Oshinsky, *Worse than Slavery*, 100, 1–133; Cobb, *The Most Southern Place on Earth*, 112–118; Holmes, "Whitecapping: Agrarian Violence in Mississippi," 166, 165–185.
6. Oshinsky, *Worse than Slavery*, 101–102, 278, n.40; Thompson, *Lynching in Mississippi*.
7. *Vicksburg Evening Post*, February 13, 1904; Oshinsky, *Worse than Slavery*, 101–102; Cobb, *Most Southern Place on Earth*, 112–118.
8. Litwack, *Been in the Storm*, Chapter 8; Oshinsky, *Worse than Slavery*, 86.
9. Franklin and Moss, *Slavery to Freedom*, 236; Wharton, *Negro in Mississippi*, 206–15.
10. Quoted in Norrell, "Understanding the Wizard," 68.
11. McMillen, *Dark Journey*, 73, 78; Wharton, *The Negro in Mississippi*, 234–255; Oshinsky, *Worse than Slavery*, 89.
12. Booker T. Washington to Emily Howland, October 13, 1901, *Booker T. Washington Papers*, Ed. by Harlan and Smock, 6: 240–241 (hereafter cited as BTWP); *New York Evening Post*, October 21, 1901 cited in BTWP, 6: 243–247.
13. Ibid., 246.
14. Ibid.
15. Washington to Theodore Roosevelt, October 16, 1901, BTWP, 6: 243; Harlan, *Making of a Black Leader*, 304.
16. Ibid., 311; for full discussion see pp. 304–324.
17. Bennett, *Before the Mayflower*, 256, 329.
18. *Jackson Clarion-Ledger*, October 24, 1901.
19. *Biloxi Daily Herald*, October 20, 1901.
20. *Jackson Clarion-Ledger*, November 7, 1901.

21. Oshinsky, *Worse than Slavery*, 87–88.
22. *Jackson Clarion-Ledger*, October 24, 1901.
23. Ibid.
24. Ibid.
25. Ibid.
26. Ibid., November 7, 1901.
27. *New York Age*, October 22, 1908.
28. *Baltimore Afro-American Ledger*, July 8, 1911; See entire study, Jackson, *A Chief Lieutenant*; Hamilton, *Beacon Lights*, 207.
29. Washington, *My Larger Education*, 207–208; Washington, "Charles Banks," 731–733; Jackson, *A Chief Lieutenant*, 1–216, especially pp. 154–155.
30. Wiggins, *The Life & Works of Paul Lawrence Dunbar*, 184; circular letter from Charles Banks to whites in adjoining counties, ca. October 5, 1912, BTWPF.
31. Charles Banks to Booker T. Washington, November 12, 1912, BTWPF; Jackson, *A Chief Lieutenant*, 45–46.
32. Charles Banks to Booker T. Washington, September 4, 1908, BTWPF.
33. Charles Banks to Booker T. Washington, August 31, 1908, BTWPF.
34. Booker T. Washington to Charles Banks, September 17, 1908, BTWPF.
35. Charles Banks to newspaper editors, September 23, 1908, BTWPF.
36. Charles Banks to Perry Howard, September 23, 1908, BTWPF.
37. Charles Banks to Emmett Scott, September 5, 1908, BTWPF.
38. Emmett Scott to Charles Banks, September 8, 1908, BTWPF.
39. Charles Banks to Booker T. Washington, September 10, 1908, BTWPF.
40. Ibid.
41. Emmett Scott to Charles Banks, September 16, 1908, BTWPF.
42. Charles Banks to Booker T. Washington, September 18, 1908, BTWPF.
43. Charles Banks to J. T. Harahan, September 16, 1908, BTWPF.
44. See itinerary in *Jackson Evening News*, ca. August 28, 1908, in BTWPF, slide 141.
45. Hine, Hine, and Harold, *African American Odyssey*, 380; Franklin and Moss, *From Slavery to Freedom*, 316; Crouthamel, "Springfield Race Riot of 1908," 164–181. For examples of Northern racism, see Loewen, *Sundown Towns*, 12, 197.
46. Miller, report, October 6, 1908, in BTWP, 9: 641; *New York Age*, October 22, 1908; Moton, *Finding a Way Out*, 180–181.
47. Harlan, *Wizard of Tuskegee*, 263; Miller, report, October 6, 1908, in BTWP, 9: 642–643; Oshinsky, *Worse than Slavery*, 85.
48. *Baltimore Afro-American Ledger*, October 17, 1908; Kealing, "Booker T. Washington's Tour through Mississippi," 20–27;

"Principal Washington's Tour of Mississippi," 1, 4; "Principal Washington's Mississippi Visit," 1, 3; "Booker T. Washington's Trip through Mississippi" [Part I], 1; "Booker T. Washington's Trip through Mississippi" [Part II], 1, 4; Hemmingway, "Booker T. Washington in Mississippi," 30, 42. Interestingly, Isaiah Montgomery does not appear to have been with Washington's contingent throughout the trip.

49. *New York Age*, October 8, 1908.

50. Washington, "A Cheerful Journey through Mississippi," BTWP, 10: 63; Kealing, "Booker T. Washington's Tour through Mississippi," BTWP, 9: 676, 678; *New York Age*, October 22, 1908; *Baltimore Afro-American Ledger*, October 17, 1908; Oshinsky, *Worse than Slavery*, 89; Lakey, *History of the CME Church*, 289.

51. Jackson, *A Chief Lieutenant*, 19; *New York Age*, October 22, 1908; Willard, "Timing Impossible Subjects," 651–655.

52. *New Orleans Picayune*, October 6, 1908; *Baltimore Afro-American Ledger*, October 10, 1908; *Memphis Commercial Appeal*, October 6, 1908; *New York Age*, October 22, 1908; Kealing, "Booker T. Washington's Tour through Mississippi," in BTWP, 9: 677, 680; Moton, "The Significance of Mr. Washington's Lecture Trip In Mississippi," 691–695; "Principal Washington's Tour of Mississippi," 1, 4; "Principal Washington's Mississippi Visit," 1, 3; "Booker T. Washington's Trip through Mississippi" [Part I], 1; "Booker T. Washington's Trip through Mississippi" [Part II], 1, 4.

53. *Baltimore Afro-American Ledger*, October 10, 1908.

54. *Indianapolis Freeman*, October 17, 1908; *Baltimore Afro-American Ledger*, October 17, 1908.

55. *New York Age*, October 22, 1908; Kealing, "Booker T. Washington's Tour through Mississippi," BTWP, 9: 677; Washington, "A Cheerful Journey," BTWP, 10: 64; "Principal Washington's Tour of Mississippi," 1, 4; "Principal Washington's Mississippi Visit," 1, 3; "Booker T. Washington's Trip through Mississippi" [Part I], 1; "Booker T. Washington's Trip through Mississippi" [Part II], 1, 4; Cooper, "William H. Holtzclaw and Utica Institute," 15–33.

56. Jackson, "Perry Wilbon Howard," 417–419; McMillen, "Perry W. Howard: Boss of Black-and-Tan Republicanism in Mississippi," 205–224.

57. *New York Age*, October 22, 1908; Washington, "A Cheerful Journey through Mississippi," 10: 66; Washington to Seth Low, October 8, 1908, BTWP, 9: 647; The *Indianapolis Freeman*, October 17, 1908, asserts that eight thousand people turned out to hear Washington of whom six hundred were "leading" whites.

58. *Indianapolis Freeman*, October 10, 1908; *New York Age*, October 22, 1908; *Baltimore Afro-American Ledger*, October 17, 1908; Reports of Pinkerton Detective F. E. Miller, October 3–December, 1908, BTWP, 9: 640–645. The *Indianapolis Freeman*, October 17,

1908, asserted that "two hundred or more people fell through to the bottom floor. In a rush for the exits there were a dozen or more, both white and colored badly mashed. Some got broken legs, some broken arms."

59. *New York Age*, October 22, 1908; *Indianapolis Freeman*, October 17, 1908; *Baltimore Afro-American Ledger*, October 24, 1908.

60. Oshinsky, *Worse than Slavery*, 87, 91, see also Chapter 4; BTWP, 7: 267, n.1.

61. Washington to Francis J. Garrison, October 10, 1908, BTWP, 9: 648–649, 646; *New York Age*, October 22, 1908; *Indianapolis Freeman*, October 17, 1908; *Baltimore Afro-American Ledger*, October 24, 1908.

62. *New York Age*, October 22, 1908; *Indianapolis Freeman*, October 17, 1908; *Baltimore Afro-American Ledger*, October 24, 1908.

63. *Hattiesburg Mississippi News*, November 23, 1909.

64. *Vicksburg Daily Herald*, October 9, 1908; Washington, "Cheerful Journey through Mississippi," BTWP, 10: 64, 66; Washington, *My Larger Education*, 196.

65. *New York Age*, October 22, 1908.

66. Ibid; *Vicksburg Daily Herald*, October 9, 1908; On Ewing, see James, James, and James, *The Mississippi Black Bankers*, 39; On Mollison, see BTWP, 6: 249, n.1. For more on Dr. Miller see McMillen, *Dark Journey*, 31, 171; and Ward, *Black Physicians*, 237, 275. Although Miller tried never to "meddle in the white man's affairs...or complain at the many acts of lawlessness" against his race, in 1918, after America's entry into World War I, and some eighteen years after he had been practicing medicine in Vicksburg, a white "vigilance committee" comprised of "leading citizens" and a policeman charged Dr. Miller with "sedition" and tarred and feathered him. After which, they paraded him through town, displayed him near City Hall, put him in jail, and then finally ran him out of Vicksburg under the threat of death. Miller migrated to Detroit, but had to sell his Vicksburg property at a great loss.

67. *Vicksburg Daily Herald*, October 9, 1908.

68. Ibid.

69. Ibid; *New York Age*, October 22, 1908; *New Orleans Picayune*, October 9, 1908.

70. Lampton died in 1910, just two years after Washington's speech. See Wright, *Bishops of the A.M.E. Church*, 251, 252; BTWP, 6: 447–448, n.3; *New York Age*, October 22, 1908.

71. Washington, "Cheerful Journey through Mississippi," BTWP, 10: 64, 66; Washington, *My Larger Education*, 196; *New York Age*, October 22, 1908.

72. Booker T. Washington, *The Negro in Business*; Willey, "Mound Bayou—A Negro Municipality," 163; Hood, *The Negro at Mound Bayou*, 10–45; Hamilton, *Black Towns and Profit*, 63, 68; McMillen,

Dark Journey, 120–121; Holmes, "Whitecapping: Agrarian Violence in Mississippi," 165–185; Meier, "Booker T. Washington and the Town of Mound Bayou," 217–223.

73. *New York Age*, October 22, 1908; *Baltimore Afro-American Ledger*, October 24, 1908; Hartshorn, *An Era of Progress and Promise*, 516; Washington, *My Larger Education*, 196–197; Hemmingway, "Booker T. Washington in Mississippi," 36; Reports of Pinkerton Detective F. E. Miller, October 10, 1908, BTWP, 9: 645. The Pinkerton report says that he spoke to about three thousand people in Mound Bayou.

74. *New York Age*, October 22, 1908; *Baltimore Afro-American Ledger*, October 24, 1908; Hartshorn, *An Era of Progress and Promise*, 516; Washington, *My Larger Education*, 196–197.

75. The townspeople in Lula said that the bodies were left hanging because none of their family members claimed them that day. For details on the lynching, see the *Memphis Commercial Appeal*, October 12–13, 1908. See also Holmes, "Whitecapping: Agrarian Violence in Mississippi," 165–185; Hemmingway, "Booker T. Washington in Mississippi," 39–42.

76. Emmett Scott to Charles Banks, October 15, 1908, BTWPF.

77. Washington, "Cheerful Journey through Mississippi," 10: 66; *New York Age*, October 22, 1908.

78. Booker T. Washington to Charles Banks, October 18, 1908, BTWPF.

79. Washington, "Cheerful Journey through Mississippi," 10: 67; see also Washington, *My Larger Education*, 197; Moton, "The Significance of Mr. Washington's Lecture Trip in Mississippi," 691–695; for further reading on the progress of Mississippi Negroes, see also Woodard's, "Negro Progress in a Mississippi Town," 3–8.

80. Emmett Scott to Charles Banks, October 15, 1908, BTWPF; *New York Age*, July 9, and October 22, 1908.

81. Roscoe C. Simmons to Charles Banks, n.d., BTWPF, slide 137; *New York Age*, July 9, 1908, October 22, 1908.

82. See, for example, *Indianapolis Freeman*, October 24, 1908; *New York Age*, October 22, 1908; *Baltimore Afro-American Ledger*, November 21, 1908.

5   Tour of the Volunteer State, November 1909

1. Jackson, *A Chief Lieutenant*, 98–99.

2. *Baltimore Afro-American Ledger*, November 20, 1909; *Nashville Tennessean*, November 11, 1909; Washington, *The Negro in Business*, 119–120; Lovett, *African American History of Nashville*, 114.

3. *Nashville American*, August 20, 1903 cited in Lamon, *Black Tennesseans*, 6; Lovett, *African American History of Nashville*, 114.

4. Booker T. Washington to James C. Napier, BTWP, 10: 193–194.
5. "Account of Washington's Tour of Tennessee," BTWP, 10: 222; *Indianapolis Freeman*, November 20, 1909.
6. "Account of Washington's Tour of Tennessee," BTWP, 10: 222; *Indianapolis Freeman*, November 20, 1909.
7. Goings and Smith, "Unhidden Transcripts," 372–394; Tucker, "Miss Ida B. Wells and Memphis Lynching," 113–116; Lamon, *Black Tennesseans*, 244–254.
8. Dray, *At the Hands of Persons Unknown*, ix, 151–152, 157–158.
9. Ibid.
10. "Account of Washington's Tour of Tennessee," BTWP, 10: 200–201, 207, 214, 222; *Baltimore Afro-American Ledger*, November 20, 1909.
11. "Account of Washington's Tour of Tennessee," BTWP, 10: 200–201.
12. *Bristol Herald Courier*, November 19, 1909; *Nashville Tennessean*, November 23, 1909.
13. *Nashville Globe*, November 19, 1909; *Bristol Herald Courier*, November 19, 1909; *Chattanooga Daily Times*, November 20, 1909; *Johnson City Comet*, November 25, 1909; *Nashville Tennessean*, November 23, 1909, Lamon, *Black Tennesseans*, 176.
14. "Account of Washington's Tour of Tennessee," BTWP, 10: 226.
15. *Indianapolis Freeman*, November 20, 1909; *Chattanooga Daily Times*, November 20, 1909; See also *Chattanooga Daily Times*, July 9, 1907; *Nashville American*, July 9, 1907; Lamon, *Black Tennesseans*, 35.
16. "Account of Washington's Tour of Tennessee," BTWP, 10: 201.
17. Ibid; *New York Age*, November 25, 1909; *Knoxville Daily Journal and Tribune*, November 19, 1909; Lamon, *Black Tennesseans*, 179.
18. "Account of Washington's Tour of Tennessee," BTWP, 10: 201–202; *Nashville Tennessean*, November 19, 1909; *Johnson City Comet*, November 25, 1909.
19. "Account of Washington's Tour of Tennessee," BTWP, 10: 202.
20. Ibid., 203; *Knoxville Daily Journal and Tribune*, November 19, 1909.
21. "Account of Washington's Tour of Tennessee," BTWP, 10: 203–204; *Knoxville Daily Journal and Tribune*, November 19, 1909.
22. "Account of Washington's Tour of Tennessee," BTWP, 10: 204; *Nashville Tennessean*, November 19, 1909; *Knoxville Daily Journal and Tribune*, November 19, 1909; *New York Age*, November 25, 1909.
23. Lamon, *Black Tennesseans*, 33, 39, 243; for population information, see *Crisis* 14 (June 1917): 89; *Knoxville Daily Journal and Tribune*, August 18, 19, 1908, cited in Lamon, *Black Tennesseans*, 134–135. In 1919, a race riot occurred in Knoxville. See discussion in Lamon, *Black Tennesseans*, 245–255.
24. "Account of Washington's Tour of Tennessee," BTWP, 10: 205; *Nashville Banner*, November 19, 1909; Lamon, *Black Tennesseans*, 33, 39.

25. "Account of Washington's Tour of Tennessee," BTWP, 10: 206–207; *Nashville Banner*, November 19, 1909; *Chattanooga Daily Times*, November 20, 1909; *Knoxville Daily Journal and Tribune*, November 21, 1909.

26. "Account of Washington's Tour of Tennessee," BTWP, 10: 205, 206.

27. *Chattanooga Daily Times*, November 20, 1909; Lamon, *Black Tennesseans*, 30, 38.

28. *Chattanooga Daily Times*, November 20, 1909.

29. Crawford, "Business Negroes of Chattanooga," 535; *Chattanooga Daily Times*, November 17, 20, 1909; Lamon, *Black Tennesseans*, 30.

30. "Account of Washington's Tour of Tennessee," BTWP, 10: 205, 206; *Chattanooga Daily Times*, November 17, 20, 21, 1909; *Knoxville Daily Journal and Tribune*, November 20, 1909.

31. "Account of Washington's Tour of Tennessee," BTWP, 10: 207, 214.

32. Ibid., 208.

33. Ibid., 208–209; *Nashville Tennessean*, November 21, 1909.

34. "Account of Washington's Tour of Tennessee," BTWP, 10: 209–210; *Nashville Tennessean*, November 21, 1909.

35. "Account of Washington's Tour of Tennessee," BTWP, 10: 209–210; Lamon, *Black Tennesseans*, 1; Faries, "Carmack versus Patterson," 332–347.

36. "Account of Washington's Tour of Tennessee," BTWP, 10: 209–210; *Nashville Banner*, November 22, 1909; *Baltimore Afro-American Ledger*, November 29, 1909.

37. "Account of Washington's Tour of Tennessee," BTWP, 10: 209–210; *Nashville Banner*, November 22, 1909; *Nashville Globe*, November 26, 1909; *Baltimore Afro-American Ledger*, November 29, 1909.

38. "Account of Washington's Tour of Tennessee," BTWP, 10: 211, 227, 229; Ward, *Black Physicians*.

39. "Account of Washington's Tour of Tennessee," BTWP, 10: 211, 227, 229.

40. Harvey, "Richard Henry Boyd: Black Business and Religion in the Jim Crow South," 51–52.

41. "Account of Washington's Tour of Tennessee," BTWP, 10: 211–212, 229; *Nashville Globe*, November 26, 1909.

42. Ibid.; *Nashville Tennessean*, November 22, 1909; Lamon, *Black Tennesseans*, 67.

43. *Nashville Globe*, November 29, 1909; *Baltimore Afro-American Ledger*, November 29, 1909.

44. *Nashville Globe*, November 26, 1909.

45. "Account of Washington's Tour of Tennessee," BTWP, 10: 214.

46. Ibid., 215; *Nashville Tennessean*, November 23, 1909; *Nashville Globe*, November 26, 1909.

47. "Account of Washington's Tour of Tennessee," BTWP, 10: 215.

48. Ibid., 215, 228.

49. *Nashville Tennessean*, November 23, 1909.

50. "Account of Washington's Tour of Tennessee," BTWP, 10: 216. The *Baltimore Afro-American Ledger*, December 4, 1909 reported that Clarksville had the "second largest tobacco market in the world."

51. "Account of Washington's Tour of Tennessee," BTWP, 10: 217.

52. Ibid.; *Nashville Banner*, November 24, 1909; *Nashville Tennessean*, November 24, 1909.

53. Lamon, *Black Tennesseans*, 2, 110, 115; Goings and Smith, "Unhidden Transcripts," 390.

54. *Memphis Commercial Appeal*, December 11, 1908, February 12, 1909; Goings and Smith, "Unhidden Transcripts," 386, 388.

55. "Account of Washington's Tour of Tennessee," BTWP, 10: 219; Wells-Barnett, "Lynch Law and All Its Phases," 654; Tucker, "Miss Ida B. Wells and Memphis Lynching," 113, 116; Dray, *At the Hands of Persons Unknown*, 61.

56. "Account of Washington's Tour of Tennessee," BTWP, 10: 219.

57. Church and Walter, *Nineteenth Century Memphis Families of Color*, 16–17.

58. "Account of Washington's Tour of Tennessee," BTWP, 10: 219–220.

59. *Memphis Commercial Appeal*, November 25, 1909; *Nashville American*, February 15, 1903.

60. *Memphis Commercial Appeal*, November 25, 1909.

61. *Boston Transcript*, December 10, 1909 cited in "Account of Washington's Tour of Tennessee," BTWP, 10: 219–220, 235.

62. "Account of Washington's Tour of Tennessee," BTWP, 10: 222; *Johnson City Comet*, November 25, 1909; *Baltimore Afro-American Ledger*, December 4, 1909.

63. *Johnson City Comet*, November 25, 1909.

64. *Chattanooga Daily Times*, November 21, 1909.

65. Robert Ogden to Booker T. Washington, December 3, 1909, BTWP, 10: 240.

66. Booker T. Washington to Sarah Newlin, December 4, 1909, BTWP, 10: 241.

67. *New York Evening Post*, December 2, 1909; Booker T. Washington to Sarah Newlin, December 4, 1909, BTWP, 10: 241.

68. James C. Napier to Booker T. Washington, December 3, 1909, BTWP, 10: 239–240.

69. *Baltimore Afro-American Ledger*, November 29, 1909.

70. *Johnson City Comet*, November 25, 1909.

71. Lamon, *Black Tennesseans*, 4.

6 TOUR OF THE TAR HEEL STATE, OCTOBER–NOVEMBER 1910

1. Lewis, *W. E. B. Du Bois, 1868–1919*, 404–411.

2. Logan, *The Negro in North Carolina, 1876–1894*, vii.

3. Gavins, "Fear, Hope, and Struggle: Recasting Black North Carolina in the Age of Jim Crow," 193.

4. Prather, "We Have Taken a City: A Centennial Essay," 16–17.

5. Ibid., 17–18.

6. Ibid., 18–19,

7. Ibid., 23, 25; Hine, Hine, and Harrold, *African American Odyssey*, 318; Hale, *Making Whiteness*, 89.

8. Prather, "We Have Taken a City," 23, 25; Hine, Hine, and Harrold, *African American Odyssey*, 318; Hale, *Making Whiteness*, 89; Coulter, *Georgia: A Short History*, 385, 392, 395, 416; Coleman, ed., *A History of Georgia*, 184, 218–221, 247, 303, 306, 310; Hall, *Revolt against Chivalry*, 43, 153, 337–338, n.66.

9. Prather, "We Have Taken a City," 23, 25; Hine, Hine, and Harrold, *African American Odyssey*, 318.

10. Ibid.; Bennett, *Before the Mayflower*, 277.

11. Ibid.

12. Hine, Hine, and Harrold, *African American Odyssey*, 318; Anderson, *Race and Politics in North Carolina: 1872–1901*, 296–312; Bennett, *Before the Mayflower*, 277.

13. Harlan, *Wizard of Tuskegee*, 290–292.

14. Ibid.

15. Ibid., 290–294; Washington, *Man Farthest Down*.

16. Harlan, *Wizard of Tuskegee*, 290–294.

17. Ibid., 293–294.

18. Kenzer, *Enterprising Southerners*, 83; Weare, *Black Business in the New South*, 144–145.

19. *New York Age*, November 3, 1910; *Baltimore Afro-American Ledger*, October 22, 1910, November 5, 1910; *Indianapolis Freeman*, October 1, 1910 and November 26, 1910; *Charlotte Daily Observer*, October 28, 1910. Considering the small number of black doctors in Durham, Moore presumably could not be away from his practice for such a lengthy period of time. Regarding the role of the African Methodist Episcopal Zion Church in North Carolina affairs, see Walls, *The African Methodist Episcopal Zion Church*. See also Montgomery, *Under Their Own Vine and Fig Tree*; Martin, *For God and Race*.

20. *Charlotte Daily Observer*, October 28, 1910; Howard N. Rabinowitz, "A Comparative Perspective on Race Relations in Southern and Northern Cities, 1860–1900, with Special Emphasis on Raleigh," 137–159, 162–163; Richardson, ed., *National Cyclopedia*, 233; Kenzer, *Enterprising Southerners*, 106.

21. *Charlotte Daily Observer*, October 26, 1910, October 27, 1910; *Indianapolis Freeman*, October 22, 1910.

22. Richardson, ed., *National Cyclopedia*, 412; See biosketch in BTWP, 4: 21, n.1. Historian Janette Greenwood in *Bittersweet Legacy*, 225 states that Clinton "never advocated Washington's strategy." This writer obviously disagrees with that interpretation.

23. *Baltimore Afro-American Ledger*, October 22, 1910.
24. *Charlotte Daily Observer*, October 29, 1910; Richardson, ed., *National Cyclopedia*, 270. The *Observer* noted that Washington himself was a Baptist.
25. Richardson, ed., *National Cyclopedia*, 270, 271; Greenwood, *Bittersweet Legacy*, 44.
26. *Baltimore Afro-American Ledger*, October 22, 1910; *Charlotte Daily Observer*, October 29, 1910.
27. Ibid., October 27, 29, 1910; November 3, 1910; Quote from J. W. Smith in the *Star of Zion*, October 2, 1902, cited in Greenwood, *Bittersweet Legacy*, 223.
28. The *Observer* says that Sanders was an attorney. *Charlotte Daily Observer*, October 29, 1910; Quotes by J. T. Sanders and J. W. Smith are found in the *Star of Zion*, October 2, 1902, cited in Greenwood, *Bittersweet Legacy*, 223. See also 136, 139.
29. *Charlotte Daily Observer*, October 27, 29, 1910; *New York Age*, November 3, 1910.
30. Ibid.
31. Ibid.
32. Ibid.
33. *Indianapolis Freeman*, November 5, 1910; *Charlotte Daily Observer*, October 29, 1910; Greenwood, *Bittersweet Legacy*, 140; Richardson, ed., *National Cyclopedia*, 412. See also Summers, *Manliness & Its Discontents*.
34. *Charlotte Daily Observer*, October 28, 1910; *New York Age*, November 3, 1910; *Indianapolis Freeman*, November 5, 1910; Fox, *The Guardian of Boston*, 159–160.
35. *Charlotte Daily Observer*, October 30, 1910; Lewis, "An Account of Washington's North Carolina Tour," in BTWP, 10: 458.
36. Ibid.
37. *Indianapolis Freeman*, November 5, 1910; Greenwood, *Bittersweet Legacy*, 140.
38. *New York Age*, November 3, 1910; *Indianapolis Freeman*, November 5, 1910; *Baltimore Afro-American Ledger*, November 5, 1910; *Charlotte Daily Observer*, October 30, 1910; Bederman, *Manliness & Civilization*.
39. *Indianapolis Freeman*, November 5, 1910; *Charlotte Daily Observer*, October 30, 1910; Lewis, "An Account of Washington's North Carolina Tour," in BTWP, 10: 458.
40. *Indianapolis Freeman*, November 5, 1910.
41. Ibid., November 2, 5, 1910; *Washington Bee*, November 5, 1910; Lewis, "An Account of Washington's North Carolina Tour," in BTWP, 10: 458–459.
42. Chafe, *Civilities and Civil Rights*, 14–16; Kipp, "Old Notable and Newcomers: The Economic and Political Elite of Greensboro, North Carolina, 1870–1920," 373–394; *Indianapolis Freeman*,

November 2, 5, 1910; *Washington Bee*, November 5, 1910. Lewis says Washington spoke to four thousand people. See Lewis, "An Account of Washington's North Carolina Tour," BTWP, 10: 459.

43. *Indianapolis Freeman*, November 12, 1910.
44. Ibid.
45. Richardson, ed., *National Cyclopedia*, 274–275; Brief information on Dudley in BTWP, 7: 272, n.1.
46. Lewis, "An Account of Washington's North Carolina Tour," in BTWP, 10: 456; Logan, *Negro in North Carolina*, 31.
47. Lewis, "An Account of Washington's North Carolina Tour," in BTWP, 10: 456; Weare, *Black Business in the New South*, 3; Washington, "Durham, North Carolina, A City of Negro Enterprises," 57; Du Bois, "The Upbuilding of Black Durham," 338.
48. Lewis, "An Account of Washington's North Carolina Tour," in BTWP, 10: 460; Washington, "Durham, North Carolina: A City of Negro Enterprises," 56; Weare, *Black Business in the New South*, 44; Du Bois, "The Upbuilding of Black Durham," 338; Tate, *Cigarette Wars*, 13, 25, 32–37.
49. Ingham, "John Merrick," 586–587; Weare, *Black Business in the New South*, 50–52, 81, 108; Weare, "Charles Clinton Spaulding," 171.
50. Weare, *Black Business in the New South*, 52–53; Richardson, ed., *National Cyclopedia*, 346; Weare, "Charles Clinton Spaulding," 171.
51. Richardson, ed., *National Cyclopedia*, 346; Weare, "Charles Clinton Spaulding," 168, 174; Weare, *Black Business in the New South*, 56, 59.
52. Lewis, "An Account of Washington's North Carolina Tour," in BTWP, 10: 460; Washington, "Durham, North Carolina: A City of Negro Enterprises," 56; Weare, *Black Business in the New South*, 3–5.
53. *BTWP*, 5: 71, n.1; Richardson, ed., *National Cyclopedia*, 268–269.
54. *Charlotte Daily Observer*, November 1, 1910; Lewis, "An Account of Washington's North Carolina Tour," in BTWP, 10: 460; Weare, *Black Business in the New South*, 258; *Washington Bee*, November 12, 1910.
55. Lewis, "An Account of Washington's North Carolina Tour," in BTWP, 10: 460–416, 583; Harlan, *Wizard of Tuskegee*, 193.
56. Lewis, "An Account of Washington's North Carolina Tour," in BTWP, 10: 461.
57. Ibid., 462; *Charlotte Daily Observer*, November 3, 6, 1910.
58. Lewis, "An Account of Washington's North Carolina Tour," in BTWP, 10: 462–463.
59. Ibid., 463.
60. *Charlotte Daily Observer*, November 5, 1910.
61. Lewis, "An Account of Washington's North Carolina Tour," in BTWP, 10: 456, 461; *Indianapolis Freeman*, November 26, 1910.
62. *New York Age*, November 3, 1910; *Indianapolis Freeman*, November 5, 1910; *Charlotte Daily Observer*, October 29, 30, 1910, November 5, 1910; *Baltimore Afro-American Ledger*, November 5, 1910.

63. *Crisis* 1:2 (December 1910).
64. *Indianapolis Freeman*, November 26, 1910.
65. Ibid.
66. Lewis, "An Account of Washington's North Carolina Tour," in BTWP, 10: 461–462.
67. *Indianapolis Freeman*, November 26, 1910.
68. Ibid.
69. *Charlotte Daily Observer*, November 5, 1910.
70. Ibid.; Lewis, "An Account of Washington's North Carolina Tour," in BTWP, 10: 456.
71. *Indianapolis Freeman*, November 26, 1910; *Charlotte Daily Observer*, November 5, 1910.

7 Tour of the Lone Star State, September–October 1911

1. Hine, Hine, and Harrold, *African American Odyssey*, 344; Weaver, *Brownsville Raid*; Berry and Blassingame, *Long Memory*, 310–311; Tinsley, "Roosevelt, Foraker, and the Brownsville Affray," 43–65; Thornbrough, "The Brownsville Episode and the Negro Vote," 469–493; Harlan, *Wizard of Tuskegee*, 318.
2. Hine, Hine, and Harrold, *African American Odyssey*, 344; Tinsley, "Roosevelt, Foraker, and the Brownsville Affray," 43–65; Thornbrough, "The Brownsville Episode and the Negro Vote," 469–493; Harlan, *Wizard of Tuskegee*, 318.
3. "A Memorandum Prepared by Emmett Jay Scott," BTWP, 10: 276; Barr, *Black Texans*, 112–113; Rice, *The Negro in Texas*, 50–52, 83–84, 95, 252; Richardson, ed., *National Cyclopedia*, 348.
4. Barr, *Black Texans*, 137, 169; Hine, Hine, and Harrold, *African American Odyssey*, 355; Bennett, *Before the Mayflower*, 341–342; Litwack, *Trouble in Mind*, 443; Bederman, *Manliness & Civilization*, 1–44.
5. Barr, *Black Texans*, 136–138.
6. Harlan, *Wizard of Tuskegee*, 379–382; N. Barnett Dodson, "An Account of the Assault on Washington," in BTWP, 11: 27–30; Gatewood, "Booker T. Washington and the Ulrich Affair," 286–302.
7. Dray, *At the Hands of Persons Unknown*, 179–182. For full story see Downey and Hyser, *No Crooked Death*.
8. *Washington Bee*, September 9, 1911.
9. Barr, *Black Texans*, 152–153; Rice, *The Negro in Texas*, 195; Pitre, "Robert Lloyd Smith," 262–268; Harris, *The Negro as Capitalist*, 237; Garrett, "He Ran His Business like a White Man," 103–109.
10. The *Dallas Express* quoted in the *Indianapolis Freeman*, September 9, 1911.
11. Slatter, "An Account of Washington's Tour of Texas," BTWP, 11: 332; Emanuel Griggs also served as state organizer for the TXSNBL.

See Bacote, *Who's Who among Colored Baptists*, 55; *The Red Book of Houston*, 180, for data on Edward L. Blackshear.

12. *El Paso Morning Times*, September 25, 1911; "An Account of Washington's Tour of Texas," BTWP, 11: 322–323, 329; Slatter, "An Account of Washington's Tour of Texas," BTWP, 11: 332.

13. "An Account of Washington's Tour of Texas," BTWP, 11: 323.

14. *El Paso Morning Times*, September 25, 1911; "An Account of Washington's Tour of Texas," BTWP, 11: 323, 329–330; Biehler and Snowman, *Psychology Applied to Teaching*, 161.

15. *El Paso Herald*, September 25, 1911; "An Account of Washington's Tour of Texas," BTWP, 11: 322, 323.

16. *El Paso Morning Times*, September 25, 1911; *El Paso Herald*, September 25, 1911; "An Account of Washington's Tour of Texas," BTWP, 11: 322, 323.

17. *El Paso Herald*, September 25, 1911; *Baltimore Afro-American Ledger*, September 30, 1911; *El Paso Morning Times*, September 26, 1911; Barr, *Black Texans*, 140.

18. Slatter, "An Account of Washington's Tour of Texas," BTWP, 11: 332.

19. Ibid., 332–333.

20. Ibid; www.sanantonio.gov/LIBRARY/texana/cityofficers.asp.

21. Slatter, "An Account of Washington's Tour of Texas," BTWP, 11: 332–333; Duster, ed., *Crusade for Justice*, 148–149; Dray, *At the Hands of Persons Unknown*, 103–104.

22. Slatter, "An Account of Washington's Tour of Texas," BTWP, 11: 333–334.

23. Ibid., 334.

24. *Indianapolis Freeman*, September 30, 1911; Slatter, "An Account of Washington's Tour of Texas," BTWP, 11: 332, 334, 342.

25. *New York Age*, October 12, 1911; Slatter, "An Account of Washington's Tour of Texas," BTWP, 11: 334, 335, 342.

26. Ibid., 336; "An Account of Washington's Tour of Texas," BTWP, 11: 326; Barr, *Black Texans*, 141.

27. Slatter, "An Account of Washington's Tour of Texas," BTWP, 11: 336; "An Account of Washington's Tour of Texas," BTWP, 11: 326.

28. *New York Age*, October 12, 1911; Slatter, "An Account of Washington's Tour of Texas," BTWP, 11: 336–337.

29. Ibid., 337.

30. "An Account of Washington's Tour of Texas," BTWP, 11: 324–325.

31. *New York Age*, October 12, 1911; Pitre, *Through Many Dangers, Toils and Snares*, 195–205; Pitre, "Robert Lloyd Smith," 262–268; Barr, *Black Texans*, 90, 148, 149, 153; Carroll, "Robert L. Smith and the Farmer's Improvement Society of Texas"; and biosketch in BTWP, 4: 297–298, n.1.

32. "An Account of Washington's Tour of Texas," BTWP, 11: 325.

33. Toppin, "Emmett Jay Scott," 753–754; See biosketch in BTWP, 4: 171–172, n.1; Barr, *Black Texans*, 160.

34. "An Account of Washington's Tour of Texas," BTWP, 11: 325.
35. Barr, *Black Texans*, 156–157.
36. "An Account of Washington's Tour of Texas," BTWP, 11: 323–324.
37. Barr, *Black Texans*, 163.
38. *Houston Chronicle* quoted in the *Baltimore Afro-American Ledger*, October 7, 1911; Thornbrough, "Booker T. Washington as Seen by His White Contemporaries," 175.
39. *New York Age*, Ocotber 12, 1911; "An Account of Washington's Tour of Texas," BTWP, 11: 326; Slatter, "An Account of Washington's Tour of Texas," BTWP, 11: 338; Barr, *Black Texans*, 161.
40. "An Account of Washington's Tour of Texas," BTWP, 11: 326; Barr, *Black Texans*, 145, 164.
41. "An Account of Washington's Tour of Texas," BTWP, 11: 327.
42. Ibid., 327–328.
43. Ibid., 328.
44. Ibid.
45. *Cleveland Gazette*, October 28, 1911.
46. *El Paso Herald*, September 25, 1911; *Crisis* 2:5 (September 1911): 187; *New York Age*, October 12, 1911; Slatter, "An Account of Washington's Tour of Texas," BTWP, 11: 338–339; *Baltimore Afro-American Ledger*, October 21, 1911; Barr, *Black Texans*, 141.
47. Slatter, "An Account of Washington's Tour of Texas," BTWP, 11: 339.
48. Ibid., 339–340.
49. *New York Age*, October 12, 1911; Slatter, "An Account of Washington's Tour of Texas," BTWP, 11: 340.
50. *New York World*, May 16, 1916; Hale, *Making Whiteness*, 215–222; Dray, *At the Hands of Persons Unknown*, 216–218. In 1916, only a few years after Washington's tour, an eighteen-year-old African American male in Waco became the victim of one of the most horrendous lynchings on record. Jesse Washington had been charged with murdering fifty-three-year-old Lucy Fryar and raping her corpse. He worked as a hired hand for the Fryars and was their neighbor. Although one writer on the subject concluded that this charge against Jesse "was attached more as the result of rumor than of evidence," and the physician who examined Fryar's body made no mention of any sexual assault, after a mere semblance of a trial, an all-white jury spent only four minutes before finding him guilty. After which, a mob seized him from court officers. Philip Dray describes what happened next:
    "As he was prodded and dragged along, [Jesse] Washington was kicked, stabbed, hit with bricks and shovels, and had most of his clothes torn off, then was forced naked onto the pyre. The chain around his neck was looped over a tree limb, and he was jerked into the air. His body was sprinkled with coal oil, as were the boxes and scraps of wood below. There was a momentary delay when it was discerned that the tree itself, which adorned the city hall square,

would be destroyed by the fire, but by now the crowd was huge [an estimated fifteen thousand people] and pressing in from all sides—students from Waco High on their lunch hour, secretaries, and businessmen had wandered over to take in the event—and there was no stopping what was about to occur."

"Washington was lowered down one last time so the participants could cut off his fingers, ears, toes, and finally his penis, then with the crowd's delirious roar and approval the oil-soaked boxes were lit and Washington's body began to be consumed by flames…When Washington was dead, a man on a horse lassoed the charred remains and dragged them through town, followed by a group of young boys. The skull eventually bounced loose and was captured by some of the boys, who pried the teeth out and offered them for sale." For full story, see Bernstein, *First Waco Horror.*

51. *New York Age,* October 12, 1911; Slatter, "An Account of Washington's Tour of Texas," BTWP, 11: 340.
52. Summers, *Manliness & Its Discontents,* 39–40.
53. *Indianapolis Freeman,* September 30, 1911.
54. *New York Age,* October 12, 1911; Slatter, "An Account of Washington's Tour of Texas," BTWP, 11: 341.
55. *New York Age,* October 12, 1911; *Baltimore Afro-American Ledger,* October 21, 1911; Slatter, "An Account of Washington's Tour of Texas," BTWP, 11: 341–342.
56. *El Paso Herald,* September 26, 1911.
57. Ibid.; Biehler and Snowman, *Psychology Applied to Teaching,* 532–533.
58. Barr, *Black Texans,* 143.
59. Goings, *The NAACP Comes of Age,* 4–6; for instance, in 1917, Houston, a city Washington had spoken so fondly of, became the scene of one of the nation's worst race riots. The Third Battalion of the 24th Infantry had recently been stationed at Camp Logan near Houston. Public facilities and streetcars were segregated in Houston, and local Hispanics and whites regularly insulted black troops calling them "niggers" and other racially derogatory terms. Once, when an African American soldier tried to stop a white policeman, Lee Sparks, from beating a black woman, the officer began to beat the soldier and incarcerated him. When another black soldier, Corporal Charles W. Baltimore (a military police), tried to find out what occurred, Houston police beat and arrested him too. Although both soldiers were later released, black troops were infuriated over the abuse. Hence around one hundred and fifty of them launched a two-hour attack on the police station, killing sixteen people, including five police officers. Sixty-three black soldiers were later charged with mutiny by the army. Nineteen of them, including Corporal Baltimore, were hanged while sixty-seven others were sent to prison. Officer Lee Sparks remained on the Houston police force and killed two African Americans by the end of the year.

8 TOUR OF THE SUNSHINE
STATE, MARCH 1912

1. Angell, *Bishop Henry McNeal Turner*, 217.
2. Jones, "The African-American Experience," 373–390; Richardson, "Florida Black Codes," 365–379; Shofner, "Custom, Law and History," 277–298; Jones, Rivers et al., "A Documented History of the Incident Which Occurred at Rosewood, Florida;" Colburn, "Rosewood and America in the Early Twentieth Century," 175–192; Jones, "The Rosewood Massacre and the Women Who Survived It," 193–208; D'Orso, *Like Judgment Day*; Ortiz, *Emancipation Betrayed*.
3. Jones, "The Rosewood Massacre," 193; Tolnay and Beck, *Festival of Violence*, 37–38; Jackson, "Forum," 377–387; Severn and Rogers, "Theodore Roosevelt Entertains Booker T. Washington," 308; Ortiz, *Emancipation Betrayed*.
4. *Jacksonville Evening Metropolis*, October 29, 1901; for complete discussion, see Severn and Rogers, "Theodore Roosevelt Entertains Booker T. Washington," 306–318; Shofner, "Custom, Law, and History," 277.
5. *Jacksonville Evening Metropolis*, October 22, 1901; Severn and Rogers, "Theodore Roosevelt Entertains Booker T. Washington," 315–317; for another example of "genetic annihilation" fears, see the *Chicago Record Herald*, October 20, 1901.
6. White, "Booker T. Washington's Florida Incident," 227–249.
7. *New York Times*, January 30, 1903; *Jacksonville Evening Metropolis*, February 2, 1903.
8. White, "Booker T. Washington's Florida Incident," 240–244.
9. *Weekly True Democrat*, April 6, 1906.
10. Ibid., June 28, 1907; for more on Lewey, see Young, "Florida's Pioneer African American Attorneys," 60–82.
11. *Tampa Tribune*, February 7, 1993; *The College Arms* 16 (March 1912). The last publication was a monthly published at Florida A&M College for students and alumni.
12. See "A Press Release on Washington's Tour of Florida," March 8, 1912, in BTWP, 4: 297–298; BTWP, 11: 483, 486; "The Florida Trip," 1; "Principal Washington's Florida Tour," 1; "Welcomed at Pensacola," 1; "Incidents of the Florida Tour," 1–2; "Ocala Welcomes Dr. Washington," 1–3; *Indianapolis Freeman*, February 17, 1912; *Gainesville Daily Sun*, March 2, 1912; Nichols and Crogman, *Progress of a Race*, 402–403; *Jacksonville Evening Metropolis*, March 4, 6, 1912; *Baltimore Afro-American-Ledger*, March 9, 1912.
13. Howard and Howard, "Family, Religion, and Education: A Profile of African American Life in Tampa, Florida, 1900–1930," 2.
14. *New York Age*, May 29, 1913.
15. Nichols and Crogman, *Progress of a Race*, 378–379; Perkins, *Who's Who in Colored Louisiana*, 125, 135–136; Williams, Green, and

Jones, *History and Manual of the Colored Knights of Pythias*, 882; Richardson, ed., *National Cyclopedia*, 182.

16. *New York Age*, May 29, 1913. Green must have taken another train to Ocala after he arrived in Jacksonville.

17. Ibid.

18. "...Violence of Mob: Supreme Colored Chancellor of Black Knights Goes After the L and N Railroad," in *The Montgomery Advertiser* in Tuskegee News Clipping Files, ca. May 20, 1913.

19. Ibid.

20. Hale, *Making Whiteness*, 129.

21. *Atlanta Constitution*, May 9, 1920.

22. Menard, *Lays in Summer Lands*, 98; Shofner, "Florida," in Suggs, ed., *The Black Press in the South*; *Jacksonville Florida Union*, May 20, 1869; "The Florida Trip," 1; "Principal Washington's Florida Tour," 1; "Welcomed at Pensacola," 1; "Incidents of the Florida Tour," 1–2; *Washington Bee*, March 9, 1912; Young, "Florida's Pioneer African American Attorneys," 60–82.

23. Washington said he chose Pensacola not because it was superior to other black communities but because he was able to secure more complete information on this community than on others. See Washington, *The Negro in Business*, 230, 231–236; Neyland, *Twelve Black Floridians*, 9–14; Brown, *Florida's Black Public Officials*, 104; Bragaw, "Status of Negroes in a Southern Port City," 294–295, 299.

24. "The Washington Tour in Florida," 199.

25. Bragaw, "Status of Negroes in a Southern Port City," 284, 296; Washington, *The Negro in Business*, 230–236.

26. *Washington Bee*, March 9, 1912; *Lakeland Evening Telegram*, March 6, 1912; *Apalachicola Times*, March 9, 1912; *New York Age*, March 14, 1912; *Indianapolis Freeman*, March 16, 1912 reported that Washington spoke to eight thousand people. Potter, "Booker T. Washington: A Visit to Florida." Potter focuses exclusively on Washington's stop in Pensacola.

27. *Lakeland Evening Telegram*, March 6, 1912; Litwack, *Been in the Storm So Long*, 338, 399. See also Chapter 8.

28. *Lakeland Evening Telegram*, March 6, 1912; *Apalachicola Times*, March 9, 1912; Bragaw, "Status of Negroes in a Southern Port City," 299.

29. "A Press Release on Washington's Tour of Florida," March 8, 1912, BTWP, 11: 483.

30. Ric Kabat and William Rogers, "Mob Violence in Tallahassee, Florida, 1909," 113, 111–122.

31. *New York Age*, March 14, 1912; *Weekly True Democrat*, February 26, 1912, March 5, 1912; *The College Arms* 16 (March 1912). For full story on Young, see Holland, *Nathan B. Young*.

32. "The Washington Tour in Florida," 200. *New York Age*, March 14, 1912; *Weekly True Democrat*, February 26, 1912, March 5, 1912;

Jacksonville Florida Times-Union, March 4, 1912; *The College Arms* 16 (March 1912). For more on Young, see Richardson, ed., *National Cyclopedia*, 420.

33. "A Press Release on Washington's Tour of Florida," BTWP, 11: 483.
34. *Weekly True Democrat*, May 19, 26, 1911.
35. Ibid., May 26, 1911.
36. *Lakeland Evening Telegram*, March 14, 1912; "A Press Release on Washington's Tour of Florida," BTWP, 11: 483–484.
37. *Jacksonville Evening Metropolis*, March 4, 1912.
38. See, for example, Jackson, "Charles Banks: 'Wizard of Mound Bayou,'" 275–276. For more detailed discussion, see Jackson, *A Chief Lieutenant*, 41–49; Harlan, "The Secret Life of Booker T. Washington," 393–416.
39. *Indianapolis Freeman*, April 23, 1892, October 15, 1892; "A Press Release on Washington's Tour of Florida," BTWP, 11: 484.
40. Ibid., 484–485; "The Washington Tour in Florida," 199.
41. "A Press Release on Washington's Tour of Florida," BTWP, 11: 484–485; *Jacksonville Evening Metropolis*, March 5, 7, 1912; *Jacksonville Florida Times-Union*, March 4, 1912; "Ocala Welcomes Dr. Washington," 1–3.
42. *Jacksonville Evening Metropolis*, March 5, 7, 1912; *Gainesville Daily Sun*, March 8, 1912; *Jacksonville Florida Times-Union*, March 4, 1912.
43. Moton, *Finding a Way Out*, 183–184.
44. Ibid., 184.
45. Ibid., 184–185.
46. *Jacksonville Evening Metropolis*, March 5, 7, 1912; *Gainesville Daily Sun*, March 8, 1912; *Jacksonville Florida Times-Union*, March 4, 1912; Moton, *Finding a Way Out*, 185.
47. *Jacksonville Evening Metropolis*, March 5, 7, 1912; *Gainesville Daily Sun*, March 8, 1912; *Jacksonville Florida Times-Union*, March 4, 1912; Richardson, "Joseph L. Wiley: A Black Florida Educator," 458, 460, 463.
48. *New York Age*, July 10, September 18, October 30, 1913; Richardson, "Joseph L. Wiley: A Black Florida Educator," 467, 470; "Ocala Welcomes Dr. Washington," 1–3.
49. See Leland Hawes's article, "Booker T. Washington Slept Here," *Tampa Tribune*, February 7, 1993; Iorio, "Colorless Primaries," 297–318.
50. Howard and Howard, "A Profile of African-American Life in Tampa," 2; See also Ortiz, *Emancipation Betrayed*.
51. Howard and Howard, "A Profile of African-American Life in Tampa," 3–8; Brown and Brown, *Family Records of the African American Pioneers of Tampa and Hillsborough County*, 14, 176–177; Hewitt, *Southern Discomfort*, 54, 87, 164, 165, 157–169.
52. *Tampa Tribune*, March 4, 5, 1912.

53. Ibid.; *Indianapolis Freeman*, March 23, 1912; *Baltimore Afro-American Ledger*, March 16, 1912. Blacks in increasingly large numbers shared Ybor City or West Tampa with black Cubans. See Howard and Howard, "A Profile of African-American Life in Tampa," 3.

54. Moton, *Finding a Way Out*, 189–190; Harlan, *Wizard of Tuskegee*, 98, 233.

55. *Lakeland Evening Telegram*, March 4, 5, 1912; *Baltimore Afro-American Ledger*, March 16, 1912; Brown, *In the Midst of All That Makes Life Worth Living*, 225.

56. "A Press Release on Washington's Tour of Florida," BTWP, 11: 485.

57. *Lakeland Evening Telegram*, March 5, 1912.

58. Ibid; *Baltimore Afro-American Ledger*, March 16, 1912.

59. *Lakeland Evening Telegram*, ca. March 6, 1912.

60. Ibid; *Jacksonville Evening Metropolis*, March 4, 1912. For another example, see *Apalachicola Times*, March 9, 1912 and *Indianapolis Freeman*, March 16, 1912.

61. "A Press Release on Washington's Tour of Florida," BTWP, 11: 485–486. For more on the Hungerford school, see Washington, *The Negro in Business*, 77–80; and Otey, *Eatonville, Florida*, 11–14, 19; *Jacksonville Florida Times-Union*, January 11, 1908.

62. "A Press Release on Washington's Tour of Florida," BTWP, 11: 485, 486; Lord, "At Home and Afield, Washington at the Hungerford School," 387–388; Moton, *Finding a Way Out*, 190. For more on Eatonville and the Hungerford School, see Washington, *The Negro in Business*, 77–80.

63. "A Press Release on Washington's Tour of Florida," BTWP, 11: 486; *Jacksonville Florida Times-Union*, March 2, 1912; *Jacksonville Evening Metropolis*, March 9, 1912; *Daytona Gazette*, March 9, 1912; *New York Age*, March 14, 1912; Neyland, *Twelve Black Floridians*, 15–24; Lempel, "The Mayor's 'Henchmen and Henchwomen, Both White and Colored,'" 277; Ludlow, "The Bethune School," 144–154; Hine, "Mary Jane McLeod Bethune," 76.

64. Brown, *Florida's Black Public Officials*, 68–69, 178–179.

65. *Jacksonville Evening Metropolis*, March 4, 5, 6, 1912; "The Washington Tour in Florida," 200.

66. *Jacksonville Evening Metropolis*, March 4, 5, 6, 1912; *Indianapolis Freeman*, September 13, 1902.

67. Phelts, *An American Beach for African Americans*, 24–36; Neyland, *Twelve Black Floridians*, 53–59; Richardson, ed., *National Cyclopedia*, 470; Schweninger, *Black Property Owners in the South*, 222.

68. Phelts, *An American Beach for African Americans*, 28; Richardson, ed., *National Cyclopedia*, 435.

69. Ibid., 463, 466–467, 471.

70. No admission fee was charged in Jacksonville for Washington's lecture. *Jacksonville Evening Metropolis*, March 7, 8, 1912.

71. Scott and Stowe, *Booker T. Washington: Builder of a Civilization*, 93–94.

72. *Jacksonville Evening Metropolis*, March 7, 8, 1912; "A Press Release on Washington's Tour of Florida," BTWP, 11: 482, 486.

73. Scott and Stowe, *Booker T. Washington: Builder of a Civilization*, 94.

74. *Jacksonville Evening Metropolis*, March 8, 1912.

75. Harlan, "Booker T. Washington and the Voice of the Negro, 1904–1907," 144–145.

76. *Jacksonville Evening Metropolis*, March 8, 1912; *St. Petersburg Daily Times*, March 9, 1912.

77. *Jacksonville Evening Metropolis*, March 5, 6, 7, 1912.

78. See Bederman, *Manliness & Civilization*, 1–76.

79. Booker T. Washington to Henry Lee Higginson, March 5, 1912, BTWP, 5: 68; "A Press Release on Washington's Tour of Florida," BTWP, 11: 482.

80. *Crisis* 3:6 (April 1912), 229.

9 CONCLUSION

1. Bederman, *Manliness & Civilization*, 18, 27, 29. While planning for Washington's visit to Jacksonville, a newspaper stated explicitly: "Ladies will not attend the collation which will be given at Odd Fellows Temple...after the speaking at the theater, in honor of Dr. Washington and party. This function will be attended by men only." See the *Jacksonville Evening Metropolis*, March 5, 1912.

2. Ibid., 20, 21; Summers, *Manliness & Its Discontents*, 35.

3. *New York Age*, November 3, 1910; Washington, *The Man Farthest Down*.

4. Thornbrough, "Booker T. Washington," 175.

5. For instance, see Graham, *The Senator and the Socialite*, 252–254. Graham provides a literal interpretation of Washington without exercising diligence in critically analyzing the Tuskegee Wizard.

6. See, for example, Harlan, *Wizard of Tuskegee*, 203–205, 308–309; Meier, *Negro Thought in America*; Harlan, *Making of a Black Leader*, 253; Graham, *The Senator and the Socialite*, 146, 170, 171–172, 252–254; Campbell, *Middle Passages*, 115.

7. Kornweibel, "*Investigate Everything*," 142–148; Lewis, *W. E. B. Du Bois, 1868–1919*, 551–560; Ellis, *Race, War, and Surveillance*, 159–182; Ellis, "'Closing Ranks' and 'Seeking Honors,'" 96, 98, 99, 108–109, 113.

8. Ibid., 110–111, 124; Ellis, *Race, War, and Surveillance*, 159–182; Kornweibel, "*Investigate Everything*," 142–148; Lewis, *W. E. B. Du Bois, 1868–1919*, 551–560.

9. Ellis, *Race, War, and Surveillance*, 159–182; Ellis, "'Closing Ranks' and 'Seeking Honors,'" 96, 98, 99, 108–109, 113; Lewis,

W. E. B. Du Bois, 1868–1919, 551–560; Kornweibel, "*Investigate Everything*," 142–148.

10. Jackson, *A Chief Lieutenant*, 41–49.
11. Bederman, *Manliness & Civilization*, 54.
12. Wells is quoted in Hine, Hine, and Harrold, *African American Odyssey*, 320–321.

Works Cited

Primary Sources

Newspapers

Apalachicola Times, 1912.
Atlanta Constitution, 1920.
Baltimore Afro-American Ledger, 1908, 1909, 1910, 1911, 1912.
Biloxi Daily Herald, 1901.
Boston Transcript, 1909.
Bristol Herald Courier, 1909.
Charlotte Daily Observer, 1910.
Chattanooga Daily Times, 1907, 1909.
Chicago Record Herald, 1901.
Cleveland Gazette, 1911.
Crisis 1, 1910.
Crisis 2, 1911.
Crisis 3, 1912.
Crisis 14, 1917.
Daytona Gazette, 1912.
El Paso Herald, 1911.
El Paso Morning Times, 1911.
Gainesville Daily Sun, 1912.
Hattiesburg Mississippi News, 1909.
Indianapolis Freeman, 1892, 1902, 1908, 1909, 1910, 1911, 1912.
Jackson Evening News, 1908.
Jackson [Mississippi] Clarion-Ledger, 1901.
Jacksonville Evening Metropolis, 1901, 1903, 1912.
Jacksonville Florida Times-Union, 1869, 1900, 1908, 1912.
Johnson City Comet, 1909.
Knoxville Daily Journal and Tribune, 1909.
Lakeland Evening Telegram, 1912.
Memphis Commercial Appeal, 1908, 1909, 1913.
Montgomery Advertiser, 1905, 1913.
Nashville American, 1903, 1907.
Nashville Banner, 1909.
Nashville Globe, 1909.
Nashville Tennessean, 1909.

New Orleans Picayune, 1908.
New York Age, 1908, 1909, 1910, 1911, 1912, 1913.
New York Evening Post, 1901, 1909.
New York Times, 1903, 1906.
New York World, 1916.
Saturday Evening Post [Philadelphia], 1905.
Springfield Republican, 1903.
St. Petersburg Daily Times, 1912.
Star of Zion, 1902.
Tampa Tribune, 1912, 1993.
Vicksburg Evening Post, 1904.
Vicksburg Daily Herald, 1908.
Washington Bee, 1910, 1911, 1912.
Weekly True Democrat, 1906, 1907, 1911, 1912.

Manuscripts, Papers, and Collections

Harlan, Louis R., and Raymond W. Smock. Eds. *Booker T. Washington Papers*. 14 vols. Urbana, IL: University of Illinois Press, 1972–1989.
National Negro Business League Papers. Microfilm Collection. Ned R. McWherter Library. University of Memphis.
Washington, Booker T. Papers Microfilm Collection. Ned R. McWherter Library, University of Memphis.

Published Works

"An Account of Washington's Tour of Texas." *Tuskegee Student* 23 (October 7, 1911): 1–4.
Allen, William F., Charles P. Ware, and Lucy M. Garrison. Eds. *Slave Songs of the United States*. Bedford, MA: Applewood Books, 1867.
Bacote, Samuel W. *Who's Who among Colored Baptists of the United States*. Kansas City: Franklin Hudson, 1913.
Banks, Charles. "Negro Town and Colony, Mound Bayou, Bolivar Co., Miss., Opportunities Open to Farmers and Settlers." Pamphlet. Mound Bayou, MS: Demonstrator Print, n.d.
Barringer, Paul B. *The American Negro: His Past and Future*. Raleigh, NC: Edwards and Broughton, 1900.
"Booker T. Washington's Trip through Mississippi." *The Tuskegee Student* 20 (October 31, 1908).
———. *The Tuskegee Student* 20 (November 7, 1908).
Bruce, John Edward. *Short Biographical Sketches of Eminent Negro Men & Women in Europe & the United States*. Yonkers, NY: Gazette Press, 1910.
Carroll, Charles. *The Negro a Beast or in the Image of God*. Miami, FL: Mnemosyne, 1900.
The College Arms. 16 (March 1912).

Crawford, R. J. "Business Negroes of Chattanooga." *Voice of the Negro* 1:11 (1904): 534–537.

Du Bois, William E. B. "The Upbuilding of Black Durham." *World's Work* 23 (January, 1912): 334–338.

———. *Black Reconstruction in America 1860–1880.* Introduction by David Levering Lewis. New York: Harcourt, Brace, 1935. Reprint, New York: Atheneum, 1992.

———. *Dusk of Dawn: An Essay toward an Autobiography of a Race Concept.* New York: Harcourt, Brace & World, 1940. Reprint, New Brunswick, NJ: Transaction Publishers, 1997.

Equiano, Olaudah. *The Interesting Narrative of the Life of Olaudah Equiano.* Reprint, Boston: Bedford Books, 1995.

"The Florida Trip." *The Tuskegee Student* 24 (February 17, 1912).

Garvey, Marcus. *Message to the People: The Course of African Philosophy.* Ed. by Tony Martin. Dover, MA: Majority Press, 1986.

Gayarre', Charles. "The Southern Question." *North American Review* 225 (November–December 1877): 472–498.

Hamilton, Green P. *The Bright Side of Memphis.* Memphis: G. P. Hamilton, 1908.

———. *Beacon Lights of the Race.* Memphis, TN: E. H. Clarke and Brother, 1911.

Hartshorn, William N. *An Era of Progress and Promise, 1863–1910.* Boston: Priscilla Publishing, 1910.

Hood, Aurelius P. *The Negro at Mound Bayou.* Nashville, TN: African Methodist Episcopal Sunday School Union, 1909.

"Incidents of the Florida Tour." *The Tuskegee Student* 24 (March 16, 1912).

Kealing, Hightower T. "Booker T. Washington's Tour through Mississippi, a New Form of University Extension." *A.M.E. Church Review* 25 (October 1908): 20–27.

Lewis, William H. "An Account of Washington's North Carolina Tour." In BTWP, Vol. 10: 455–468.

Lord, Nathalie. "At Home and Afield: Washington at the Hungerford School." *Southern Workman* 41 (June 1912): 387–388.

Ludlow, Helen W. "The Bethune School." *Southern Workman* 41 (March 1912): 144–154.

Menard, John W. *Lays in Summer Lands.* Ed. by Larry E. Rivers, Richard Matthews, and Canter Brown, Jr. Tampa, FL: University of Tampa Press, 2002.

Moton, Robert R. "The Significance of Mr. Washington's Lecture Trip in Mississippi." *Southern Workman* (December 1908): 691–695.

———. *Finding a Way Out: An Autobiography.* Garden City, NY: Doubleday, 1921.

Nichols, J. L., and William H. Crogman. *Progress of a Race.* Naperville, IL: J. L. Nichols, 1920; Reprint, New York: Arno Press, 1969.

"Ocala Welcomes Dr. Washington." *The Tuskegee Student* 24 (March 16, 1912).

Perkins, Archie E. *Who's Who in Colored Louisiana.* Baton Rouge, LA: Douglas Loan Company, 1930.

Ponton, Mungo M. *Life and Times of Henry M. Turner.* Atlanta, GA: A. B. Caldwell Publishing, 1917.

"Principal Washington's Tour of Mississippi." *The Tuskegee Student* 20 (October 10, 1908).

"Principal Washington's Mississippi Visit." *The Tuskegee Student* 20 (October 17 and 24, 1908).

"Principal Washington's Florida Tour." *The Tuskegee Student* 24 (March 2, 1912).

The Red Book of Houston: A Compendium of Social, Professional, Religious, Educational and Industrial Interests of Houston's Colored Population. Houston: Sotex [1915?].

Richardson, Clement. *The National Cyclopedia of the Colored Race.* Montgomery, AL: National Publishing, 1919.

Scott, Emmett Jay, and Lyman B. Stowe. *Booker T. Washington: Builder of a Civilization.* Garden City, NJ: Doubleday, 1916.

Shufeldt, Robert W. *The Negro: A Menace to Civilization* (Boston: Gorham Press, 1907).

Simmons, William J. *Men of Mark: Eminent, Progressive and Rising.* Cleveland, OH: George M. Rewell, 1887. Reprint, Chicago: Johnson Publishing, 1970.

Slatter, Horace D. "An Account of Washington's Tour of Texas." *Tuskegee Student* 23 (October 14, 1911): 1–4.

"The Washington Tour of Florida." *Southern Workman* 41 (April 1912): 198–200.

Washington, Booker T. *Up from Slavery.* New York: Doubleday, 1901. Reprint, New York: Penguin, 1986.

———. *The Negro in Business.* Boston and Chicago: Hertel, Jenkins, 1907. Reprint, New York: AMS Press, 1971.

———. "Industrial Education Is the Solution." In *Black Workers: A Documentary History from Colonial Times to the Present.* Ed. by Philip S. Foner and Ronald L. Lewis. Philadelphia: Temple University Press, 1989.

———. "A Cheerful Journey through Mississippi." *World's Work*, February 1909. Reprint, BTWP, 10: 60–68.

———. "Charles Banks." *American Magazine* 81 (March 1911): 731–733.

———. "Durham, North Carolina, a City of Negro Enterprises." *Independent* 70 (March 30, 1911): 642–650.

———. *My Larger Education: Being Chapters from My Experience.* New York: Doubleday, 1911.

———. *The Man Farthest Down: A Record of Observation and Study in Europe.* New York: Doubleday, 1912.

Wells-Barnett, Ida B. "Lynch Law in All Its Phases." In *African Intellectual Heritage: A Book of Sources.* Ed. by Molefi K. Asante and Abu S. Abarry. Philadelphia: Temple University Press, 1996.

Wiggins, Lida K. *The Life & Works of Paul Lawrence Dunbar*. Naperville, IL, and Memphis, TN: J. L. Nichols, 1907. Reprint; Nashville, TN: Winston-Derek Publishers, 1992.

Willey, Day Allen. "Mound Bayou—A Negro Municipality." *Alexander's Magazine*, July 15, 1907.

Williams, Ephie A., S. W. Green, and Joseph L. Jones. *History and Manual of the Colored Knights of Pythias North America, South America, Europe, Asia, Africa, and Australia*. Nashville, TN: National Baptist Publishing Board, 1917.

Woodard, D. W. "Negro Progress in a Mississippi Town." Pamphlet. Committee of Twelve for the Advancement of the Interests of the Negro Race. Philadelphia: Biddle Press, 1909.

Work, Monroe N. Ed. *Negro Year Book and Annual Encyclopedia of the Negro*. Nashville, TN: Sunday School Union Print, 1912.

Secondary Sources

Published Works

Anderson, Eric. *Race and Politics in North Carolina 1872–1901: The Black Second*. Baton Rouge, LA: Louisiana State University Press, 1981.

Anderson, James D. *The Education of Blacks in the South, 1860–1935*. Chapel Hill, NC: University of North Carolina Press, 1988.

Angell, Stephen W. *Bishop Henry McNeal Turner and African-American Religion in the South*. Knoxville, TN: University of Tennessee Press, 1992.

Barr, Alwyn. *Black Texans: A History of African Americans in Texas, 1528–1995*. Norman: University of Oklahoma Press, 1996.

Barr, Alwyn, and Robert A. Calvert. Eds. *Black Leaders: Texans for Their Times*. Texas State Historical Association, 1990.

Bay, Mia. *The White Image in the Black Mind: African-American Ideas about White People, 1830–1925*. New York: Oxford University Press, 2000.

Bederman, Gail. *Manliness & Civilization: A Cultural History of Gender and Race in the United States, 1880–1917*. Chicago: University of Chicago Press, 1995.

Bennett, Jr., Lerone. *Before the Mayflower: A History of Black America*. New York: Penguin Books, 1984.

Berry, Mary F., and John W. Blassingame. *Long Memory: The Black Experience in America*. New York: Oxford University Press, 1982.

Bernstein, Patricia. *The First Waco Horror: The Lynching of Jesse Washington and the Rise of the NAACP*. College Station, TX: Texas A&M University Press, 2005.

Biehler, Robert F., and Jack Snowman. *Psychology Applied to Teaching*. 5th edition. Boston: Houghton Mifflin, 1986.

Blassingame, John. *The Slave Community: Plantation Life in the Antebellum South*. New York: Oxford University Press, 1979.

Blight, David W. *Race and Reunion: The Civil War in American Memory.* Cambridge, MA: Belknap Press, 2001.

Bradford, Phillips V., and Harvey Blume. *Ota Benga: The Pygmy in the Zoo.* New York: St. Martin's Press, 1992.

Bragaw, Donald H. "Status of Negroes in a Southern Port City in the Progressive Era: Pensacola, 1896–1920." *Florida Historical Quarterly* 51 (January 1973): 282–303.

Brinkley, Alan. *American History: A Survey, Vol. II: Since 1865.* New York: McGraw-Hill College, 1999.

Brown, Jr., Canter. *Florida's Black Public Officials, 1867–1924.* Tuscaloosa, AL: University of Alabama Press, 1998.

———. *In the Midst of All That Makes Life Worth Living: Polk County, Florida, to 1940.* Tallahassee, FL: Sentry Press, 2001.

Brown, Jr., Canter, and Barbara G. Brown. *Family Records of the African American Pioneers of Tampa and Hillsborough County.* Tampa, FL: University of Tampa Press, 2003.

Calista, Donald. "Booker T. Washington: Another Look." *Journal of Negro History* 49 (October 1964): 240–255.

Campbell, James T. *Middle Passages: African American Journeys to Africa, 1787–2005.* New York: Penguin Press, 2006.

Chafe, William H. *Civilities and Civil Rights: Greensboro, North Carolina, and the Black Struggle for Freedom.* New York: Oxford University Press, 1981.

Church, Roberta, and Ronald Walter. *Nineteenth Century Memphis Families of Color, 1850–1900.* Memphis, TN: Murdock Printing, 1989.

Clarke, John H. *Critical Lessons in Slavery and the Slave Trade.* Richmond, VA: Native Sun Publishers, 1996.

Clinton, Catherine. *The Plantation Mistress: Woman's World in the Old South.* New York: Pantheon Books, 1982.

Cobb, James C. *The Most Southern Place on Earth: The Mississippi Delta and the Roots of Regional Identity.* New York: Oxford University Press, 1992.

Colburn, David R. "Rosewood and America in the Early Twentieth Century." *Florida Historical Quarterly* 76 (Fall 1997): 175–192.

Coleman, Kenneth. Ed. *A History of Georgia.* Athens, GA: University of Georgia Press, 1991.

Cone, James H. *The Spirituals & the Blues: An Interpretation.* New York: Seabury Press, 1972.

Cooper, Arnie. " 'We Rise upon the Structure We Ourselves Have Builded': William H. Holtzclaw and Utica Institute, 1903–1915." *Journal of Mississippi History* 47 (February 1985): 15–33.

Coulter, E. Merton. *Georgia: A Short History.* Chapel Hill, NC: University of North Carolina Press, 1947.

Crockett, Norman L. *The Black Towns.* Lawrence, KS: Regents Press of Kansas, 1979.

Crouthamel, James L. "Springfield Race Riot of 1908." *Journal of Negro History* 45 (July 1960): 164–181.

Dagbovie, Pero Gaglo. "Exploring a Century of Historical Scholarship on Booker T. Washington." *Journal of African American History* 92 (Spring 2007): 239–264.

Daniel, Pete. "Up from Slavery and Down to Peonage: The Alonzo Bailey Case." *Journal of American History* 57 (December 1970): 654–670.

———. *The Shadow of Slavery: Peonage in the South, 1901–1969*. Urbana, IL: University of Illinois Press, 1972.

Davis, David B. *Inhuman Bondage: The Rise and Fall of Slavery in the New World*. New York: Oxford University Press, 2006.

Denton, Virginia L. *Booker T. Washington and the Adult Education Movement*. Gainesville, FL: University Press of Florida, 1993.

D'Orso, Michael. *Like Judgment Day: The Ruin And Redemption of a Town Called Rosewood*. New York: Berkeley Publishing, 1996.

Downey, Dennis B., and Raymond M. Hyser. *No Crooked Death: Coatesville, Pennsylvania, and the Lynching of Zachariah Walker*. Urbana, IL: University of Illinois Press, 1990.

Dray, Philip. *At the Hands of Persons Unknown: The Lynching of Black America*. New York: Random House, 2002.

Duster, Alfreda M. Ed. *Crusade for Justice: The Autobiography of Ida B. Wells*. Chicago: University of Chicago Press, 1972.

Ellis, Mark. "'Closing Ranks' and 'Seeking Honors': W. E. B. Du Bois in World War I." *Journal of American History* 79 (June 1992): 96–124.

———. *Race, War, and Surveillance: African Americans and the United States Government during World War I*. Bloomington, IN: Indiana University Press, 2001.

Ellsworth, Scott. *Death in a Promised Land: The Tulsa Race Riot of 1921*. Baton Rouge, LA: Louisiana State University Press, 1982.

Faries, Clyde J. "Carmack versus Patterson: The Genesis of a Political Feud." *Tennessee Historical Quarterly* 38 (Fall 1979): 332–347.

Flynn, John P. "Booker T. Washington: Uncle Tom or Wooden Horse." *Journal of Negro History* 54 (July 1969): 262–274.

Foner, Eric. *Reconstruction: America's Unfinished Revolution, 1863–1877*. New York: Harper & Row, 1988.

———. *Freedom's Lawmakers: A Directory of Black Officeholders during Reconstruction*. Baton Rouge: Louisiana State University Press, 1996.

Fox, Stephen. *The Guardian of Boston: William Monroe Trotter*. New York: Atheneum, 1970.

Franklin, John H. and Alfred A. Moss, Jr. *From Slavery to Freedom: A History of Negro Americans*. 6th edition. New York: Alfred A. Knopf, 1988.

Fredrickson, George M. *White Supremacy a Comparative Study in American & South African History*. New York: Oxford University Press, 1981.

———. *The Black Image in the White Mind: The Debate on Afro-American Character and Destiny, 1817–1914*. Hanover, NH: Wesleyan University Press, 1987.

Gatewood, Willard. "Booker T. Washington and the Ulrich Affair." *Phylon*, 30 (Fall 1969): 286–302.

―――. *Aristocrats of Color: The Black Elite, 1880–1920*. Bloomington, IN: Indiana University Press, 1993.

Gavins, Raymond. "Fear, Hope, and Struggle: Recasting Black North Carolina in the Age of Jim Crow." In *Democracy Betrayed: The Wilmington Race Riot of 1898 and Its Legacy*. Ed. by David S. Cecelski and Timothy B. Tyson. Chapel Hill, NC: University of North Carolina Press, 1998.

Goings, Kenneth W. *The NAACP Comes of Age: The Defeat of Judge John J. Parker*. Bloomington, IN: Indiana University Press, 1990.

―――. *Mammy and Uncle Mose: Black Collectibles and American Stereotyping*. Bloomington, IN: Indiana University Press, 1994.

Goings, Kenneth W., and Gerald L. Smith. "'Unhidden' Transcripts: Memphis and African-American Agency, 1862–1920." *Journal of Urban History* 21 (March 1995): 372–394.

Graham, Lawrence O. *The Senator and the Socialite: The True Story of America's First Black Dynasty*. New York: HarperCollins, 2006.

Greenwood, Janette T. *Bittersweet Legacy: The Black and White "Better Classes" in Charlotte, 1850–1910*. Chapel Hill, NC: University of North Carolina Press, 1994.

Hale, Grace E. *Making Whiteness: The Culture of Segregation in the South, 1890–1940*. New York: Random House, 1998.

Hall, Jacquelyn D. *Revolt against Chivalry: Jessie Daniel Ames and the Women's Campaign against Lynching*. New York: Columbia University Press, 1993.

Hamilton, Kenneth M. *Black Towns and Profit: Promotion and Development in the Trans-Appalachian West, 1877–1915*. Urbana, IL: University of Illinois Press, 1991.

Harlan, Louis R. "The Secret Life of Booker T. Washington." *Journal of Southern History* 37 (August 1971): 393–416.

―――. *Booker T. Washington: The Making of a Black Leader, 1856–1901*. New York: Oxford University Press, 1972.

―――. "Booker T. Washington and the Politics of Accommodation." In *Black Leaders of the Twentieth Century*. Ed. by John Hope Franklin and August Meier. Urbana, IL: University of Illinois Press, 1982.

―――. *Booker T. Washington: The Wizard of Tuskegee, 1901–1915*. New York: Oxford University Press, 1983.

―――. "Booker T. Washington and the Voice of the Negro, 1904–1907." In *Booker T. Washington in Perspective: Essays of Louis R. Harlan*. Ed. by Raymond W. Smock. Jackson, MS: University Press of Mississippi, 1988.

Harris, Abram L. *The Negro as Capitalist*. Philadelphia: American Academy of Political and Social Science, 1936.

Harvey, Paul. "Richard Henry Boyd: Black Business and Religion in the Jim Crow South." In *Portraits in African American Life since 1865*. Ed. by Nina Mjagkij. Wilmington, DE: Scholarly Resources, 2003.

Haskins, James. *Black Music in America: A History through Its People*. New York: HarperCollins, 1987.

Hemmingway, Theodore. "Booker T. Washington in Mississippi, October, 1908." *Journal of Mississippi History* 46 (February 1984): 29–42.

Hewitt, Nancy A. *Southern Discomfort: Women's Activism in Tampa, Florida, 1880s–1920s.* Urbana, IL: University of Illinois Press, 2001.

Higginbotham, Evelyn B. "African-American Women's History and the Metalanguage of Race." *Signs: Journal of Women in Culture and Society* 17 (Winter 1992): 251–274.

Hine, Darlene Clark. "Mary Jane McLeod Bethune." In *African American Lives.* Ed. by Henry Louis Gates, Jr., and Evelyn Brooks Higginbotham. New York: Oxford University Press, 2004.

Hine, Darlene Clark, William C. Hine, and Stanley Harrold. *The African-American Odyssey.* Upper Saddle River, NJ: Pearson Education, 2003.

Hoberman, John. *Darwin's Athletes: How Sport Has Damaged Black America and Preserved the Myth of Race.* Boston: Houghton Mifflin, 1997.

Holland, Antonio F. *Nathan B. Young and the Struggle over Black Higher Education.* Columbia, MO: University of Missouri Press, 2006.

Holmes, William F. "Whitecapping: Agrarian Violence in Mississippi, 1902–1906." *Journal of Southern History* 35 (May 1969): 97–115.

———. *The White Chief: James Kimble Vardaman.* Baton Rouge, LA: Louisiana State University Press, 1970.

Honey, Michael. "Class, Race, and Power in the New South: Racial Violence and the Delusions of White Supremacy." In *Democracy Betrayed: The Wilmington Race Riot of 1898 and Its Legacy.* Ed. by David S. Cecelski and Timothy B. Tyson. Chapel Hill, NC: University of North Carolina Press, 1998.

Howard, Walter T., and Virginia M. Howard. "Family, Religion, and Education: A Profile of African-American Life in Tampa, Florida, 1900–1930." *Florida Historical Quarterly* 79 (Winter 1994): 1–17.

Ingham, John N. "John Merrick." In *African American Lives.* Ed. by Henry Louis Gates, Jr., and Evelyn Brooks Higginbotham. New York: Oxford University Press, 2004.

Iorio, Pam. "Colorless Primaries: Tampa's White Municipal Party." *Florida Historical Quarterly* 79 (Winter 2001): 297–318.

Jackson, Jr., David H. "Charles Banks: 'Wizard of Mound Bayou.'" *Journal of Mississippi History* 62 (Winter 2000): 269–294.

———. "Forum." *Florida Historical Quarterly* 79 (Winter 2001): 377–387.

———. *A Chief Lieutenant of the Tuskegee Machine: Charles Banks of Mississippi.* Gainesville, FL: University Press of Florida, 2002.

———. "Perry Wilbon Howard." In *African American Lives.* Ed. by Henry Louis Gates, Jr., and Evelyn Brooks Higginbotham. New York: Oxford University Press, 2004.

———. "The Growth of African American Cultural and Social Institutions." In *A Companion to African American History.* Ed. by Alton Hornsby, Jr., Malden, MA: Blackwell, 2005.

James, Arthur, Jimmie James, Jr., and Robert James. *The Mississippi Black Bankers and Their Institutions* (n.p., 1996).

Johnson, Sylvester A. *The Myth of Ham in Nineteenth-Century American Christianity: Race, Heathens, and the People of God.* New York: Palgrave Macmillan, 2004.

Jones, Maxine D. "The Rosewood Massacre and the Women Who Survived It." *Florida Historical Quarterly* 76 (Fall 1997): 193–208.

———. "The African-American Experience in Twentieth-Century Florida." In *The New History of Florida.* Ed. by Michael Gannon. Gainesville, FL: University Press of Florida, 1996.

Jones, Maxine D., Larry E. Rivers, David R. Colburn, Tom Dye, and William R. Rogers. "A Documented History of the Incident Which Occurred at Rosewood, Florida in January 1923." Submitted to the Florida Board of Regents, December 22, 1993.

Kabat, Ric, and William Rogers. "Mob Violence in Tallahassee, Florida, 1909." In *Florida's Heritage of Diversity: Essays in Honor of Samuel Proctor.* Ed. by Mark I. Greenberg, William W. Rogers, and Canter Brown, Jr. Tallahassee, FL: Sentry Press, 1997.

Kenzer, Robert C. *Enterprising Southerners: Black Economic Success in North Carolina, 1865–1915.* Charlottesville, VA: University Press of Virginia, 1997.

Kipp, III, Samuel M. "Old Notables and Newcomers: The Economic and Political Elite of Greensboro, North Carolina: 1880–1920." *Journal of Southern History* 43 (August 1977): 373–394.

Kolchin, Peter. *American Slavery 1619–1877.* New York: Hill and Wang, 1993.

Kornweibel, Jr., Theodore. *"Investigate Everything": Federal Efforts to Compel Black Loyalty during World War I.* Bloomington, IN: Indiana University Press, 2002.

Lakey, Othal H. *The History of the CME Church.* Memphis: CME Publishing House, 1985.

Lamon, Lester C. *Black Tennesseans, 1900–1930.* Knoxville, TN: University of Tennessee Press, 1977.

———. *Blacks in Tennessee, 1791–1970.* Knoxville, TN: University of Tennessee Press, 1981.

Lempel, Leonard R. "The Mayor's 'Henchmen and Henchwomen, Both White and Colored': Edward H. Armstrong and the Politics of Race in Daytona Beach, 1900–1940." *Florida Historical Quarterly* 79 (Winter 2001): 267–296.

Levine, Lawrence W. *Black Culture and Black Consciousness: Afro-American Folk Thought from Slavery to Freedom.* New York: Oxford University Press, 1977.

Lewis, David L. *W. E. B. Du Bois, 1868–1919: Biography of a Race.* New York: Henry Holt, 1993. Litwack, Leon F. *Been in the Storm So Long: The Aftermath of Slavery.* New York: Vintage Books, 1980.

———. "Trouble in Mind: The Bicentennial and the Afro-American Experience." *Journal of American History* 74 (September 1987): 315–337.

———. *Trouble in Mind: Black Southerners in the Age of Jim Crow.* New York: Vintage Books, 1999.

Loewen, James W. *Sundown Towns: A Hidden Dimension of American Racism.* New York: New Press, 2005.

Logan, Frenise A. *The Negro in North Carolina, 1876–1894.* Chapel Hill, NC: University of North Carolina Press, 1964.

Logan, Rayford W. *The Betrayal of the Negro: From Rutherford B. Hayes to Woodrow Wilson.* New York: Collier Books, 1965. Reprint, New York: Da Capo Press, 1997.

Lovett, Bobby L. *The African-American History of Nashville, Tennessee, 1780–1930.* Fayetteville, AR: University of Arkansas Press, 1999.

———. "James Carroll Napier (1845–1940): From Plantation to the City." In *The Southern Elite and Social Change.* Ed. by Randy Finley and Thomas A. DeBlack. Fayetteville, AR: University of Arkansas Press, 2002.

Martin, Sandy D. *For God and Race: The Religious and Political Leadership of AMEZ Bishop James Walker Hood.* Columbia, SC: University of South Carolina Press, 1999.

McMillen, Neil R. "Perry W. Howard, Boss of Black-and-Tan Republicanism in Mississippi, 1924–1960." *Journal of Southern History* 48 (May 1982): 205–224.

———. *Dark Journey: Black Mississippians in the Age of Jim Crow.* Urbana, IL: University of Illinois Press, 1990.

Meier, August. *Negro Thought in America, 1880–1915: Racial Ideologies in the Age of Booker T. Washington.* Ann Harbor, MI: University of Michigan Press, 1963.

———. "Booker T. Washington and the Town of Mound Bayou." In *Along the Color Line: Explorations in the Black Experience.* Ed. by August Meier and Elliott Rudwick. Urbana, IL: University of Illinois Press, 1976.

Montgomery, William E. *Under Their Own Vine and Fig Tree: The African American Church in the South, 1865–1900.* Baton Rouge, LA: Louisiana State University Press, 1993.

Moore, Jacqueline M. *Leading the Race: The Transformation of the Black Elite in the Nation's Capital, 1880–1920.* Charlottesville, VA: University Press of Virginia, 1999.

———. *Booker T. Washington, W. E. B. Du Bois, and the Struggle for Racial Uplift.* Wilmington, DE: Scholarly Resources, 2003.

Neyland, Leedell W. *Twelve Black Floridians.* Tallahassee, FL: Florida A&M University Foundation, 1970.

Norrell, Robert J. "Understanding the Wizard: Another Look at the Age of Booker T. Washington." In *Booker T. Washington and Black Progress: Up from Slavery 100 Years Later.* Ed. by W. Fitzhugh Brundage. Gainesville, FL: University Press of Florida, 2003.

Ortiz, Paul. *Emancipation Betrayed: The Hidden History of Black Organizing and White Violence in Florida from Reconstruction to the Bloody Election of 1920*. Berkeley, CA: University of California Press, 2005.

Oshinsky, David M. *"Worse than Slavery:" Parchman Farm and the Ordeal of Jim Crow Justice*. New York: Free Press Paperbacks, 1997.

Otey, Frank. *Eatonville, Florida: A Brief History*. Winter Park, FL: Four-G Publishers, 1989.

Patterson, Orlando. *Rituals of Blood: Consequences of Slavery in Two American Centuries*. New York: Basic Civitas, 1998.

Phelts, Marsha D. *An American Beach for African Americans*. Gainesville, FL: University Press of Florida, 1997.

Pinn, Anthony B. *Why, Lord? Suffering and Evil in Black Theology*. New York: Continuum, 1995.

Pitre, Merline. "Robert Lloyd Smith." *Phylon* 46 (3rd Qtr., 1985): 262–268.

———. *Through Many Dangers, Toils and Snares: Black Leadership in Texas, 1870–1890*. Austin, TX: Eakin Press, 1997.

Potter, Richard C. "Booker T. Washington: A Visit to Florida." *Negro History Bulletin*, n.d., Booker T. Washington File, Florida A&M University, Black Archives.

Prather, Sr., H. Leon. "We Have Taken A City: A Centennial Essay." In *Democracy Betrayed: The Wilmington Race Riot of 1898 and Its Legacy*. Ed. by David S. Cecelski and Timothy B. Tyson. Chapel Hill, NC: University of North Carolina Press, 1998.

Rabinowitz, Howard N. *Race Relations in the Urban South, 1865–1890*. Urbana, IL: University of Illinois Press, 1980.

———. "A Comparative Perspective on Race Relations in Southern and Northern Cities, 1860–1900, with Special Emphasis on Raleigh." In *Black Americans in North Carolina and the South*. Ed. by Jeffrey J. Crow and Flora J. Hatley. Chapel Hill, NC: University of North Carolina Press, 1984.

Rice, Lawrence D. *The Negro in Texas 1874–1900*. Baton Rouge, LA: Louisiana State University Press, 1971.

Richardson, Joe M. "Florida Black Codes." *Florida Historical Quarterly* 47 (April 1969): 365–379.

———. "Joseph L. Wiley: A Black Florida Educator." *Florida Historical Quarterly* 71 (April 1993): 458–472.

Schweninger, Loren. *Black Property Owners in the South, 1790–1915*. Urbana, IL: University of Illinois Press, 1997.

Severn, John K., and William W. Rogers. "Theodore Roosevelt Entertains Booker T. Washington: Florida's Reaction to the White House Dinner." *Florida Historical Quarterly* 54 (January 1976): 306–318.

Sewell, George A. *Mississippi Black History Makers*. Jackson, MS: University of Mississippi Press, 1977.

Shofner, Jerrell H. "Custom, Law and History: The Enduring Influence of Florida's 'Black Code,'" *Florida Historical Quarterly* 55 (January 1977): 277–298.

————. "Florida." In *The Black Press in the South, 1865–1979*. Ed. by Henry L. Suggs. Westport, CT: Greenwood Press, 1983.

Simkins, Francis B. *Pitchfork Ben Tillman: South Carolinian*. Columbia, SC: University of South Carolina Press, 2002.

Spivey, Donald. *Schooling for the New Slavery: Black Industrial Education, 1868–1915*. Westport, CT: Greenwood Press, 1978.

Stampp, Kenneth M. *The Peculiar Institution: Slavery in the Ante-Bellum South*. New York: Vintage Books, 1989.

Summers, Martin. *Manliness & Its Discontents: The Black Middle Class & the Transformation of Masculinity, 1900–1930*. Chapel Hill, NC: University of North Carolina Press, 2004.

Tate, Cassandra. *Cigarette Wars: The Triumph of "The Little White Slaver."* New York: Oxford University Press, 1999.

Thomas, Hugh. *The Slave Trade: The Story of the Atlantic Slave Trade: 1440–1870*. New York: Touchstone, 1997.

Thompson, Julius E. *Lynchings in Mississippi: A History, 1865–1965*. Jefferson, NC: McFarland, 2001.

Thornbrough, Emma L. "The Brownsville Episode and the Negro Vote." *Mississippi Valley Historical Review* 44 (December 1957): 469–483.

————. "Booker T. Washington as Seen by His White Contemporaries." *Journal of Negro History* 53 (April 1968): 161–182.

Tinsley, James A. "Roosevelt, Foraker, and the Brownsville Affray." *Journal of Negro History* 41 (January 1956): 43–65.

Tolnay, Stewart E., and E. M. Beck, *Festival of Violence: An Analysis of Southern Lynchings, 1882–1930*. Urbana, IL: University of Illinois Press, 1995.

Toppin, Edgar A. "Emmett Jay Scott." In *African American Lives*. Ed. by Henry Louis Gates, Jr., and Evelyn Brooks Higginbotham. New York: Oxford University Press, 2004.

Tucker, David M. "Miss Ida B. Wells and Memphis Lynching." *Phylon* 32 (Summer 1971): 112–122.

Turner, Patricia A. *Ceramic Uncles & Celluloid Mammies: Black Images and Their Influence on Culture*. New York: Anchor Books, 1994.

Walker, Juliet, E. K. *The History of Black Business in America: Capitalism, Race, Entrepreneurship*. New York: Macmillan, 1998.

Walker, Randolph M. *The Metamorphosis of Sutton E. Griggs: The Transition from Black Radical to Conservative, 1913–1933*. Memphis, TN: Walker, 1991.

Walls, William J. *The African Methodist Episcopal Zion Church: Reality of the Black Church*. Charlotte: AME Zion Publishing House, 1974. Ward, Jr., Thomas J. *Black Physicians in the Jim Crow South*. Fayetteville, AR: University of Arkansas Press, 2003.

Washington, Harriet A. *Medical Apartheid: The Dark History of Medical Experimentation on Black Americans from Colonial Times to the Present*. New York: Doubleday, 2006.

Watkins, Mel. *On the Real Side: Laughing, Lying, and Signifying—The Underground Tradition of African-American Humor That Transformed American Culture, from Slavery to Richard Pryor.* New York: Touchstone Book, 1994.

Weare, Walter B. "Charles Clinton Spaulding: Middle-Class Leadership in the Age of Segregation." In *Black Leaders of the Twentieth Century.* Ed. by John Hope Franklin and August Meier. Urbana, IL: University of Illinois Press, 1982.

————. *Black Business in the New South: A Social History of the North Carolina Mutual Life Insurance Company.* Durham, NC: Duke University Press, 1993.

Weaver, John D. *The Brownsville Raid.* College Station, TX: Texas A&M University Press, 1992.

Welsing, Frances Cress. *The Isis Papers: The Keys to the Colors.* Chicago: Third World Press, 1991.

West, Michael R. *The Education of Booker T. Washington: American Democracy and the Idea of Race Relations.* New York: Columbia University Press, 2006.

Wharton, Vernon L. *The Negro in Mississippi 1865–1890.* New York: Harper Touchbooks, 1965.

White, Arthur O. "Booker T. Washington's Florida Incident, 1903–1904." *Florida Historical Quarterly* 51 (January 1973): 227–249.

Wiggins, Lida K. *The Life & Works of Paul Lawrence Dunbar.* Napierville, IL, and Memphis: J. L. Nichols, 1907. Reprint; Nashville, TN: Winston-Derek Publishers, 1992.

Willard, Carla. "Timing Impossible Subjects: The Marketing Style of Booker T. Washington." *American Quarterly* 53 (December 2001): 624–669.

Williams, David A. *Bricks Without Straw: A Comprehensive History of African Americans in Texas.* Austin, TX: Eakin Press, 1997.

Wright, Richard R. *The Bishops of the African Methodist Episcopal Church.* Nashville: AME Sunday School Union, 1963.

Unpublished Works

Borchert, James A. "The National Negro Business League, 1900–1915: Business as a Solution to the Negro Problem." Master's thesis, University of Cincinnati, 1966.

Burrows, John H. "The Necessity of Myth: A History of the National Negro Business League, 1900–1945." Ph.D. dissertation, Auburn University, 1977.

Carroll, Robert. "Robert L. Smith and the Farmer's Improvement Society of Texas." Master's thesis, Baylor University, 1974.

Clark, Herbert L. "The Public Career of James Carroll Napier: Businessman, Politician, and Crusader for Racial Justice, 1845–1940." D.A. dissertation, Middle Tennessee State University, 1980.

Garrett, Shennette M. "He Ran His Business like a White Man: Race, Entrepreneurship, and the Early National Negro Business League in the New South." Master's thesis, University of Texas, 2006.

Young, Darius J. "Florida's Pioneer African American Attorneys during the Post–Civil War Era." Master's thesis, Florida A&M University, 2005.

INDEX

Bennett College, 105, 115
Berry O'Kelly Training Center, 105
Bethune, Mary McLeod, 170
Biddle, Henry, *wife of,* 108
Biddle University, 105, 107, 108
Biloxi Daily Herald, 57
Birmingham Age-Herald, 75
Birth of a Nation, 14, 18, 51
Bishop College, 146
Black codes, 17, 151
Black press, 9, 10
Black progress, 7, 8, 52, 55, 65, 66, 67,
    69, 73, 74, 75, 77, 78, 85, 88, 108,
    109, 113, 116, 118–119, 120, 122,
    123, 132, 133, 136, 138, 142, 146,
    148, 149, 157, 162, 167–168, 170,
    175, 177, 178, 179, 180, 184, 185,
    186–187
Black psychology, 10
Black Second, 12, 103
Black survival strategy. *See* Black
    survivalism
Black survivalism, 33, 35, 37, 39, 40,
    42, 47, 59, 116, 133, 138, 152,
    162, 165, 168, 185
Black Texans, 148
Black Victorians, 66–67
Blackness, 21
Blackshear, Edward L., 131, 222n.11
Blassingame, John, 35
Blight, David, 7–8
Blodgett, Joseph Haygood, 171, 172
Blodgett Villa, 171
Bookerites. *See* Washington, Booker T.
Boston Guardian, 183
Boston Transcript, 95–96, 111
Boyd, Henry Allen, 89
Boyd, James E., 114
Boyd, Richard Henry, 78, 81, 88–89
Boyd, Robert F., 81, 87–88
Boyden, Archibald H., 112
Brackenridge, George W., 135
Bradley, Charles W., 132
Brainard Institute, 107
Bristol Negro Business League, 81–82
Bristol Normal Institute, 80
Bronx Zoo, 27–28
Brooklyn (New York), 29
Brooks, John M., 84
Brooks, Samuel Palmer, 145
Brook's Band, 70
Brown, William Wells, 35
Brown University, 132

Browne, Jefferson B., 152
Brown's Opera House, 120
Brownsville Affair, 127, 138
Bruce, Blanche K., 12
Bruce, John Edward, 7
Brunson, A. L., 168
Bullock, William S., 162–163
Burbage, George E., 82
Burge, J. B., 96
Burns, Tommy, 128
Burroughs, Ambrose H., 82–83
Burroughs, Betsy, 82–83
Burroughs, James, 82
Burton, Walter M., 12
Bush, John E., 80
Bynum, W. P., 114

Calhoun, Russell C., 169
Calista, Donald, 33, 43
Call, R. M., 174
Callagan, Bryan, 134–135
Calvary Baptist Church, 28
Campbell, James T., 182
Campbell, Lee Lewis, 131
Cardozo, Thomas W., 12
Carmack, Edward W., 87
Carnegie Library, 107, 112, 137
Carriger, W. H., 83
Carroll, Charles, 23–24
Carroll, Richard, 111
Carter, A. L., 84
Carver, George Washington, 2
Central High School, 146
Central Texas College, 145
Chafe, William, 113–114
Charleston West Virginia Advocate, 75
Charlotte Clothing Cleaning Company,
    109
Charlotte Daily Observer, 106, 107, 110,
    113, 120, 122, 124
Charlotte Negro Business League, 109
Chattanooga Daily Times, 85
Chattanooga Negro Business League, 85
Chautauqua salute, 159–160
Chicago (Illinois), 72, 154, 155, 174
Christian Recorder, 75
Church, Sr., Robert R., 80–81, 94
Church's Park, 94
Civil War, 11, 13, 21, 54, 74, 108, 112,
    132, 157, 167
Civilization, 22, 23, 112, 135, 174, 180,
    181, 185, 186
The Clansman, 14, 49, 51